Frommer's®

Y0-CAV-195

Chinese
Phrasebook &
Culture Guide

1st Edition

WILEY
Wiley Publishing, Inc.

Published by:

Wiley Publishing, Inc.

111 River St.
Hoboken, NJ 07030-5774

ISBN-13: 978-0-470-22857-9

Editor: Jennifer Polland
Chinese Editor: Wendy Abraham
Series Editor: Maureen Clarke
Travel Tips & Culture Guide: Wendy Abraham
Illustrations: Maciek Albrecht
Photo Editor: Richard H. Fox

Translation, Copyediting, Proofreading, Production, and Layout by:
Lingo Systems, 15115 SW Sequoia Pkwy, Ste 200, Portland, OR 97224

For information on our other products and services or to obtain technical support,
please contact our Customer Care Department within the U.S. at 800/762-2974, outside the U.S. at 317/572-3993 or fax 317/572-4002.
Wiley also publishes its books in a variety of electronic formats. Some content that
appears in print may not be available in electronic formats.

Manufactured in the United States of America

5 4 3 2 1

Contents

An Invitation to the Reader

In researching this book, we discovered many wonderful sayings and terms useful to travelers in Chinese-speaking countries. We're sure you'll find others. Please tell us about them so we can share them with your fellow travelers in upcoming editions. If you were disappointed about any aspect of this book, we'd like to know that, too. Please write to:

Frommer's Chinese Phrasebook & Culture Guide, 1st Edition
Wiley Publishing, Inc.
111 River St. • Hoboken, NJ 07030-5774

An Additional Note

The packager, editors and publisher cannot be held responsible for the experience of readers while traveling. Your safety is important to us, however, so we encourage you to stay alert and aware of your surroundings. Keep a close eye on cameras, purses, and wallets, all favorite targets of thieves and pickpockets.

Frommers.com

Now that you have the language for a great trip, visit our website at **www.frommers.com** for travel information on more than 3,600 destinations. With features updated regularly, we give you instant access to the most current trip-planning information available. At Frommers.com you'll also find the best prices on airfares, accommodations, and car rentals—and you can even book travel online through our travel booking partners. Frommers.com also features:

- Online updates to our most popular guidebooks
- Vacation sweepstakes and contest giveaways
- Newsletter highlighting the hottest travel trends
- Online travel message boards with featured travel discussions

INTRODUCTION: HOW TO USE THIS BOOK

Given China's population of more than 1.3 billion, it is safe to say that close to a quarter of humanity speaks Chinese, primarily in the People's Republic of China (PRC), the Republic of China (ROC, or Taiwan), Hong Kong, and Singapore. A member of the Sino-Tibetan language family, found in East Asia, Chinese is unique in that its written language can be read and understood by all who speak Chinese, whereas its spoken language has literally hundreds of different local and regional dialects—each mutually incomprehensible without the written word that has bound them together for thousands of years. The easiest Chinese dialect to learn is standard Mandarin, based on the northern dialect, which has only four tones (as opposed to other dialects with nine or even eleven tones in several different registers). Mandarin is the official dialect of both the PRC and Taiwan and is the dialect whose pronunciation and tones this book will highlight.

Our intention is not to teach you Chinese; we figure you'll find an audio program for that. Our aim is to provide a portable travel tool that's easy to use. The problem with most phrasebooks is that you practically have to memorize the contents before you know where to look for a term you might need on the spot. This phrasebook is designed for fingertip referencing, so you can whip it out and find the words you need fast. The extensive PhraseFinder dictionary at the back is an additional perk, and one to which we're guessing you'll appreciate having instant access.

Like most phrasebooks, part of this book organizes terms by chapters, like the chapters in a Frommer's guide—getting a room, getting a good meal, etc. Within those sections, we tried to organize phrases intuitively, according to how frequently most readers would be likely to use them. But let's say you're in a cab and you've received the wrong change, and you forget which chapter covers money. With Frommer's PhraseFinder, you can quickly look up "change" in the dictionary, and learn how to say "Sorry, but this isn't the correct change."

To make the best use of this book, we recommend that you spend some time flipping through it before you depart for your trip. Familiarize yourself with the order of the chapters. Read through the pronunciations section in chapter one and practice pronouncing random phrases throughout the book. Try looking up a few phrases in the phrasebook section as well as in the dictionary. This way, you'll be able to locate phrases faster and speak them more clearly when you need them.

What will make this book most practical? What will make it easiest to use? These are the questions we asked ourselves constantly as we assembled these travel terms.

Our immediate goal was to create a phrasebook as indispensable as your passport. Our far-ranging goal, of course, is to enrich your experience of travel. And with that, we wish you: *Yí lù píng an*. (Bon voyage!).

CHAPTER ONE

SURVIVAL CHINESE

If you tire of toting around this phrasebook, tear out this chapter. You should be able to navigate your destination with only the terms found in the next 32 pages.

BASIC GREETINGS

For a full list of greetings, see p103.

Hello.	您好。
	nín hǎo。
How are you?	您好吗?
	nín hǎo ma?
I'm fine, thanks.	我很好，谢谢。
	wǒ hěn hǎo, xiè xiè。
And you?	您呢?
	nín ne?
My name is ____.	我叫_____。
	wǒ jiào _____。
And yours?	您呢?
	nín ne?
It's a pleasure to meet you.	见到您很愉快。
	jiàn dào nín hěn yú kuài。
Please.	请。
	qǐng。
Thank you.	谢谢您。
	xiè xiè nín。
Yes.	是的。
	shì de。
No.	不是。
	bù shì。

1

Okay.	好。
	hǎo。
No problem.	没问题。
	méi wèn tí。
I'm sorry, I don't understand.	很抱歉，我不懂。
	hěn bào qiàn, wǒ bù dǒng。
Would you speak slower please?	您能再说慢点吗？
	nín néng zài shuō màn diǎn ma?
Would you speak louder please?	您能大点声说吗？
	nín néng dà diǎn shēng shuō ma?
Do you speak English?	您说英语吗？
	nín shuō yīng yǔ ma?
Do you speak any other languages?	您说其他语言吗？
	nín shuō qí tā yǔ yán ma?
I speak ____ better than Chinese.	我的_____语说得比汉语好。
	wǒ de _____ yǔ shuō dé bǐ hàn yǔ hǎo。
Would you spell that?	请问它怎么写？
	qǐng wèn tā zěn me xiě?
Would you please repeat that?	请再说一遍好吗？
	qǐng zài shuō yī biàn hǎo ma?
Would you point that out in this dictionary?	您能在这本字典里把它指给我看吗？
	nín néng zài zhè běn zì diǎn lǐ bǎ tā zhǐ gěi wǒ kàn ma?

THE KEY QUESTIONS

With the right hand gestures, you can get a lot of mileage from the following list of single-word questions and answers.

Who?	谁?
	shuí?
What?	什么?
	shén me?
When?	什么时候?
	shén me shí hou?
Where?	哪里?
	nǎ lǐ?
To where?	到哪里?
	dào nǎ lǐ?
Why?	为什么?
	wéi shén me?
How?	怎么样?
	zěn me yàng?
Which?	哪一个?
	nǎ yī gè?
How many? / How much?	多少?
	duō shǎo?

THE ANSWERS: WHO

For full coverage of pronouns, see p22.

I	我
	wǒ
you	你 / 您 / 你们
(familiar, formal, plural)	*nǐ / nín / nǐ mén*
him	他
	tā
her	她
	tā
us	我们
	wǒ mén
them	他们
	tā mén

THE ANSWERS: WHEN

For full coverage of time, see p12.

now	现在
	xiàn zài
later	稍后
	shāo hòu
in a minute	马上
	mǎ shàng
today	今天
	jīn tiān
tomorrow	明天
	míng tiān
yesterday	昨天
	zuó tiān
in a week	一周内
	yī zhōu nèi
next week	下周
	xià zhōu
last week	上周
	shàng zhōu
next month	下个月
	xià gè yuè
At ____	在____
	zài ____
ten o'clock this morning.	今天上午十点。
	jīn tiān shàng wǔ shí diǎn。
two o'clock this afternoon.	今天下午两点。
	Jīn tiān xià wǔ liǎng diǎn。
seven o'clock this evening.	今天晚上七点。
	Jīn tiān wǎn shàng qī diǎn。

For full coverage of numbers, see p7.

THE ANSWERS: WHERE

here	这里
	zhè lǐ
there	那里
	nà lǐ
near	附近
	fù jìn
closer	较近
	jiào jìn
closest	最近
	zuì jìn
far	远
	yuǎn
farther	较远
	jiào yuǎn
farthest	最远
	zuì yuǎn
across from	在…对面
	zài … duì miàn
next to	紧邻
	jǐn lín
behind	后面
	hòu miàn
straight ahead	一直向前
	yī zhí xiàng qián
left	左边
	zuǒ biān
right	右边
	yòu biān
up	上边
	shàng biān
down	下边
	xià biān
lower	较低
	jiào dī

higher	较高
	jiào gāo
forward	前面
	qián miàn
back	后面
	hòu miàn
around	周围
	zhōu wéi
across the street	街对面
	jiē duì miàn
down the street	沿着街道
	yán zhe jiē dào
on the corner	在拐角处
	zài guǎi jiǎo chù
kitty-corner	斜对角
	xié duì jiǎo
____ blocks from here	离这里_____条街远的地方
	lí zhè lǐ _____ tiáo jiē yuǎn de dì fāng

For a full list of numbers, see the next page.

THE ANSWERS: WHICH

this one	这个
	zhè gè
that (that one)	那个
	nà gè
these	这些
	zhè xiē
those (those there, close by)	那些
	nà xiē

NUMBERS & COUNTING

one	一 *yī*	seventeen	十七 *shí qī*
two	二 *èr*	eighteen	十八 *shí bā*
three	三 *sān*	nineteen	十九 *shí jiǔ*
four	四 *sì*	twenty	二十 *èr shí*
five	五 *wǔ*	twenty-one	二十一 *èr shí yī*
six	六 *liù*	thirty	三十 *sān shí*
seven	七 *qī*	forty	四十 *sì shí*
eight	八 *bā*	fifty	五十 *wǔ shí*
nine	九 *jiǔ*	sixty	六十 *liù shí*
ten	十 *shí*	seventy	七十 *qī shí*
eleven	十一 *shí yī*	eighty	八十 *bā shí*
twelve	十二 *shí èr*	ninety	九十 *jiǔ shí*
thirteen	十三 *shí sān*	one hundred	一百 *yī bǎi*
fourteen	十四 *shí sì*	two hundred	二百 *èr bǎi*
fifteen	十五 *shí wǔ*	one thousand	一千 *yī qiān*
sixteen	十六 *shí liù*		

FRACTIONS & DECIMALS

one eighth	八分之一 *bā fēn zhī yī*
one quarter	四分之一 *sì fēn zhī yī*
one third	三分之一 *sān fēn zhī yī*
one half	二分之一 *èr fēn zhī yī*
two thirds	三分之二 *sān fēn zhī èr*
three quarters	四分之三 *sì fēn zhī sān*
double	两倍 *liǎng bèi*
triple	三倍 *sān bèi*
one tenth	十分之一 *shí fēn zhī yī*
one hundredth	百分之一 *bǎi fēn zhī yī*
one thousandth	千分之一 *qiān fēn zhī yī*

MATH

addition	加 *jiā*
2 + 1	二加一 *èr jiā yī*
subtraction	减 *jiǎn*
2 − 1	二减一 *èr jiǎn yī*

multiplication	乘 *chéng*
2 × 3	二乘以三 *èr chéng yǐ sān*
division	除 *chú*
6 ÷ 3	六除以三 *liù chú yǐ sān*

ORDINAL NUMBERS

first	第一 *dì yī*
second	第二 *dì èr*
third	第三 *dì sān*
fourth	第四 *dì sì*
fifth	第五 *dì wǔ*
sixth	第六 *dì liù*
seventh	第七 *dì qī*
eighth	第八 *dì bā*
ninth	第九 *dì jiǔ*
tenth	第十 *dì shí*
last	最后 *zuì hòu*

MEASUREMENTS

Measurements will usually be metric, though you may need a few American measurement terms.

inch	英寸
	yīng cùn
foot	英尺
	yīng chǐ
mile	英里
	yīng lǐ
millimeter	毫米
	háo mǐ
centimeter	分米
	fēn mǐ
meter	米
	mǐ
kilometer	千米
	qiān mǐ
hectare	公顷
	gōng qǐng
squared	平方
	píng fāng
short	短
	duǎn
long	长
	cháng

VOLUME

milliliters	毫升
	háo shēng
liter	升
	shēng
kilo	千
	qiān
ounce	盎司
	àng sī

cup	杯
	bēi
pint	品脱
	pǐn tuō
quart	夸脱
	kuā tuō
gallon	加仑
	jiā lún

QUANTITY

some	一些
	yī xiē
none	一个也没有
	yī gè yě méi yǒu
all	全部
	quán bù
many / much	许多
	xǔ duō
a little bit (can be used for quantity or for time)	一点
	yī diǎn
dozen	一打
	yī dá

SIZE

small	小的
	xiǎo de
the smallest	最小的
	zuì xiǎo de
medium	中等的
	zhōng děng de
big	大的
	dà de
fat	胖的
	pàng de

wide	宽的
	kuān de
narrow	窄的
	zhǎi de

TIME

When the Chinese tell time, the period of the day is stated before the exact hour (early morning, noon, afternoon and evening). All of China is officially on one time zone, despite the great distances from one province to the next.

For full coverage of number terms, see p7.

HOURS OF THE DAY

What time is it?	现在几点钟?
	xiàn zài jǐ diǎn zhōng?
At what time?	在几点钟?
	zài jǐ diǎn zhōng?
For how long?	多长时间?
	duō cháng shí jiān?
It's one o'clock.	现在一点钟。
	xiàn zài yī diǎn zhōng.
It's two o'clock.	现在两点钟。
	xiàn zài liǎng diǎn zhōng.
It's two thirty.	现在两点半。
	xiàn zài liǎng diǎn bàn.
It's two fifteen.	现在两点一刻。
	xiàn zài liǎng diǎn yī kè.
It's a quarter to three.	现在两点四十五分。
	xiàn zài liǎng diǎn sì shí wǔ fēn.
It's noon.	现在是中午。
	xiàn zài shì zhōng wǔ.
It's midnight.	现在是午夜。
	xiàn zài shì wǔ yè.
It's early.	现在还早。
	xiàn zài hái zǎo.

It's late.	现在晚了。 *xiàn zài wǎn le。*
in the morning	在上午 *zài shàng wǔ*
in the afternoon	在下午 *zài xià wǔ*
at night	在晚上 *zài wǎn shàng*
dawn	黎明 *lí míng*

DAYS OF THE WEEK

Sunday	星期日 *xīng qī rì*
Monday	星期一 *xīng qī yī*
Tuesday	星期二 *xīng qī èr*
Wednesday	星期三 *xīng qī sān*
Thursday	星期四 *xīng qī sì*
Friday	星期五 *xīng qī wǔ*
Saturday	星期六 *xīng qī liù*
today	今天 *jīn tiān*
tomorrow	明天 *míng tiān*
yesterday	昨天 *zuó tiān*
the day before yesterday	前天 *qián tiān*
one week	一周 *yī zhōu*

next week	下周
	xià zhōu
last week	上周
	shàng zhōu

MONTHS OF THE YEAR

January	一月
	yī yuè
February	二月
	èr yuè
March	三月
	sān yuè
April	四月
	sì yuè
May	五月
	wǔ yuè
June	六月
	liù yuè
July	七月
	qī yuè
August	八月
	bā yuè
September	九月
	jiǔ yuè
October	十月
	shí yuè
November	十一月
	shí yī yuè
December	十二月
	shí èr yuè
next month	下个月
	xià gè yuè
last month	上个月
	shàng gè yuè

SEASONS OF THE YEAR

spring	春季
	chūn jì
summer	夏季
	xià jì
autumn	秋季
	qiū jì
winter	冬季
	dōng jì

CHINESE GRAMMER BASICS

THE ALPHABET

While there is no alphabet in Chinese, each morpheme (the smallest unit of meaning in a language) is represented by one syllable, which in turn consists of an initial sound and a final sound, and which is always uttered in one of the four tones which characterize the Mandarin dialect.

PRONUNCIATION GUIDE
INITIAL SOUNDS

In Chinese, initials are always comprised of consonants, which are much more numerous than the final vowel sounds, and are represented in the pinyin Romanization system as follows:

Initial	Sound	Pronunciation
b	baw	*bore*
p	paw	*pour*

PINYIN AND CHINA'S WRITTEN LANGUAGE

The official Romanization system of the People's Republic of China (PRC), "pinyin" literally means "to spell the way it sounds." Adopted in the 1950s, it became China's official Romanization system in 1979. While English is not commonly found on street signs or storefronts in China, pinyin is ubiquitous, so boning up on the basics in advance of your trip is well worth the effort. Since Chinese written characters don't necessarily give any indication of pronunciation, the Chinese themselves are taught pinyin in school in addition to the characters. In the Republic of China a mixture of various Romanization systems, including pinyin, is currently used.

As a point of reference, Chinese characters date to the earliest dynasty with archaeological evidence, the Shang (1766–1122 BC), and were originally used for divination purposes.

They can be read left to right, right to left, or top to bottom. The four most common types of characters, reflecting

m	maw	*mourn*
f	faw	*four*
d	duh	*dull*
t	tuh	*ton*
n	nuh	*null*
l	luh	*lull*
g	guh	*gum*
k	kuh	*come*
h	huh	*hum*
j	gee	*gee*
q	chee	*cheese*
x	she	*she*
z	dzuh	*"ds" as in suds*

meanings and sounds, include: **pictographs**, which are formed according to the shape of the objects themselves, such as the sun and the moon, and indicate the meaning of the character rather than the sound; **ideographs**, which represent more abstract concepts; **complex ideographs**, which are combinations of simpler characters; and phonetic compounds, also called **logographs**, formed by two elements—one hinting at the meaning of the word and the other giving a clue as to the sound. This last category accounts for over 80% of all Chinese characters.

To simplify the Chinese writing system so that the vast majority of Chinese could attain an adequate level of literacy, which hovered around 15% in 1949 when the PRC was established, the number of strokes required to create many characters was greatly reduced. These are known as "simplified" characters, and are used in the PRC today, where the literacy rate has climbed to 85%. "Traditional" (long form) characters are still taught and used in Taiwan. Using simplified characters in Taiwan can be construed as making a political statement, and would best be avoided if you are having business material translated into Chinese and printed for use in Taiwan.

c	tsuh	*"ts" as in cuts*
s	suh	*son*
zh	jir	*germ*
ch	chir	*chirp*
sh	shir	*shirt*
r	ir	*"er" as in larger*
w	wuh	*what*
y	yuh	*yum*

FINAL SOUNDS

There are only six vowels sounds in standard Mandarin: a, o, e, i, u, and ü. Pronouncing the vowels in sequence, your mouth will start off very wide and your tongue will start off very low. Vowels can be combined to form compound vowels, listed below:

Final	Sound	Pronunciation
a	ah	*not*
ai	i	*eye*
ao	ow	*chow*
an	ahn	*on*
ang	ahng	*thong*
o	aw	*draw*
ong	oong	*too+ng*
ou	oh	*toe*
e	uh	*bush*
ei	ay	*way*
en	un	*none*
eng	ung	*strung*
er	ar	*star*
i	ee	*bee*
ia	ya	*gotcha*
iao	yaow	*meow*
ie	yeh	*yet*
iu	yo	*leo*
ian	yan	*Cheyenne*

iang	yahng	*y+angst*
in	een	*seen*
ing	eeng	*ping*
iong	yoong	*you+ng*
u	oo	*too*
ua	wa	*suave*
uo	waw	*war*
ui	way	*sway*
uai	why	*why*
uan	wan	*want*
un	one	*won*
uang	wahng	*wan+ng*
ueng	wung	*one+ng*
ü	yew	*ewe*
üe	yweh	*you+eh*
üan	ywan	*you+wan*
ün	yewn	*you+n*

TONES

In the pinyin system of Romanization, Tone marks always appear above the vowel. If there are consecutive vowels, the Tone mark appears above the first vowel in that sequence. The only exception to this is for the vowels iu and ui, where the Tone mark falls on the second vowel.

In a spoken language with a great number of homophones, Tones are the key to understanding the meaning of what is being said. Even so, any given syllable with a specific Tone can also often have more than one meaning. Ultimately only by viewing the written character can the meaning be deduced on the spot. When dealing with spoken Chinese, the meaning must be deduced in large part from the context of what else is being said.

Mandarin has the following four Tones:

First tone: High level. This tone should be as high as your individual pitch range can be, and is indicated by a horizontal line above the vowel: ā

Second tone: Rising. This tone should have your voice going up as if asking a question, and is indicated by a line which rises from left to right above the vowel: á

Third tone: Dipping then rising. This tone starts in the middle level of your voice range and then falls before slightly rising again at the end. It is indicated by a reverse triangle without the horizontal line on top, located above the vowel: ǎ

Fourth tone: Falling. This tone sounds as if you're giving an order, falling from the high pitch level it starts at. It is indicated by a line dropping from left to right above the vowel: à

Other Tonal Rules

Two Consecutive Third Tones: When one third tone is followed by another, the first third tone is spoken like a second tone (rising), and only the second third tone exhibits the characteristics of a full third tone (falling and then rising again).

Half-Third Tones: When one third tone is followed by any other tone, only the first half (the falling half) of the tone is pronounced before the remaining syllables are pronounced with their respective tones. It sounds more like a low, level tone.

Neutral Tones: Although there are four primary tones in Mandarin, a fifth tone exists which is actually toneless, or neutral. There is no tone mark above a fifth tone, and you say it only when you attach it to grammatical particles or the second character of repetitive syllables such as bàba (father) or māma (mother).

Tonal Changes in Yī and Bù

Yī (one) and **bù** (not or no) are unusual in that their tones may change depending on what comes after them. Yī by itself is pronounced with the first tone, but when a first, second or third tone follows it, **yī** is spoken with a fourth tone, such as in **yìzhāng zhǐ** (a piece of paper). If a fourth tone follows yī it automatically becomes a second tone, such as in the word **yíyàng** (the same).

THE MONOSYLLABLE MYTH

Since each Chinese character is pronounced as a single syllable, the myth that Chinese is monosyllabic is often believed to be the case. The truth is that most Chinese words are polysyllabic and are written in clusters of characters. Most words in modern Chinese are two syllables (two characters). For example, míng means "clear, bright" and bái means "white, blank." Put together, míngbái means "understand, clear."

TERMS FOR MANDARIN

Standard Mandarin, the official language of both the PRC and the ROC, is referred to as **pǔtōnghuà** ("the common language") in the PRC, and **guóyǔ** ("national speech") in the ROC.

ELEMENTS OF CHINESE GRAMMAR

In general the way to tell how one part of a Chinese sentence relates to another is by the use of particles and the order of the words (syntax) rather than morphology (changes in the form of the word through inflection).

The basic word order of Chinese is exactly the same as in English: Subject-Verb-Object:

Subject	Verb	Object
I (wǒ)	love (xǐ huān)	spinach (bōcài)
You (nǐ)	read (kàn)	books (shū)

While Chinese word order resembles English, most everything else about the language differs. There are no gender-specific nouns in Chinese, no distinction between singular and plural, no verb conjugation, no such thing as first, second, or third person, no such thing as active or passive voices, or even past or present tense. Additionally, one word can function as both subject and object. Context is often the only way one knows when an action may have taken place.

PERSONAL PRONOUNS

English	Pinyin	Pronunciation
I	wǒ	waw
You	nǐ	nee
He / She / It	tā	tah
We	wǒ mén	waw-mun
You (Plural)	nǐ mén	nee-mun
They	tā mén	tah-mun

CLASSIFIERS

Classifiers, also referred to as measure words, help classify particular nouns, and are located in between a number (or a demonstrative pronoun such as "this" or "that") and a noun. They're similar to English words such as a "gaggle" of geese or a "school" of fish. While English doesn't use classifiers nearly as often as Chinese, in Chinese they can be found wherever a number is followed by a noun, or an implied noun. The most common classifier is "ge" (guh), which can safely be used when in doubt.

Classifier	Pinyin	Pronunciation
Printed and bound things (such as books or magazines)	běn	bun
Stick-like things, such as string or blades of grass	gēn	gun
Things with flat surfaces such as tables or beds	zhāng	jahng
Round, tiny things such as pearls	kē	kuh

Subject	Verb	Number	Classifier	Object
I	want	a / one		book
Wǒ	yào	yī	bēn	shū
You	buy	three		tables
Nǐ	mǎi	sān	zhāng	zhuō zi

THIS & THAT

English	Pinyin	Pronunciation
This	zhè (ge)	jay (guh)
That	nà (ge)	nah (guh)
These	zhè xiē	jay-shyeh
Those	nà xiē	nay-shyeh

DEFINITE VS. INDEFINITE ARTICLES

Equivalents to the English articles "a," "an," and "the" do not exist in Chinese. The only way to tell if something is being referred to specifically (definite) or just generally (indefinite) is by the word order.

Nouns that refer specifically to something are usually found at the beginning of a sentence before the verb:

yǐ zi zài nàr. (The chairs are there.)

hái zi xǐ huān tā. (The child likes him.)

dāo zài zhuō zi shàng. (The knife / knives are on the table.)

Nouns that refer to something more general are usually found at the end of the sentence, after the verb:

nǎ r yǒu shū? (Where are some books? / Where is there a book?)

nà r yǒu shū. (There are some books over there.)

zhè ge yǒu wèn tí. (There's a problem with this. / There are some problems with this.)

EXCEPTIONS TO DEFINITE VS. INDEFINITE ARTICLES

Several exceptions to the above rules on definite vs. indefinite articles exist in Chinese:

- If a noun is at the beginning of a sentence it might refer to something indefinite if the sentence makes a general comment (as opposed to relating an entire story), like when the verb **shì** is part of the comment: **xióng māo shì dòng wù.** (Pandas are animals.)

- If an adjective appears after the noun it might also indicate an indefinite article: **pú tao hěn tián**. (Grapes are very sweet.)

- If an auxiliary verb exists it might also indicate an indefinite article: **māo huì zhuā lǎo shǔ.** (Cats can catch mice.)

- If a verb indicates that the action occurs habitually it may indicate an indefinite article: **niú chī cǎo.** (Cows eat grass.)

- Nouns preceded by a numeral and a classifier are considered definite: **wǔ gè xué sheng dōu hěn cōng ming.** (The five students are all quite smart.)

- If the word **yǒu** (to exist) comes before the noun and is then followed by a verb, it can also indicate an indefinite article: **yǒu shū zài zhuō zi shàng.** (There are books on top of the table.)

- Finally, if the word **zhè** (this) or **nà** (that), plus a classifier is used when a noun comes after the verb, it indicates a definite reference: **wǒ yào mǎi nà zhāng huà.** (I want to buy that painting.)

ADJECTIVES

If an adjective is pronounced with only one syllable it appears immediately in front of the noun it qualifies:

lǜ chá (green tea)

cháng gǔ tóu (long bone)

If the adjective has two syllables, however, the possessive particle de (duh) is placed between it and whatever it qualifies:

gàn jìng de yī fu (clean clothes)

chǎo nào de hái zi (noisy child / children)

If a numeral is followed by a classifier, those should both go in front of the adjective and whatever it qualifies:

yī jiàn xīn yī fu (a [piece of] new clothing)

sì běn yǒu qù de shū (four interesting books)

Finally, when an adjective is also the predicate, appearing at the end of a sentence, it follows the subject or the topic without needing the verb shì (shir; to be):

tā de fáng zi hěn gān jìng. (His house [is] very clean.)

nà jiàn yī fu tài jiù. (That piece of clothing [is] too old.)

VERBS

There is no conjugation of verbs in Chinese. The verb in the sentence "They eat Chinese food" is said the same way as in the sentence "He eats Chinese food." There are ways to indicate tense in Chinese sentences, but these are noted in the section on "Aspect Markers" below. The verb itself is never inflected. Below are some of the most common verbs in Chinese:

English	Pinyin	Pronunciation
To read	kàn	kahn
I read books.	wǒ kàn shū.	Waw kahn shoo.
To have	yǒu	yo
We have books.	wǒ mén yǒu shū.	Waw mun yo shoo.
To want	yào	yow
She wants cake.	tā yào dàn gāo.	Tah yow dahn gow.
To Be	shì	shir
We are Chinese.	wǒ mén shì zhōng guó rén.	Waw mun shir joong gwaw run.
To study	xué xí	shweh she
You study Chinese.	nǐ xué xí hàn yǔ.	Nee shweh she hahn yew.
To know	zhī dào	jir dow
I know him.	wǒ zhī dào tā.	Waw jir dow tah.

NOTE: The verb **yǒu** (to have) can also be translated as "there is" or "there are." Examples: **yǒu hěn duō hái zi** (There are many children); **wǒ yǒu hěn duō hái zi**. (I have many children.)

ASPECT MARKERS (EXPRESSIONS OF TENSE)

Aspects characterize the Chinese language in place of tense and refer to how a speaker views an event or a state of being. There are only two aspects in Chinese: complete and continuous, as opposed to English, which has many different aspects such as indefinite, continuous, perfect, perfect continuous, etc.

Le

Le indicates an action has been completed if it's used as a suffix to a verb:

English	Pinyin	Pronunciation
You bought many books.	nǐ mǎi le hěn duō shū.	Nee my luh hun dwaw shoo.
He brought his umbrella.	tā dài le tā de yǔ sǎn.	Tah dye luh tah duh yew sahn.

Le in Questions

To turn statements with le into questions, add meiyou at the end of them, which automatically negates the action completed by le:

English	Pinyin	Pronunciation
You bought many books.	nǐ mǎi le hěn duō shū.	Nee my luh hun dwaw shoo.
Did he bring his umbrella?	tā yǒu méi yǒu dài tā de yǔ sǎn?	Tah yo mayo dye tah duh yew sahn?

Guò

Guò indicates that something has been done at one time or another, even though it is not currently happening.

English	Pinyin	Pronunciation
He has been to France.	tā qù guò fǎ guó.	Tah chyew gwaw fah gwaw.
We have eaten French food.	wǒ mén chī guò fǎ guó cài.	Waw mun chir gwaw fah gwaw tsye.

Zài

Zài indicates if an action is currently happening as you speak. You can also add the word **zhèng** in front of it to add emphasis, which can be translated as "to be right in the middle of" doing something.

English	Pinyin	Pronunciation
We are eating.	wǒ mén zài chī fàn.	Waw mun dzye chir fahn.
We're in the middle of eating.	wǒ mén zhèng zài chī fàn.	Waw mun juhng dzye chir fahn.
Your father is cooking.	nǐ bà ba zài zuò fàn.	Nee bah bah dzye dzwaw fahn.
Your father is right in the middle of cooking.	nǐ bà ba zhèng zài zuò fàn.	Nee bah bah juhng dzye dzwaw fahn.

Zhe

To indicate continual action resulting from something else, add the syllable **zhe** to the end of the verb:

English	Pinyin	Pronunciation
He's wearing a red hat.	tā dài zhe yī dǐng hóng mào zi.	Tah dye juh ee deeng hoong maow dzuh.
You're wearing a yellow shirt.	nín chuān zhe yī jiàn huáng chèn shān.	Nee chwahn juh ee jyan hwahng chun shahn.

Zhe can also indicate two actions occurring at the same time:

English	Pinyin	Pronunciation
She's sitting and eating.	tā zài zuò zhe chī fàn.	Tah dzye dzwaw juh chir fahn.
He's singing while he walks.	tā zǒu zhe chàng gē.	Tah dzoe juh chahng guh.

NEGATION

Bù

Bù can negate something done in the past, present or anticipated for the future.

English	Pinyin	Pronunciation
She didn't like to eat spinach when she was young.	tā xiǎo de shí hòu bù xǐ huān chī bō cài.	Tah shyaow duh shir ho boo she hwahn chir baw tsye.
They don't want to sing.	tā men bú yào chàng gē.	Tah mun boo yow chahng guh.
The restaurant won't be open on Friday.	fàn diàn xīng qī wǔ bù kāi mén.	Fahn dyan sheeng chee woo boo kye mun.

Méi yǒu

To negate the verb **yǒu**, the usual negative prefix **bù** cannot be used. Instead you must use the prefix **méi**.

English	Pinyin	Pronunciation
We don't have books.	wǒ mén méi yǒu shū.	Waw mun may yo shoo.
They don't have dogs.	tā mén méi yǒu gǒu.	Tah mun may yo go.

QUESTIONS

The simplest way to ask a question in Chinese is to end any statement with the particle **ma**.

English	Pinyin	Pronunciation
Does he read?	tā kàn shū ma?	Tah kahn shoo mah?
Do you speak English?	nǐ shuō yīng yǔ ma?	Nee shwaw eeng yew mah?

Alternate choice questions

Another way to pose questions is by repeating the verb in its negative form by inserting **bù** in between the repeating verbs. This form can only be used for a yes or no question.

English	Pinyin	Pronunciation
Are you an American?	nǐ shì bù shì měi guó rén?	Nee shir boo shir may gwaw run?
Does she want children?	tā yào bù yào hái zi?	Ta yow boo yow hi dzuh?

POSSESSIVES

The particle **de** is attached to the end of a pronoun or other modifier to indicate possession.

English	Pinyin	Pronunciation
My computer has Internet.	wǒ de jì suàn jī yǒu yīn tè wǎng.	Waw duh dyan now yo een tuh wahng.
Does yours?	nǐ de ne?	Nee duh nuh?

Interrogative Pronouns

Another way to ask questions in Chinese is by using the following interrogative pronouns:

English	Pinyin	Pronunciation
Who / whom	shéi	shay
Whose	shéi de	shay duh
What	shénme	shummah
Which	nǎ (+ classifier)	nah
Where	nǎr	nar

FUN FACTS

Government   Socialist Republic

Capital   Beijing

Largest City   Shanghai (9.8 million people)

Official Currency   Yuán (¥)

Official Dialect   There are hundreds of Chinese dialects, but Mandarin is the official language.

Surface Area   3.7 million square miles ($1/15$ of the world's land mass)

Population   1.3 billion, making it the world's most populous country.

Number of Cell Phones   440 million

Economy   China has seen a breathtaking 9% average annual GDP growth rate since reforms began in 1979. More than $3 billion in business transactions are conducted annually between the U.S. and China, with U.S. investments totaling over $15 billion.

History   Two of China's 12 major dynasties were ruled by non-Chinese: The Mongols under Genghis and Kublai Khan ruled the Yuan dynasty (1279-1368), and the Manchus of Manchuria ruled China's last dynasty, the Qing (1644-1911).

Literature   Noel Coward penned "Private Lives" at the Cathay Hotel (now known as the Peace Hotel) along the Bund in Shanghai in 1930.

GREAT MOMENTS

Strolling Past the Old Russian Architecture in Harbin   At the heart of the Russian-built city, Zhongyang Dajie's unexpected cupola-topped Art Nouveau mansions are reminders of the 1920s and 1930s, when Harbin was the liveliest stop on this leg of the Trans-Siberian Railroad.

Exploring the Forbidden City's Forgotten Corners (Beijing)   No one fails to be impressed by the grandeur of the Forbidden City's central axis, which is all most visitors see. But the quieter maze of pavilions, gardens, courtyards, and theaters to either side have the greater charm.

Dining on Shanghai's Bund China's most famous waterfront street of colonial architecture, the Bund, has become the toniest address in town, with the redevelopment of a few formerly stodgy old buildings into some of the city's finest shopping and dining establishments. These rooftop restaurants offer unsurpassed views of Shanghai, old and new.

Cycling the City Wall in Xi'an The largest city walls in China have been much pierced for modern purposes and can be tackled in a modern way, too, with a breezy, traffic-light-free ride above the rooftops on rented bicycles and tandems. Behold views of remnants of vernacular architecture, clustered around small temples.

Exploring Li Jiang's Old Town Built over 800 years ago and partly rebuilt after a massive 1996 earthquake, Li Jiang's old town, with its maze of cobblestone streets, gurgling streams, and original and reconstructed traditional Naxi houses, is one of the most atmospheric places in China, hordes of tourists notwithstanding. Rise before the sun, then watch its golden rays filter through the gray winding streets, lighting up the dark wooden houses.

Walking on the Great Wall from Jinshanling to Simatai (Beijing) The Great Wall, winding snakelike through the mountains, was meant to be walked. This magnificent 3-hour hike follows China's greatest monument through various states of repair, from freshly restored to thoroughly crumbling, over steep peaks and gentle flats, and through patches of wilderness and rugged farmland, with over two dozen watchtowers along the way.

Riding the Star Ferry (Hong Kong) There's no better way to get acquainted with Hong Kong than to ride the cheapest cruise in China. The century-old green-and-white Star ferries weave between tugs, junks, and oceangoing vessels in a 5-minute harbor crossing, and thanks to the wonderful Suzy Wong novel, remain one of the territories' premier attractions.

Exploring the karst scenery around Yangshuo The cruise down the now polluted Li River between Guilin and Yangshuo may be overexposed and overpriced, but the scenery area remains captivating. Avoid the pricey taxis and motorbike rentals and explore instead in traditional Chinese style, by bicycle. Both the Yulong River and the Jin Bao are still relatively peaceful as they flick lazily through serrated hills like dragon's teeth.

Unwinding in a Sichuan Teahouse One of the great pleasures of being in Sichuan is drinking tea at a neighborhood teahouse. On any given afternoon at Qingyang Gong in Chengdu, for instance, seniors can be found playing mahjong with friends while their caged songbirds sit in nearby trees providing ambient music. As patrons eat watermelon seeds, nuts, dried squid, or beef jerky, attendants appear at regular intervals to refill their cups from copper kettles. For an afternoon of perfect relaxation, stop by and forget about sightseeing for a few hours.

Gazing at the Sea of Terra-Cotta Warriors at the Tomb of Qin Shi Huang (Xi'an) The first sight of the tomb, in a hangarlike building, leaves many visitors stunned and awed. This destination is at the top of almost every visitor's list, and it does not disappoint.

Strolling in Shanghai's French Concession The domain of the French community up until 1949 was colonial Shanghai's trendiest area, and it remains full of tree-lined boulevards, colonial mansions, and Art Deco masterpieces, now bundled up with phone lines and pole-hung washing. Some of the city's best shopping is also here. Just beyond the former concession is one of modern Shanghai's trendiest areas, the mega-development of restaurants and shops known as Xin Tiandi.

Getting Lost in the lanes around Beijing's Back Lakes No other city in the world has anything quite like the hutong, narrow lanes once "as numberless as the hairs on an ox." Now rapidly vanishing, the best-preserved hutong are found around a pair of man-made lakes in the city center. This area is almost the last repository of Old Beijing's gritty, low-rise charm, dotted with tiny temples, hole-in-the-wall noodle shops, and quiet courtyard houses whose older residents still wear Mao suits.

Strolling the Old Neighborhoods of Kashgar   The dusty alleys, colorful residential doorways, and mud-brick walls remain as they have been for decades. Kids with henna-dyed feet and fingernails will approach you speaking a few words of Chinese and English; men with donkey carts trudge down narrow passages; bakers arrange round large slabs of nan in coal ovens built into the ground. Spending hours watching how citizens of Kashgar live is one of the most rewarding experiences along the Silk Road.

Taking a "Peapod" Boat on Shennong Stream (Yangzi River)   Best of the Three Gorges cruise excursions, this 2-hour journey through a long, narrow canyon takes passengers to one of the famous suspended coffins of the Ba people, then returns them downstream in a fraction of the time. Along the way, howler monkeys may be spotted swinging through the trees, small waterfalls appear from the rocks, and swallows and other small birds flit about. The water in this small tributary is surprisingly clear, and the scenery and silence are thoroughly calming.

CHAPTER TWO

GETTING THERE & GETTING AROUND

This section deals with every form of transportation. Whether you've just reached your destination by plane or you're renting a car to tour the countryside, you'll find the phrases you need in the next 25 pages.

AT THE AIRPORT

I am looking for ____	我在找_____
	wǒ zài zhǎo _____
a porter.	行李搬运工。
	xíng li bān yùn gōng。
the check-in counter.	值机柜台。
	zhí jī guì tái。
the ticket counter.	售票台。
	shòu piào tái。
arrivals.	飞机到达处。
	fēi jī dào dá chù。
departures.	飞机起飞处。
	fēi jī qǐ fēi chù。
gate number ____.	登机口号_____。
	dēng jī kǒu hào _____。

For full coverage of numbers, see p7.

the waiting area.	等候处。
	děng hòu chù。
the men's restroom.	男洗手间。
	nán xǐ shǒu jiān。
the women's restroom.	女洗手间。
	nǚ xǐ shǒu jiān。
the police station.	警察局。
	jǐng chá jú。
a security guard.	保安。
	bǎo ān。

the smoking area.	吸烟区。
	xī yān qū。
the information booth.	问讯台。
	wèn xùn tái。
a public telephone.	公用电话。
	gōng yòng diàn huà。
an ATM.	**ATM**。
	ATM。
baggage claim.	行李领取处。
	xíng li lǐng qǔ chù。
a luggage cart.	行李手推车。
	xíng li shǒu tuī chē。
a currency exchange.	货币兑换处。
	huò bì duì huàn chù。
a café.	咖啡馆。
	kā fēi guǎn。
a restaurant.	饭店。
	fàn diàn。
a bar.	酒吧。
	jiǔ bā。
a bookstore or newsstand.	书店或报亭。
	shū diàn huò bào tíng。
a duty-free shop.	免税商店。
	miǎn shuì shāng diàn。

Is there Internet access here?	这能上网吗?
	zhè néng shàng wǎng ma?
I'd like to page someone.	我想呼叫某人。
	wǒ xiǎng hū jiào mǒu rén。
Do you accept credit cards?	可以用信用卡吗?
	ké yǐ yòng xìn yòng kǎ ma?

CHECKING IN

| I would like a one-way ticket to ____. | 我想要一张到____的单程票。 |
| | *wǒ xiǎng yào yī zhāng dào ____ de dān chéng piào。* |

I would like a round trip ticket to ____.

我想要一张到_____的往返票。

wǒ xiǎng yào yī zhāng dào _____ de wǎng fǎn piào。

How much are the tickets?

这些票多少钱?

zhè xiē piào duō shǎo qián?

Do you have anything less expensive?

有便宜一些的吗?

yǒu pián yi yī xiē de ma?

How long is the flight?

飞行时间有多长?

fēi xíng shí jiān yǒu duō cháng?

For full coverage of number terms, see p7.
For full coverage of time, see p12.

What time does flight ____ leave?

_____航班什么时候起飞?

_____ háng bān shén me shí hòu qǐ fēi?

What time does flight ____ arrive?

_____航班什么时候到达?

_____ háng bān shén me shí hòu dào dá?

Do I have a connecting flight?

我需要中转航班吗?

wǒ xū yào zhōng zhuǎn háng bān ma?

Do I need to change planes?

我需要转机吗?

wǒ xū yào zhuǎn jī ma?

My flight leaves at __:__.

我的航班在__:__起飞。

wǒ de háng bān zài __:__ qǐ fēi。

For full coverage of numbers, see p7.

What time will the flight arrive?

航班何时到达?

háng bān hé shí dào dá?

Is the flight on time?

此次航班准时吗?

cǐ cì háng bān zhǔn shí ma?

Is the flight delayed?

此次航班延误了吗?

cǐ cì háng bān yán wù le ma?

From which terminal is flight ____ leaving?

航班_____从哪个航站起飞?

háng bān _____ cóng nǎ gè háng zhàn qǐ fēi?

Common Airport Signs

飞机进港	Arrivals
飞机出港	Departures
候机楼	Terminal
登机口	Gate
票务	Ticketing
海关	Customs
行李领取处	Baggage Claim
推	Push
拉	Pull
禁止吸烟	No Smoking
入口	Entrance
出口	Exit
男洗手间	Men's
女洗手间	Women's
机场巴士	Shuttle Buses
出租车	Taxis

From which gate is flight ____ leaving?	航班 _____ 从哪个登机口起飞？ *háng bān _____ cóng nǎ gè dēng jī kǒu qǐ fēi?*
How much time do I need for check-in?	我需要花多长时间办理登机手续？ *wǒ xū yào huā duō cháng shí jiān bàn lǐ dēng jī shǒu xù?*
Is there an express check-in line?	是否有快速登机队列？ *shì fǒu yǒu kuài sù dēng jī duì liè?*
Is there electronic check-in?	可以进行电子登机吗？ *kě yǐ jin xíng diàn zǐ dēng jī ma?*

Seat Preferences

I would like ____ ticket(s) in ____
  first class.
	我要买_____张_____票。
	wǒ yào mǎi ____ zhāng ____piào。
	  头等舱
	  tóu děng cāng

business class.	商务舱 *shāng wù cāng*
economy class.	经济舱 *jīng jì cāng*
I would like ____	我想要____ *wǒ xiǎng yào* ____
Please don't give me ____	请不要给我____ *qǐng bù yào gěi wǒ* ____
a window seat.	靠窗的座位。 *kào chuāng de zuò wèi。*
an aisle seat.	靠过道的座位。 *kào guò dào de zuò wèi。*
an emergency exit row seat.	靠应急舱门的座位。 *kào yìng jí cāng mén de zuò wèi。*
a bulkhead seat.	第一排靠前挡板的座位。 *dì yī pái kào qián dǎng bǎn de zuò wèi。*
a seat by the restroom.	卫生间旁的座位。 *wèi shēng jiān páng de zuò wèi。*
a seat near the front.	靠前的座位。 *kào qián de zuò wèi。*
a seat near the middle.	靠中间的座位。 *kào zhōng jiān de zuò wèi。*
a seat near the back.	靠后的座位。 *kào hòu de zuò wèi。*
Is there a meal on the flight?	航班上是否供应膳食? *háng bān shàng shì fǒu gōng yìng shàn shí?*
I'd like to order ____	我想订____ *wǒ xiǎng dìng* ____
a vegetarian meal.	一套素餐。 *yī tào sù cān。*
a kosher meal.	一套犹太教徒餐。 *yī tào yóu tài jiào tú cān。*
a diabetic meal.	一套糖尿病人餐。 *yī tào táng niào bìng rén cān。*

GETTING THERE

I am traveling to ____.	我要前往_____。
	wǒ yào qián wǎng _____。
I am coming from ____.	我来自_____。
	wǒ lái zì _____。
I arrived from ____.	我从_____来。
	wǒ cóng _____ lái。

For full coverage of country terms, see English / Chinese dictionary.

I'd like to change / cancel / confirm my reservation.	我想更改 / 取消 / 确认我的预定。
	wǒ xiǎng gēng gǎi / qǔ xiāo / què rèn wǒ de yù dìng。
I have ____ bags to check.	我有_____个旅行袋需要托运。
	wǒ yǒu _____ gè lǚ xíng dài xū yào tuō yùn。

For full coverage of numbers, see p7.

Passengers with Special Needs

Is that wheelchair accessible?	可以使用那个轮椅吗?
	kě yǐ shǐ yòng nà gè lún yǐ ma?
May I have a wheelchair / walker please?	我可以用轮椅 / 助行器吗?
	wǒ kě yǐ yòng lún yǐ / zhù xíng qì ma?
I need some assistance boarding.	我需要登机帮助。
	wǒ xūyào dēng jī bāng zhù。
I need to bring my service dog.	我需要带上我的帮助犬。
	wǒ xū yào dài shàng wǒ de bāng zhù quǎn。
Do you have services for the hearing impaired?	有为听障人士提供的服务吗?
	yǒu wéi tīng zhàng rén shì tí gōng de fú wù ma?
Do you have services for the visually impaired?	有为视障人士提供的服务吗?
	yǒu wéi shì zhàng rén shì tí gōng de fú wù ma?

Trouble at Check-In

How long is the delay?	延误时间有多长?
	yán wù shí jiān yǒu duō cháng?

My flight was late.	我的航班晚点了。
	wǒ de háng bān wǎn diǎn le。
I missed my flight.	我错过了航班。
	wǒ cuò guò le háng bān。
When is the next flight?	下一次航班是什么时间?
	xià yī cì háng bān shì shén me shí jiān?
May I have a meal voucher?	可以给我一张就餐优惠券吗?
	kě yǐ gěi wǒ yī zhāng jiù cān yōu huì quàn ma?
May I have a room voucher?	可以给我一张客房优惠券吗?
	kě yǐ gěi wǒ yī zhāng kè fáng yōu huì quàn ma?

AT CUSTOMS / SECURITY CHECKPOINTS

I'm traveling with a group.	我随团旅行。
	wǒ suí tuán lǚ xíng。
I'm on my own.	我单独旅行。
	wǒ dān dú lǚ xíng。
I'm traveling on business.	我因公旅行。
	wǒ yīn gōng lǚ xíng。
I'm on vacation.	我在休假。
	wǒ zài xiū jià。
I have nothing to declare.	我没有要申报的东西。
	wǒ méi yǒu yào shēn bào de dōng xi。
I would like to declare ____.	我要申报_____。
	wǒ yào shēn bào _____。
I have some liquor.	我带了一些白酒。
	wǒ dài le yī xiē bái jiǔ。
I have some cigars.	我带了一些雪茄。
	wǒ dài le yī xiē xuě jiā。
They are gifts.	这些都是礼物。
	zhè xiē dōu shì lǐ wù。
They are for personal use.	这些都是个人物品。
	zhè xiē dōu shì gè rén wù pǐn。

That is my medicine.	那是我的药。
	nà shì wǒ de yào.
I have my prescription.	我有处方。
	wǒ yǒu chǔ fāng.
My children are traveling on the same passport.	我的孩子与我持同一本护照旅行。
	wǒ de hái zi yǔ wǒ chí tóng yī běn hù zhào lǚ xíng.
I'd like a male / female officer to conduct the search.	我需要一名男 / 女官员进行搜查。
	wǒ xū yào yī míng nán / nǚ guān yuán jìn xíng sōu chá.

Trouble at Security

Help me. I've lost _____	帮帮我。我丢了_____
	bāng bāng wǒ. wǒ diū le _____
my passport.	我的护照。
	wǒ de hù zhào.
my boarding pass.	我的登机牌。
	wǒ de dēng jī pái.

Listen Up: Security Lingo

请脱掉您的鞋。	Please remove your shoes.
qǐng tuō diào nín de xié.	
脱掉您的上衣 / 毛衣。	Remove your jacket / sweater.
tuō diào nín de shàng yī / máo yī.	
摘下您的首饰。	Remove your jewelry.
zhāi xià nín de shǒu shì.	
把您的包放在传送带上。	Place your bags on the conveyor belt.
bǎ nín de bāo fàng zài chuán sòng dài shàng.	
走到这边。	Step to the side.
zǒu dào zhè biān.	
我们必须进行手工搜查。	We have to do a hand search.
wǒ mén bì xū jìn xíng shǒu gōng sōu chá.	

my identification.	我的身份证。
	wǒ de shēn fèn zhèng。
my wallet.	我的钱夹。
	wǒ de qián jiā。
my purse.	我的钱包。
	wǒ de qián bāo。
Someone stole	有人偷了我的钱包 / 钱夹!
my purse / wallet!	yǒu rén tōu le! wǒ de qián bāo /
	qián jiā!

IN-FLIGHT

It's unlikely you'll need much Chinese on the plane, but these phrases will help if a bilingual flight attendant is unavailable or if you need to talk to a Chinese-speaking neighbor.

I think that's my seat.	我想这是我的座位。
	wǒ xiǎng shì wǒ de zuò wèi。
May I have _____	可以给我_____
	kě yǐ gěi wǒ _____
water?	水吗?
	shuǐ ma?
sparkling water?	汽水吗?
	qì shuǐ ma?
orange juice?	橙汁吗?
	chéng zhī ma?
soda?	苏打水吗?
	sū dá shuǐ ma?
diet soda?	减肥苏打水吗?
	jiǎn féi sū dá shuǐ ma?
a beer?	啤酒吗?
	pí jiǔ ma?
wine?	葡萄酒吗?
	pú tao jiǔ ma?

For a complete list of drinks, see p87.

a pillow?	一个枕垫吗?
	yī gè zhěn diàn ma?

GETTING THERE

a blanket?	一条毯子吗？
	yī tiáo tǎn zi ma?
a hand wipe?	一张手纸帕吗？
	yī zhāng shǒu zhǐ pà ma?
headphones?	耳机吗？
	ěr jī ma?
a magazine or newspaper?	一本杂志或报纸吗？
	yī běn zá zhì huò bào zhǐ ma?
When will the meal be served?	什么时候供餐？
	shén me shí hou gòng cān?
How long until we land?	还有多长时间着陆？
	hái yǒu duō cháng shí jiān zhuó lù?
May I move to another seat?	我可以移到另一个座位吗？
	wǒ kě yǐ yí dào lìng yī gè zuò wèi ma?
How do I turn the light on / off?	我怎样开 / 关灯？
	wǒ zěn yàng kāi / guān dēng?

Trouble In-Flight

These headphones are broken.	这些耳机坏了。
	zhè xiē ěr jī huài le.
I spilled.	我把___弄洒了。
	wǒ bǎ ___ nòng sǎ le.
My child spilled.	我的孩子把___弄洒了。
	wǒ de hái zǐ bǎ ___ nòng sǎ le.
My child is sick.	我的孩子病了。
	wǒ de hái zi bìng le.
I need an airsickness bag.	我需要一个呕吐袋。
	wǒ xū yào yī gè ǒu tù dài.
I smell something strange.	我闻到奇怪的味道。
	wǒ wén dào qí guài de wèi dào.
That passenger is behaving suspiciously.	那个乘客的行为很可疑。
	nà gè chéng kè de xíng wéi hěn kě yí.

BAGGAGE CLAIM

Where is baggage claim for flight ____?	在哪里领取航班 ____ 的行李? *zài nǎ lǐ lǐng qǔ háng bān ____ de xíng li?*
Would you please help with my bags?	您能帮我拿一下这些袋子吗? *nín néng bāng wǒ ná yī xià zhè xiē dài zi ma?*
I am missing ____ bags.	我丢失了一个 ____ 袋子。 *wǒ diū shī le gè ____ dài zi.*

For full coverage of numbers, see p7.

My bag is ____ 我的包 ____
wǒ de bāo ____

lost. 丢了。
diū le.

damaged. 坏了。
huài le.

stolen. 被盗了。
bèi dào le.

a suitcase. 是一只手提箱。
shì yī zhī shǒu tí xiāng.

a briefcase. 是一个公文包。
shì yī gè gōng wén bāo.

a carry-on. 是手提行李。
shì shǒu tí xíng li.

a suit bag. 是衣服袋。
shì yī fu dài.

a trunk. 是大衣箱。
shì dà yī xiāng.

golf clubs. 是高尔夫球包。
shì gāo ěr fū qiú bāo.

For full coverage of color terms, see English / Chinese Dictionary.

hard. 很硬。
hěn yìng.

made out of ____ 是用____
shì yòng ____

canvas.	帆布做的。 *fān bù zuò de。*
vinyl.	乙烯树脂做的。 *yǐ xī shù zhī zuò de。*
leather.	皮革做的。 *pí gé zuò de。*
hard plastic.	硬塑料做的。 *yìng sù liào zuò de。*
aluminum.	铝做的。 *lǚ zuò de。*

RENTING A VEHICLE

Is there a car rental agency in the airport?	机场有汽车租赁公司吗？ *jī chǎng yǒu qì chē zū lìn gōng sī ma?*
I have a reservation.	我已预定。 *wǒ yǐ yù dìng。*

Vehicle Preferences

I would like to rent ____	我要租用_____ *wǒ yào zū yòng _____*
an economy car.	一辆经济型轿车。 *yī liàng jīng jì xíng jiào chē。*
a midsize car.	一辆中型轿车。 *yī liàng zhōng xíng jiào chē。*
a sedan.	箱式小轿车。 *xiāng shì xiǎo jiào chē。*
a convertible.	一辆敞篷汽车。 *yī liàng chǎng péng qì chē。*
a van.	面包车。 *miàn bāo chē。*
a sports car.	一辆跑车。 *yī liàng pǎo chē。*
a 4-wheel-drive vehicle.	一辆四轮驱动汽车。 *yī liàng sì lún qū dòng qì chē。*
a motorcycle.	一辆摩托车。 *yī liàng mó tuō chē。*

a scooter.

一辆踏板车。

yī liàng tà bǎn chē.

Do you have one with _____

您的车有_____

nín de chē yǒu _____

air conditioning?

空调吗？

kōng tiáo ma?

a sunroof?

天窗吗？

tiān chuāng ma?

a CD player?

CD 播放器吗？

CD bō fàng qì ma?

satellite radio?

卫星广播吗？

wèi xīng guǎng bō ma?

satellite tracking?

卫星定位吗？

wèi xīng dìng wèi ma?

an onboard map?

车载地图吗？

chē zǎi dì tú ma?

a DVD player?

DVD 播放器吗？

DVD bō fàng qì ma?

child seats?

儿童座椅吗？

ér tóng zuò yǐ ma?

Do you have a _____

您有_____

nín yǒu _____

smaller car?

小一点的车吗？

xiǎo yī diǎn de chē ma?

bigger car?

大一点的车吗？

dà yī diǎn de chē ma?

cheaper car?

便宜一点的车吗？

pián yi yī diǎn de chē ma?

Do you have a non-smoking car?

您有非吸烟车吗？

nín yǒu fēi xī yān chē ma?

I need an automatic transmission.

我需要带自动变速器的。

wǒ xū yào dài zì dòng biàn sù qì de.

A standard transmission is okay.	有标准变速器就可以了。 *yǒu biāo zhǔn biàn sù qì jiù kě yǐ le.*
May I have an upgrade?	我可以要求升级吗？ *wǒ kě yǐ yāo qiú shēng jí ma?*

Money Matters

What's the daily / weekly / monthly rate?	日 / 周 / 月租金是多少？ *rì / zhōu / yuè zū jīn shì duō shǎo?*
What is the mileage rate?	里程运价费是多少？ *lǐ chéng yùn jià fèi shì duō shǎo?*
How much is insurance?	保险是多少？ *bǎo xiǎn shì duō shǎo?*
Are there other fees?	还有其他费用吗？ *hái yǒu qí tā fèi yòng ma?*
Is there a weekend rate?	有周末价吗？ *yǒu zhōu mò jià ma?*

Technical Questions

What kind of fuel does it take?	使用什么汽油？ *shǐ yòng shén me qì yóu?*
Do you have the manual in English?	有英语的手册吗？ *yǒu yīng yǔ de shǒu cè ma?*
Do you have a booklet in English with the local traffic laws?	有英文的地方交通法规手册吗？ *yǒu yīng wén de dì fāng jiāo tōng fǎ guī shǒu cè ma?*

Car Troubles

The ＿＿＿ doesn't work.	＿＿＿坏了。 ＿＿＿ *huài le.*

See diagram on p51 for car parts.

It is already dented.	这里已经凹进去了。 *zhè lǐ yǐ jīng āo jìn qù le.*
It is scratched.	这里有刮痕。 *zhè lǐ yǒu guā hén.*

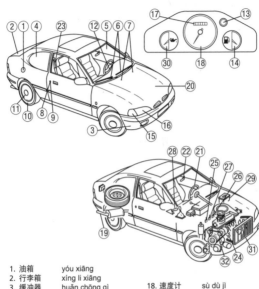

1. 油箱	yóu xiāng	18. 速度计	sù dù jì
2. 行李箱	xíng li xiāng	19. 消声器	xiāo shēng qì
3. 缓冲器	huǎn chōng qì	20. 引擎罩	yǐn qíng zhào
4. 车窗	chē chuāng	21. 方向盘	fāng xiàng pán
5. 挡风玻璃	dǎng fēng bō li	22. 后视镜	hòu shì jìng
6. 风档雨雪刷	fēng dàng yǔ xuě shuā	23. 安全带	ān quán dài
7. 洗涤壶	xǐ dí hú	24. 发动机	fā dòng jī
8. 车门	chē mén	25. 加速器	jiā sù qì
9. 车门锁	chē mén suǒ	26. 离合器	lí hé qì
10. 轮胎	lún tāi	27. 刹车	shā chē
11. 轮毂罩	lún gū zhào	28. 手制动器	shǒu zhì dòng qì
12. 方向盘	fāng xiàng pán	29. 蓄电池	xù diàn chí
13. 应急灯	yìng jí dēng	30. 机油压力表	jī yóu yā lì biǎo
14. 油量计	yóu liàng jì	31. 散热器	sàn rè qì
15. 转弯灯	zhuǎn wān dēng	32. 风扇皮带	fēng shàn pí dài
16. 前灯	qián dēng		
17. 里程表	lǐ chéng biǎo		

Please fill it up with _____. 请帮我加满
qǐng bāng wǒ jiā mǎn

   regular. 普通汽油
pǔ tōng qì yóu

   unleaded. 无铅汽油
wú qiān qì yóu

   diesel. 柴油
chái yóu

The tires look low. 轮胎好像要没气了。
lún tāi hǎo xiàng yào méi qì le。

It has a flat tire. 爆胎了。
bào tāi le。

It won't start. 这辆汽车发动不起来。
zhè liàng qì chē fā dòng bù qǐ lái。

It's out of gas. 车没油了。
chē méi yóu le。

The Check Engine light 引擎检验灯是亮的。
is on. *yǐn qíng jiǎn yàn dēng shì liàng de。*

The oil light is on. 机油灯是亮的。
jī yóu dēng shì liàng de。

The brake light is on. 刹车灯是亮的。
shā chē dēng shì liàng de。

It runs rough. 运转不平稳。
yùn zhuǎn bù píng wěn。

The car is over-heating. 汽车过热。
qì chē guò rè。

Asking for Directions

Excuse me, please. 打扰您一下。
dǎ rǎo nín yī xià。

How do I get to _____? 到_____怎么走?
dào _____ zěn me zǒu?

Go straight. 直走。
zhí zǒu。

Turn left. 向左转。
xiàng zuǒ zhuǎn。

Continue right.	继续向右。
	jì xù xiàng yòu。
It's on the right.	在右侧。
	zài yòu cè。
Can you show me on the map?	您能在地图上指给我看吗?
	nín néng zài dì tú shàng zhǐ gěi wǒ kàn ma?
How far is it from here?	那里离这有多远?
	nà lǐ lí zhè yǒu duō yuǎn?
Is this the right road for ____?	这是到_____的路吗?
	zhè shì dào _____ de lù ma?
I've lost my way.	我迷路了。
	wǒ mí lù le。
Would you repeat that?	请您再重复一遍好吗?
	qǐng nín zài chóng fù yī biàn hǎo ma?
Thanks for your help.	谢谢您的帮助。
	xiè xiè nín de bāng zhù。

For full coverage of direction-related terms, see p5.

Road Signs

限速	Speed Limit
停止	Stop
避让	Yield
危险	Danger
无出口	No Exit
单行线	One Way
不准驶入	Do Not Enter
道路封闭	Road Closed
通行费	Toll
只收现金	Cash Only
禁止停车	No Parking
停车费	Parking Fee
停车场	Parking Garage

Sorry, Officer

What is the speed limit?	限速是多少？
	xiàn sù shì duō shǎo?
I wasn't going that fast.	我没有开那么快。
	wǒ méi yǒu kāi nà me kuài.
How much is the fine?	罚款是多少？
	fá kuǎn shì duō shǎo?
Where do I pay the fine?	我在哪里交罚款？
	wǒ zài nǎ lǐ jiāo fá kuǎn?
Do I have to go to court?	我必须要上法庭吗？
	wǒ bì xū yào shàng fǎ tíng ma?
I had an accident.	我出了事故。
	wǒ chū le shì gù.
The other driver hit me.	我被别的车撞了。
	wǒ bèi bié de chē zhuàng le.
I'm at fault.	我是过错方。
	wǒ shì guò cuò fāng.

BY TAXI

Where is the taxi stand?	出租车站在哪里？
	chū zū chē zhàn zài nǎ lǐ?
Is there a limo / bus / van for my hotel?	有豪华大巴 / 公共汽车 / 面包车到宾馆吗？
	yǒu háo huá dà bā / gōng gòng qì chē / miàn bāo chē dào bīn guǎn ma?
I need to get to ____.	我要去_____。
	wǒ yào qù _____.
How much will that cost?	这需要多少钱？
	zhè xū yào duō shǎo qián?
How long will it take?	需要多长时间？
	xū yào duō cháng shí jiān?
Can you take me / us to the train / bus station?	您能带我 / 我们到火车 / 公共汽车站吗？
	nín néng dài wǒ / wǒ mén dào huǒ chē / gōng gòng qì chē zhàn ma?

Listen Up: Taxi Lingo

请上车！ *qǐng shàng chē!*	Please get in!
您可以把行李放在这，我来处理。 *nín kě yǐ bǎ xíng li fàng zài zhè,* *wǒ lái chǔ lǐ。*	Leave your luggage here. I got it.
每个包付 10 元人民币。 *měi gè bāo fù shí yuán rén mín bì。*	It's 10 RMB for each bag.
多少乘客？ *duō shǎo chéng kè?*	How many passengers?
您很着急吗？ *nín hěn zháo jí ma?*	Are you in a hurry?

I am in a hurry.	我很着急。 *wǒ hěn zháo jí。*
Slow down.	慢点开。 *màn diǎn kāi。*
Am I close enough to walk?	不用走多远就能到那里吗？ *bú yòng zǒu duō yuǎn jiù néng dào* *nà lǐ ma?*
Let me out here.	我就在这下车。 *wǒ jiù zài zhè xià chē。*
That's not the correct change.	找的钱不对。 *zhǎo de qián bù duì。*

BY TRAIN

How do I get to the train station?	我怎样到火车站？ *wǒ zěn yàng dào huǒ chē zhàn?*
Would you take me to the train station?	可以带我去火车站吗？ *kě yǐ dài wǒ qù huǒ* *chē zhàn ma?*

How long is the trip to ____?	到_____要花多长时间?
	dào _____ yào huā duō cháng shí jiān?
When is the next train?	下一班火车是什么时间?
	xià yī bān huǒ chē shì shén me shí jiān?
Do you have a schedule / timetable?	您有时刻表吗?
	nín yǒu shí kè biǎo ma?
Do I have to change trains?	我需要换车吗?
	wǒ xū yào huàn chē ma?
a one-way ticket	单程票
	dān chéng piào
a round-trip ticket	往返票
	wǎng fǎn piào
Which platform does it leave from?	从哪个站台驶离?
	cóng nǎ gè zhàn tái shǐ lí?
Is there a bar car?	有酒吧车吗?
	yǒu jiǔ bā chē ma?
Is there a dining car?	有餐车吗?
	yǒu cān chē ma?
Which car is my seat in?	我的座位在哪节车厢?
	wǒ de zuò wèi zài nǎ jié chē xiāng?
Is this seat taken?	这个座位有人吗?
	zhè gè zuò wèi yǒu rén ma?
Where is the next stop?	下一站是哪里?
	xià yī zhàn shì nǎ lǐ?
How many stops to ____?	到_____有几站?
	dào _____ yǒu jǐ zhàn?
What's the train number and where is the destination?	这列火车的车次是什么? 目的地是哪里?
	zhè liè huǒ chē de chē cì shì shén me? mù dì dì shì nǎ lǐ?

BY BUS

How do I get to the bus station?	我怎样到公共汽车站？ *wǒ zěn yàng dào gōng gòng qì chē zhàn?*
Would you take me to the bus station?	可以带我去公共汽车站吗？ *kě yǐ dài wǒ qù gōng gòng qì chē zhàn ma?*
May I have a bus schedule?	有公共汽车时刻表吗？ *yǒu gōng gòng qì chē shí kè biǎo ma?*
Which bus goes to ____?	哪一班车到_____？ *nǎ yī bān chē dào _____?*
Where does it leave from?	这车从哪里驶离？ *zhè chē cóng nǎ lǐ shǐ lí?*
How long does the bus take?	这车多长时间到？ *zhè chē duō cháng shí jiān dào?*
How much is it?	车票是多少钱？ *chē piào shì duō shǎo qián?*
Is there an express bus?	有快速公交吗？ *yǒu kuài sù gōng jiāo ma?*
Does it make local stops?	当地有站吗？ *dāng dì yǒu zhàn ma?*
Does it run at night?	夜间有车吗？ *yè jiān yǒu chē ma?*
When does the next bus leave?	下一班公共汽车什么时间离开？ *xià yī bān gōng gòng qì chē shén me shí jiān lí kāi?*

a one-way ticket	单程票
	dān chéng piào
a round-trip ticket	往返票
	wǎng fǎn piào
How long will the bus be stopped?	这班公共汽车将停多长时间？
	zhè bān gōng gòng qì chē jiāng tíng duō cháng shí jiān?
Is there an air conditioned bus?	有空调公共汽车吗？
	yǒu kōng tiáo gōng gòng qì chē ma?
Is this seat taken?	这个座位有人吗？
	zhè gè zuò wèi yǒu rén ma?
Where is the next stop?	下一站是哪里？
	xià yī zhàn shì nǎ lǐ?
Please tell me when we reach ____.	到____时请告诉我。
	dào ____ shí qǐng gào sù wǒ.
Let me off here.	我就在这下车。
	wǒ jiù zài zhè xià chē.

BY BOAT OR SHIP

Would you take me to the port?	可以带我去港口吗？
	kě yǐ dài wǒ qù gǎng kǒu ma?
When does the ship sail?	轮船什么时间启航？
	lún chuán shén me shí jiān qǐ háng?
How long is the trip?	航行时间有多长？
	háng xíng shí jiān yǒu duō cháng?
Where are the life preservers?	救生用具在哪里？
	jiù shēng yòng jù zài nǎ lǐ?
I would like a private cabin.	我要一个私人舱。
	wǒ yào yī gè sī rén cāng.
Is the trip rough?	此次航行艰险吗？
	cǐ cì háng xíng jiān xiǎn ma?
I feel seasick.	我晕船。
	wǒ yùn chuán.
I need some seasick pills.	我需要一些晕船药。
	wǒ xū yào yī xiē yūn chuán yào.

Where is the bathroom?	浴室在哪里?
	yù shì zài nǎ lǐ?
Does the ship have a casino?	轮船上有赌场吗?
	lún chuán shàng yǒu dǔ chǎng ma?
Will the ship stop at ports along the way?	轮船在沿线各港口都停吗?
	lún chuán zài yán xiàn gè gǎng kǒu dōu tíng ma?

BY SUBWAY

Where's the subway station?	地铁站在哪里?
	dì tiě zhàn zài nǎ lǐ?
Where can I buy a ticket?	我在哪里买票?
	wǒ zài nǎ lǐ mǎi piào?

SUBWAY TICKETS

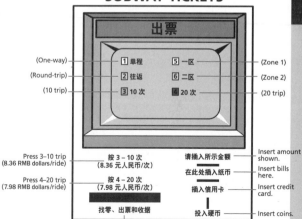

出票

(One-way) — 1 单程	5 一区 — (Zone 1)
(Round-trip) — 2 往返	6 二区 — (Zone 2)
(10 trip) — 3 10 次	4 20 次 — (20 trip)

Press 3–10 trip (8.36 RMB dollars/ride) — 按 3 – 10 次 (8.36 元人民币/次)

Press 4–20 trip (7.98 RMB dollars/ride) — 按 4 – 20 次 (7.98 元人民币/次)

找零、出票和收据 — (Take change, tickets, receipt)

请插入所示金额 — Insert amount shown.

在此处插入纸币 — Insert bills here.

插入信用卡 — Insert credit card.

投入硬币 — Insert coins.

Could I have a map of the subway?	能给我一张地铁路线图吗？
	néng gěi wǒ yī zhāng dì tiě lù xiàn tú ma?
Which line should I take for ____?	到_____应乘几号线？
	dào _____ yīng chéng jǐ hào xiàn?
Is this the right line for ____?	这是到_____的正确路线吗？
	zhè shì dào _____ de zhèng què lù xiàn ma?
Which stop is it for ____?	到_____是哪一站？
	dào _____ shì nǎ yī zhàn?
How many stops is it to ____?	到_____有几站？
	dào _____ yǒu jǐ zhàn?
Is the next stop ____?	下一站是_____吗？
	xià yī zhàn shì _____ ma?
Where are we?	我们在哪里？
	wǒ mén zài nǎ lǐ?
Where do I change to ____?	我到_____在哪里换乘？
	wǒ dào _____ zài nǎ lǐ huàn chéng?
What time is the last train to ____?	到_____的最后一班火车是什么时间？
	dào _____ de zuì hòu yī bān huǒ chē shì shén me shí jiān?

CONSIDERATIONS FOR TRAVELERS WITH SPECIAL NEEDS

Do you have wheelchair access?	有轮椅通道吗？
	yǒu lún yǐ tōng dào ma?
Do you have elevators? Where?	有电梯吗？在哪儿？
	yǒu diàn tī ma? zài nǎ ér?
Do you have ramps? Where?	有坡道吗？在哪儿？
	yǒu pō dào ma? zài nǎ ér?

Are the restrooms wheelchair accessible?

轮椅可以进入洗手间吗?

lún yǐ kě yǐ jìn rù xǐ shǒu jiān ma?

Do you have audio assistance for the hearing impaired?

可以为听障人士提供声频帮助吗?

kě yǐ wèi tīng zhàng rén shì tí gōng shēng pín bāng zhù ma?

I am deaf.

我是听障人士。

wǒ shì tīng zhàng rén shì。

May I bring my service dog?

我可以带上我的帮助犬吗?

wǒ kě yǐ dài shàng wǒ de bāng zhù quǎn ma?

I am blind.

我是视障人士。

wǒ shì shì zhàng rén shì。

I need to charge my power chair.

我需要为我的电动轮椅充电。

wǒ xū yào wèi wǒ de diàn dòng lún yǐ chōng diàn。

GETTING THERE

PRE-DEPARTURE CHECK LIST

Do you have:

- A current **passport that is valid for six months beyond your expected stay**? Make sure your leave a copy of the identification page (the one with your photo and passport number) with someone at home, or bring a copy with you and store it separate from your passport.
- The necessary **visas** to visit China? All Americans need visas to visit China.
- The address and phone number of your country's **embassy or consulate**?
- A copy of your **itinerary**, with contact numbers, that you can leave with someone at home?
- Your health **insurance card**?
- Do you have any **necessary vaccinations**? (Although no vaccinations are currently required for travel to China, it is best to check with your local doctor for individual needs and the most recent health advisories.)
- Documentation for your **e-ticket** (a printout of the reservation confirmation and your itinerary)?
- A safe, accessible place to store **cash**?
- The **credit card** you used to buy your plane ticket when you check in at a kiosk?
- Your credit card **PIN numbers**?
- A current **ATM card**? Have you checked your daily ATM withdrawal limit?
- Documentation for **traveler's checks** you might have purchased, stored separately from the checks.
- Enough **prescription medicine** to last the duration of your trip? The generic names of medicines?
- An extra pair of **glasses and/or contact lenses**?

PASSPORTS & VISAS

Check that your passport is valid for at least six months beyond the length of your intended stay in China. Your visit must begin within 90 days of the issue date. Be sure to obtain a visa in advance of your trip, since they are not granted at the border. It generally takes 3-5 days to process visas at a local Chinese Consulate, although an extra fee can expedite the process. For the most up-to-date visa application information and downloadable forms, consult the China National Tourist Office website, www.cnto.org/chinavisa.asp.

GETTING THERE

The majority of U.S. travelers purchase online tickets to China through the following three online travel agencies: www.Expedia.com, www.Orbitz.com and www.Travelocity.com. In Canada, travelers should try www.Expedia.ca or www.Travelocity.ca. U.K. residents most often use www.Expedia.co.uk and www.Opodo.co.uk. All travelers should check major airline websites for web-only specials.

The major airlines serving China are:

Air China (People's Republic of China)   © 800/982-8802; www.airchina.com

American Airlines   © 800/433-7300; www.aa.com

British Airways   © 800/247-9297 in the U.S.; © 010/8511-5599 in Beijing; www.britishairways.com

Cathay Pacific   © 800/233-2742 in the U.S.; © 010/8486-8532 in Beijing; www.cathaypacific.com

China Airlines (Taiwan)   © 800/227-5118; www.china-airlines.com

Continental Airlines   © 800/231-0856; www.continental.com

Delta Airlines   © 800/241-4141; www.delta.com

Northwest Airlines   © 800/225-2525; www.nwa.com

United Airlines   © 800/538-2929; www.united.com

Tourism Offices

Check with your local branch of the **China National Tourist Office** (www.cnto.org) for information about China:

In the United States: © 888/760-8218 or © 800/670-2228

In Canada: © 416/599-6636

In the United Kingdom: © 020-7935-9787

In Australia: © 02/9299-4057

GETTING AROUND

By Plane
Most long distance travel within China is done by plane. The country is so large that overnight train travel from a city in the north, such as Beijing, to one in the south, such as Canton, is just not feasible. The **Civil Aviation Administration of China** (CAAC) was China's only civil airline through the late 1980s, overseeing all air travel within the country. It has since divided into three major state-owned groups of **Air China, China Southern,** and **China Eastern Airlines** (www.ce-air.com). Since 2005, several budget carriers have also emerged. Chinese airlines now use aircraft from Western companies such as Boeing and Airbus, so their safety record has improved greatly from years past. People traveling through China solo can book tickets through the local **China International Travel Service** (CITS), or buy tickets at some hotel travel desks. The months of April, May, September and October are particularly coveted for travel within China, so plane tickets should be purchased well in advance of those months. Seats must be confirmed before travel.

By Train
Though in backwater areas, slow trains can be primitive, intercity trains are universally air-conditioned and mostly kept very clean. Nor is the system in general backward, with a computerized signaling system and a good safety record. There are 200kmph (125-mph) trains between Shenzhèn and Guangzhou, 300kmph (188-mph) trains and tilting trains using British technology under trial; the world's highest line is under construction to Lhasa; and the world's first commercial maglev (magnetic levitation) line runs from Shànghai to the Pudong airport.

By Bus
China's highway system, nonexistent 20 years ago, is growing rapidly, and journey times by road between many cities have been dramatically cut to the point where on a few routes, buses are now faster than trains. Although most buses are

fairly battered, in some areas they offer a remarkable level of luxury—particularly on the east coast, where there are the funds to pay for a higher quality of travel. Some buses even have on-board toilets and free bottled water.

Buses usually depart punctually, pause at a checking station where the number of passengers is compared with the number of tickets sold in advance, then dither while empty seats are filled with groups who wait at the roadside and bargain for a lower fare. Sleeper buses, although cheaper, should generally be avoided when an overnight train is an alternative. Usually they have three rows of two-tier berths, which are extremely narrow and do not recline fully.

Transport can vary widely in quality in rural and remoter areas, but it is usually dirty and decrepit, and may be shared with livestock.

By Car (Taxi)

While foreign residents of China go through the necessary paperwork, with the exception of one hire operation at Beijing's Capital Airport, self-drive for foreign visitors is not possible, and without previous experience, the no-holds-barred driving style of China is nothing you want to tackle. Renting a vehicle is nevertheless commonplace, but it comes with a driver. Hong Kong and Macau are so small that there's simply no point in hiring a car and facing navigational and parking difficulties, when there are plentiful, well-regulated taxis available.

TIPPING

Tipping is a Western custom, and is rare in China. Don't tip cabdrivers or most restaurant servers. Hotel workers are among the few who are used to tips, but much lower ones than in the U.S. A good tip for a bellman is ¥1 for a large suitcase. Never tip unless you feel you received very special service.

CHAPTER THREE

LODGING

This chapter will help you find the right accommodations, at the right price, and the amenities you might need during your stay.

ROOM PREFERENCES

Please recommend _____	请推荐_____
	qǐng tuī jiàn_____
a clean hostel.	干净的旅社。
	gān jìng de lǚ shè。
a moderately priced hotel.	价格适中的酒店。
	jià gé shì zhōng de jiǔ diàn。
a moderately priced B&B.	价格适中的 B&B (床位加早餐)酒店。
	jià gé shì zhōng de B&B (chuáng wèi jiā zǎo cān) jiǔ diàn。
a good hotel / motel.	好的酒店 / 汽车旅馆。
	hǎo de jiǔ diàn / qì chē lǚ guǎn。
Does the hotel have _____	酒店有_____
	jiǔ diàn yǒu _____
a pool?	游泳池吗?
	yóu yǒng chí ma?
suites?	套房吗?
	tào fáng ma?
a balcony?	阳台吗?
	yáng tái ma?
a fitness center?	健身中心吗?
	jiàn shēn zhōng xīn ma?
a spa?	水疗吗?
	shuǐ liáo ma?
a private beach?	私人海滩吗?
	sī rén hǎi tān ma?

a tennis court?	网球场吗？
	wǎng qiú chǎng ma?
I would like a room for ____.	我要一间房用来_____。
	wǒ yào yī jiān fáng yòng lái _____。

For full coverage of number terms, see p7.

I would like ____	我想要___
	wǒ xiǎng yào ___
a king-sized bed.	一张特大号床。
	yī zhāng tè dà hào chuáng。
a double bed.	一张双人床。
	yī zhāng shuāng rén chuáng。
a twin bed.	一张单人床。
	yī zhāng dān rén chuáng。
adjoining rooms.	毗连的房间。
	pí lián de fáng jiān。
a smoking room.	一间吸烟客房。
	yī jiān xī yān kè fáng。
a non-smoking room.	一间非吸烟客房。
	yī jiān fēi xī yān kè fáng。
a private bathroom.	独立浴室。
	dúlì yù shì。
a shower.	淋浴。
	lín yù。
a bathtub.	浴缸。
	yù gāng。

LODGING

Listen Up: Reservations Lingo

我们没有空房。	We have no vacancies.
wǒ mén méi yǒu kōng fáng。	
您将停留多长时间？	How long will you be staying?
nín jiāng tíng liú duō cháng shí jiān?	
吸烟还是不吸烟？	Smoking or non smoking?
xī yān hái shì bù xī yān?	

air conditioning.	空调。 _kōng tiáo。_
television.	电视。 _diàn shì。_
cable.	有线电视。 _yǒu xiàn diàn shì。_
satellite TV.	卫星电视。 _wèi xīng diàn shì。_
a telephone.	一部电话。 _yī bù diàn huà。_
Internet access.	网络接口。 _wǎng luò jiē kǒu。_
high-speed Internet access.	高速网络接口。 _gāo sù wǎng luò jiē kǒu。_
a refrigerator.	一台电冰箱。 _yī tái diàn bīng xiāng。_
a beach view.	海滩景观。 _hǎi tān jǐng guān。_
a city view.	城市景观。 _chéng shì jǐng guān。_
a kitchenette.	一间小厨房。 _yī jiān xiǎo chú fáng。_
a balcony.	一个阳台。 _yī gè yáng tái。_
a suite.	一个套间。 _yī gè tào jiān。_
a penthouse.	顶楼房间。 _dǐng lóu fáng jiān。_
I would like a room ____	我要一间_____ _wǒ yào yī jiān _____
on the ground floor.	一楼客房。 _yī lóu kè fáng。_
near the elevator.	靠近电梯的房间。 _kào jìn diàn tī de fáng jiān。_

near the stairs.	靠近楼梯的房间。 *kào jìn lóu tī de fáng jiān。*
near the pool.	靠近游泳池的房间。 *kào jìn yóu yǒng chí de fáng jiān。*
away from the street.	远离街道的房间。 *yuǎn lí jiē dào de fáng jiān。*
I would like a corner room.	我想要一间角房。 *wǒ xiǎng yào yī jiān jiǎo fáng。*
Do you have _____	有_____ *yǒu _____*
a crib?	婴儿床吗? *yīng ér chuáng ma?*
a foldout bed?	折叠床吗? *zhé dié chuáng ma?*

FOR GUESTS WITH SPECIAL NEEDS

I need a room with _____	我需要一间_____ *wǒ xū yào yī jiān _____*
wheelchair access.	有轮椅通道的房间。 *yǒu lún yǐ tōng dào de fáng jiān。*
services for the visually impaired.	为视障人士提供服务的房间。 *wéi shì zhàng rén shì tí gōng fú wù de fáng jiān。*
services for the hearing impaired.	为听障人士提供服务的房间。 *wéi tīng zhàng rén shì tí gōng fú wù de fáng jiān。*
I am traveling with a service dog.	我带着帮助犬旅行。 *wǒ dài zhe bāng zhù quǎn lǚ xíng。*

MONEY MATTERS

I would like to make a reservation.	我想预定。 *wǒ xiǎng yù dìng。*

LODGING

How much per night?	每晚多少钱?
	měi wǎn duō shǎo qián?
Do you have a ____	您有_____
	nín yǒu_____
weekly / monthly rate?	周 / 月房价吗?
	zhōu / yuè fáng jià ma?
a weekend rate?	有周末价吗?
	yǒu zhōu mò jià ma?
We will be staying for ____ days / weeks.	我们将停留 _____ 天 / 周。
	wǒ mén jiāng tíng liú _____ tiān / zhōu。

For full coverage of number terms, see p7.

When is checkout time?	什么时间退房?
	shén me shí jiān tuì fáng?

For full coverage of time-related terms, see p12.

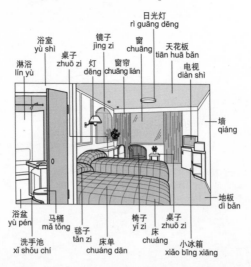

日光灯
rì guāng dēng

镜子
jìng zi

窗
chuāng

天花板
tiān huā bǎn

电视
diàn shì

浴室
yù shì

桌子
zhuō zi

灯
dēng

窗帘
chuāng lián

淋浴
lín yù

墙
qiáng

地板
dì bǎn

浴盆
yù pén

马桶
mǎ tǒng

毯子
tǎn zi

床单
chuáng dān

椅子
yǐ zi

床
chuáng

桌子
zhuō zi

洗手池
xǐ shǒu chí

小冰箱
xiǎo bīng xiāng

Do you accept credit cards / travelers checks?	可以用信用卡 / 旅行支票吗？
	kě yǐ yòng xìn yòng kǎ / lǚ xíng zhī piào ma?
May I see a room?	我可以看一下房间吗？
	wǒ kě yǐ kàn yī xià fáng jiān ma?
How much are taxes?	税是多少？
	shuì shì duō shǎo?
Is there a service charge?	有服务费吗？
	yǒu fú wù fèi ma?
I'd like to speak with the manager.	我想与经理谈谈。
	wǒ xiǎng yǔ jīng lǐ tán tán。

IN-ROOM AMENITIES

I'd like ____	我想_____
	wǒ xiǎng _____
to place an international call.	打一个国际电话。
	dǎ yī gè guó jì diàn huà。
to place a long-distance call.	打一个长途电话。
	dǎ yī gè cháng tú diàn huà。
directory assistance in English.	要英文的目录帮助。
	yào yīng wén de mù lù bāng zhù。
room service.	要客房服务。
	yào kè fáng fú wù。
maid service.	要女仆服务。
	yào nǚ pú fú wù。

LODGING

Instructions for Dialing the Hotel Phone

要呼叫另一个房间，拨打房间号。 *yào hū jiào lìng yī gè fáng jiān, bō dǎ fáng jiān hào。*	To call another room, dial the room number.
要拨打本地电话，先拨 **9**。 *yào bō dǎ běn dì diàn huà, xiān bō 9。*	To make a local call, first dial 9.
要呼叫接线员，拨 **0**。 *yào hū jiào jiē xiàn yuán, bō 0。*	To call the operator, dial 0.

the front desk ATT operator.	找前台 **ATT** 接线员。 *zhǎo qián tái ATT jiē xiàn yuán.*
Do you have room service?	有客房服务吗？ *yǒu kè fáng fú wù ma?*
When is the kitchen open?	厨房什么时间开放？ *chú fáng shén me shí jiān kāi fàng?*
When is breakfast served?	什么时间供应早餐？ *shén me shí jiān gōng yìng zǎo cān?*

For full coverage of time-related terms, see p12.

Do you offer massages?	提供按摩服务吗？ *tí gōng àn mó fú wù ma?*
Do you have a lounge?	有休息室吗？ *yǒu xiū xī shì ma?*
Do you have a business center?	有商务中心吗？ *yǒu shāng wù zhōng xīn ma?*
Do you serve breakfast?	提供早餐吗？ *tí gōng zǎo cān ma?*
Do you have Wi-Fi?	有无线保真 **(Wi-Fi)** 吗？ *yǒu wú xiàn bǎo zhēn (Wi-Fi) ma?*
May I have a newspaper in the morning?	早晨有报纸吗？ *zǎo chén yǒu bào zhǐ ma?*
Do you offer a tailor service?	提供裁剪服务吗？ *tí gōng cái jiǎn fú wù ma?*
Do you offer laundry service?	提供洗衣服务吗？ *tí gōng xǐ yī fú wù ma?*
Do you offer dry cleaning?	提供干洗服务吗？ *tí gōng gān xǐ fú wù ma?*
May we have _____	可以_____ *kě yǐ _____*
clean sheets today?	给我们换今天的床单吗？ *gěi wǒ mén huàn jīn tiān de chuáng dān ma?*
more towels?	多给我们几条毛巾吗？ *duō gěi wǒ mén jǐ tiáo máo jīn ma?*

more toilet paper?	多给我们一些卫生纸吗？
	duō gěi wǒ mén yī xiē wèi shēng zhǐ ma?
extra pillows?	多给我们几个枕头吗？
	duō gěi wǒ mén jǐ gè zhěn tóu ma?
Do you have an ice machine?	有制冰机吗？
	yǒu zhì bīng jī ma?
Did I receive any _____	有我的_____
	yǒu wǒ de _____
messages?	留言吗？
	liú yán ma?
mail?	邮件吗？
	yóu jiàn ma?
faxes?	传真吗？
	chuán zhēn ma?
A spare key, please.	请给我一份备用钥匙。
	qǐng gěi wǒ yī fèn bèi yòng yào shi。
More hangers please.	请多提供些衣架。
	qǐng duō tí gōng xiē yī jià。
I am allergic to down pillows.	我对羽绒枕过敏。
	wǒ duì yǔ róng zhěn guò mǐn。
I'd like a wake up call.	我想要电话叫醒服务。
	wǒ xiǎng yào diàn huà jiào xǐng fú wù。

For full coverage of how to tell time, see p12.

Do you have alarm clocks?	有闹钟吗？
	yǒu nào zhōng ma?
Is there a safe in the room?	房间有保险箱吗？
	fáng jiān yǒu bǎo xiǎn xiāng ma?
Does the room have a hair dryer?	房间有吹风机吗？
	fáng jiān yǒu chuī fēng jī ma?

LODGING

HOTEL ROOM TROUBLE

May I speak with the manager?	我可以与经理谈谈吗?
	wǒ kě yǐ yǔ jīng lǐ tán tán ma?
The ____ does not work.	____出问题了。
	____*chū wèn tí le。*
television	电视
	diàn shì
telephone	电话
	diàn huà
air conditioning	空调
	kōng tiáo
Internet access	网络接口
	wǎng luò jiē kǒu
cable TV	有线电视
	yǒu xiàn diàn shì
There is no hot water.	没有热水。
	méi yǒu rè shuǐ。
The toilet is over-flowing!	马桶溢水了!
	mǎ tǒng yì shuǐ le!
This room is ____	房间____
	fáng jiān ____
too noisy.	太吵。
	tài chǎo。
too cold.	太冷。
	tài lěng。

too warm.	太热。 tài rè。
This room has ____	房间有_____ fáng jiān yǒu _____
bugs.	虫子。 chóng zi。
mice.	老鼠。 lǎo shǔ。
I'd like a different room.	我想要另一间房。 wǒ xiǎng yào lìng yī jiān fáng。
Do you have a bigger room?	有大一点的房间吗? yǒu dà yī diǎn de fáng jiān ma?
I locked myself out of my room.	我把自己锁在房间外面了。 wǒ bǎ zì jǐ suǒ zài fáng jiān wài miàn le。
Do you have any fans?	有风扇吗? yǒu fēng shàn ma?
The sheets are not clean.	床单不干净。 chuáng dān bù gān jìng。
The towels are not clean.	毛巾不干净。 máo jǐn bù gān jìng。
The room is not clean.	房间不干净。 fáng jiān bù gān jìng。
The guests next door / above / below are being very loud.	隔壁 / 楼上 / 楼下的客人正大声喧哗。 gé bì / lóu shàng / lóu xià de kè rén zhèng dà shēng xuān huá。

CHECKING OUT

I think this charge is a mistake.	我认为这项收费有误。 wǒ rèn wéi zhè xiàng shōu fèi yǒu wù。
Please explain this charge to me.	请向我解释这项收费。 qǐng xiàng wǒ jiě shì zhè xiàng shōu fèi。

LODGING

Thank you, we enjoyed our stay.	谢谢您，我们在这里住得很愉快。
	xiè xiè nín, wǒ mén zài zhè lǐ zhù dé hěn yú kuài.
The service was excellent.	服务非常好。
	fú wù fēi cháng hǎo.
The staff is very professional and courteous.	员工很专业，也很有礼貌。
	yuán gōng hěn zhuān yè, yě hěn yǒu lǐ mào.
Please call a cab for me.	请为我招一辆出租车。
	qǐng wéi wǒ zhāo yī liàng chū zū chē.
Would someone please get my bags?	有人愿意帮我拿包吗？
	yǒu rén yuàn yì bāng wǒ ná bāo ma?

HAPPY CAMPING

I'd like a site for ____	我想找个地方_____
	wǒ xiǎng zhǎo ge dì fāng _____
a tent.	搭帐篷。
	dā zhàng péng.
a camper.	露营。
	lù yíng.
Are there ____	有_____
	yǒu _____
bathrooms?	浴室吗？
	yù shì ma?
showers?	淋浴吗？
	lín yù ma?
Is there running water?	有自来水吗？
	yǒu zì lái shuǐ ma?
Is the water drinkable?	这水可以喝吗？
	zhè shuǐ kě yǐ hē ma?
Where is the electrical hookup?	电线板在哪？
	diàn xiàn bǎn zài nǎ?

CHINESE HOTEL BASICS

China's booming economy has become a magnet for foreign businesses, and scores of foreign business people have begun taking up residence there. Since living in mainland China can be quite expensive and most decent apartments have very long wait lists, many foreigners opt to stay in a permanent hotel room or a serviced apartment connected to a foreign-run hotel. Since most people in China do not speak English, always remember to take a hotel card when you leave your hotel, so that you can show it to a taxi driver when you want to return.

Government Ratings

The Chinese star-rating system is basically meaningless. Five-star ratings are awarded by the Beijing authorities, whereas four-star and lower ratings depend upon provincial approval. As a result, some four-star hotels must have a pool, others a bowling alley, and others a tennis court, none of which may be in working condition, and all of which may have been approved by inspectors appropriately banqueted. Chinese hotels receive almost no maintenance once they open.

Hotel Amenities

In joint-venture hotels, amenities are typically excellent. In Chinese-owned hotels, fitness equipment may be broken and inadequately supervised and pool hygiene poor, so proceed with caution. Unexpected phone calls occur often. When you pick up, the caller may hang up if you're a woman; if you're a man, a massage may be offered, and that, as it were, is only the tip of the iceberg.

Hong Kong Hotels

Hong Kong is particularly well stocked with hotels that regularly make their way onto lists of the world's best, such as the Peninsula Hotel in Kowloon. Service is extraordinary, and they are worth flying halfway around the world to experience. Most of what we say about mainland Chinese hotels does not apply to Hong Kong hotels.

LODGING

TIPS FOR SAVING ON YOUR HOTEL ROOM

The rack rate is the maximum rate a hotel charges for a room. In China these rates are nothing more than the first bid in a bargaining discussion, designed to keep the final price you will actually pay as high as possible. You will almost never pay more than 90%, usually not more than 70%, frequently not more than 50%, and sometimes as little as 30% of this first asking price. Here are some tips to lower the cost of your room:

Book Online   Major hotel chains operating in China often have their best published rates on their own websites. It makes sense to keep checking, as these rates fluctuate constantly according to demand, sometimes hourly. Prices for any time of year booked far in advance will always appear uninviting. They'll be much cheaper closer to your scheduled arrival, unless some major event is taking place (not to mention some extraordinary event such as the Olympics in Beijing in 2008). Ordinary hotels, if they have a website at all, will just quote rack rates.

Dial Central Booking Numbers   Contrary to popular opinion, as the better hotels manage their rates with increasing care, the central booking number is likely to have a rate as good as or better than the rate you can get by calling the hotel directly, and the call is usually toll-free.

Avoid Chinese Online Agencies   Avoid booking through Chinese hotel agencies and websites specializing in Chinese hotels. The discounts they offer are precisely what you can get for yourself, and you can in fact beat them because you won't be paying their mark-up. Many of these have no allocations at all, and simply jump on the phone to book a room as soon as they hear from you.

CHINA'S BEST LOCAL ACCOMMODATIONS

Beijing

Lusong Yuan Binguan   Of all Beijing's traditional courtyard-style hotels, this former imperial residence has the most character, recalling the opulence of China's "feudal" era, but with a more lived-in feel than you'll find elsewhere (© 010/6401-8823).

Dunhuang

Dunhuang Shanzhuang (The Silk Road Dunhuang Hotel) The finest hotel on the Silk Routes, with views of the Mingsha Shan Dunes, this imposing fortress is surrounded by stylishly renovated courtyard houses (© 0937/888-2088; www.dunhuangresort. com).

Gulang Yu

Ye Baihe Binguan (Night Lily Guest House) One of the latest, and certainly one of the most successful conversions of early colonial architecture. A fascinating combination of Qing dynasty furniture and modern interior-design styles, although the antique beds have been causing a few problems for very tall foreign visitors whom they were definitely not designed for in the first place (© 0592/206-0920).

Harbin

Longmen Guibin Lou Built by the Russian-controlled Chinese Eastern Railroad in 1901, the Longmen has served as a hospital, the Russian embassy, and a cheap hostel for migrant workers. In the 1930s and 1940s, it was part of the illustrious Japanese-owned Yamato Hotel chain. The Chinese Railway Bureau renovated the building in 1996, preserving the original Russian woodwork and restoring much of its turn-of-the-20th-century atmosphere. Rooms are palatial and decorated with period furniture. (© 0451/8679-1888).

Hong Kong

The Peninsula Built in 1928 and retaining the atmosphere of its colonial past, The Peninsula has long been the grand old hotel of Hong Kong. It boasts an ornate lobby popular for people-watching, some of Hong Kong's best restaurants, and gorgeous rooms with sweeping views of Victoria Harbour. (© 800/462-7899; www.peninsula.com).

LODGING

Kashgar

Seman Binguan   Set on the grounds of the former Russian consulate, this has merely two government-issued stars and poor service, but standard rooms and suites in the original and beautifully decorated consulate buildings, with their high ceilings and dramatic oil paintings, can be bargained down to low prices. This is the nearest you'll get to experiencing some "Great Game" ambience. (© **0998/255-2861**).

Pingyao

Deju Yuan & Tian Yuan Kui   These are the top two courtyard guesthouses in a town full of ancient architecture. The Deju Yuan has rooms decorated with calligraphy and furnished with dark wooden Ming-style tables and chairs and traditional heated brick beds (© **0354/568-5366**). The Tian Yuan Kui also offers occasional opera performances on hot summer nights when the guesthouse is full and the performers available (© **0354/568-0069**).

Shanghai

The Peace Hotel   the best of Shanghai's historic hotels—built in 1929 as the Cathay Hotel—features a lobby that is an Art Deco masterpiece and splendid public areas. Rooms have been modernized, but the service has lapsed. Go for lunch or a drink. (© **021/6321-6888**; www.shanghaipeacehotel.com).

Yangshuo

Yangshuo Shèngdi (Mountain Retreat)   Situated in one of the area's most picturesque settings, this small but luxurious hotel is a world away from the usual trials and tribulations of traveling in China. This is the kind of place where you will want to extend your vacation indefinitely (© **0773/877-7091**).

CHAPTER FOUR

DINING

This chapter includes a menu reader and the language you need to communicate in a range of dining establishments and food markets.

FINDING A RESTAURANT

Would you recommend a good ____ restaurant?	您能否推荐一个好的____饭店? *nín néng fǒu tuī jiàn yī gè hǎo de ____ fàn diàn?*
Cantonese	粤式 *yuè shì*
Szechuan	川味 *chuān wèi*
Japanese	日本 *rì běn*
Thai	泰国 *tài guó*
Malaysian	马来 *mǎ lái*
Vietnamese	越南 *yuè nán*
Italian	意大利 *yì dà lì*
French	法国 *fǎ guó*
pizza	比萨饼 *bǐ sà bǐng*
steakhouse	牛排 *niú pái*
family	家庭式 *jiā tíng shì*

seafood	海鲜 *hǎi xiān*
vegetarian	素食 *sù shí*
buffet-style	自助式 *zì zhù shì*
budget	经济型 *jīng jì xíng*

Which is the best restaurant in town?	城里哪家饭店最好? *chéng lǐ nǎ jiā fàn diàn zuì hǎo?*
Is there a late-night restaurant nearby?	附近有夜宵饭店吗? *fù jìn yǒu yè xiāo fàn diàn ma?*
Is there a restaurant that serves breakfast nearby?	附近有提供早饭的饭店吗? *fù jìn yǒu tí gōng zǎo fàn de fàn diàn ma?*
Is it very expensive?	很贵吗? *hěn guì ma?*
Do I need a reservation?	我需要预定吗? *wǒ xū yào yù dìng ma?*
Do I have to dress up?	我需要穿正装吗? *wǒ xū yào chuān zhèng zhuāng ma?*
Do they serve lunch?	他们提供午餐吗? *tā mén tí gōng wǔ cān ma?*
What time do they open for dinner?	几点开始供应晚餐? *jǐ diǎn kāi shǐ gōng yīng wǎn cān?*
For lunch?	午餐? *wǔ cān?*
What time do they close?	他们几点钟关门? *tā mén jǐ diǎn zhōng guān mén?*
Do you have a take out menu?	你们有没有外卖菜单? *nǐ mén yǒu méi yǒu wài mài cài dān?*

Do you have a bar?	你们有酒吧吗？
	nǐ mén yǒu jiǔ bā ma?
Is there a café nearby?	附近有咖啡馆吗？
	fù jìn yǒu kā fēi guǎn ma?

GETTING SEATED

Are you still serving?	你们还提供服务吗？
	nǐ mén hái tí gōng fú wù ma?
How long is the wait?	需要等多长时间？
	xū yào děng duō cháng shí jiān?
Do you have a no-smoking section?	有无烟区吗？
	yǒu wú yān qū ma?
A table for ____, please.	请给我们一张———人用餐的餐桌。
	qǐng gěi wǒ mén yī zhāng _____ rén yòng cān de cān zhuō.

For a full list of numbers, see p7.

Do you have a quiet table?	餐馆里有没有安静的地方？
	cān guǎn lǐ yǒu méi yǒu ān jìng de dì fāng?
May we sit outside / inside please?	我们能坐在外面／里面吗？
	wǒ mén néng zuò zài wài miàn / lǐ miàn ma?
May we sit at the counter?	我们能坐在吧台吗？
	wǒ mén néng zuò zài bā tái ma?
A menu please?	请给份菜单。
	qǐng gěi fèn cài dān.

ORDERING

Do you have a special tonight?	你们今晚有什么特色菜？
	nǐ mén jīn wǎn yǒu shén me tè sè cài?
What do you recommend?	您推荐什么？
	nín tuī jiàn shén me?
May I see a wine list?	我可以看一下酒单吗？
	wǒ kě yǐ kàn yī xià jiǔ dān ma?
Do you serve wine by the glass?	您是否卖单杯的酒？
	nín shì fǒu mài dān bēi de jiǔ?

Listen up: Restaurant Lingo

吸烟区还是无烟区？
xī yān qū hái shì wú yān qū?

Smoking or nonsmoking?

您要穿西装戴领带。
*nín yào chuān xī zhuāng dài
lǐng dài。*

You'll need a tie and jacket.

对不起，饭店内不允许
穿短裤。
*duì bù qǐ, fàn diàn nèi bù yǔn
xǔ chuān duǎn kù。*

I'm sorry, no shorts are allowed.

请问，想喝些什么？
*qǐng wèn, xiǎng hē xiē
shén me?*

May I bring you something to drink?

您是否要看一下酒单？
*nín shì fǒu yào kàn yī xià
jiǔ dān?*

Would you like to see a wine list?

您是否想知道我们的特色菜？
*nín shì fǒu xiǎng zhī dào wǒ
mén de tè sè cài?*

Would you like to hear our specials?

您可以点菜了吗？
nín kě yǐ diǎn cài le ma?

Are you ready to order?

对不起，先生，您的信用卡
被拒收了。
*duì bù qǐ, xiān shēng, nín de
xìn yòng kǎ bèi jù shōu le。*

I'm sorry, sir, your credit card was declined.

May I see a drink list?	我能否看一下饮料单?
	wǒ néng fǒu kàn yī xià yǐn liào dān?
I would like it cooked ____	请将牛排_____
	qǐng jiāng niú pái _____
rare.	烤得一分熟。
	kǎo dé yī fēn shú.
medium rare.	烤得三分熟。
	kǎo dé sān fēn shú.
medium.	烤得五分熟。
	kǎo dé wǔ fēn shú.
medium well.	烤得七分熟。
	kǎo dé qī fēn shú.
well.	烤得全熟。
	kǎo dé quán shú.
charred.	烤焦。
	kǎo jiāo.
Do you have a ____ menu?	您有_____菜单吗?
	nín yǒu _____ cài dān ma?
diabetic	适合糖尿病人的
	shì hé táng niào bìng rén de
kosher	犹太教徒
	yóu tài jiào tú
vegetarian	素食
	sù shí
children's	儿童
	ér tóng
What is in this dish?	这道菜里都有什么?
	zhè dào cài lǐ dōu yǒu shén me?
How is it prepared?	这道菜是怎么做的?
	zhè dào cài shì zěn me zuò de?
What kind of oil is that cooked in?	这道菜是用什么油炒的?
	zhè dào cài shì yòng shén me yóu chǎo de?
Do you have any low-salt dishes?	你们有低盐菜吗?
	nǐ mén yǒu dī yán cài ma?

On the side, please.

请放在旁边。

qǐng fàng zài páng biān.

May I make a substitution?

我能换道菜吗?

wǒ néng huàn dào cài ma?

I'd like to try that.

我想试试那个。

wǒ xiǎng shì shì nà gè.

Is that fresh?

是新鲜的吗?

shì xīn xiān de ma?

Waiter!

服务员!

fú wù yuán!

Extra butter, please.

请多给我一些牛油。

qǐng duō gěi wǒ yī xiē niú yóu.

No butter, thanks.

不要牛油,谢谢。

bù yào niú yóu, xiè xiè.

Dressing on the side, please.

请把沙拉酱放在边上。

qǐng bǎ shā lā jiàng fàng zài biān shàng.

No salt, please.

请不要放盐。

qǐng bù yào fàng yán.

May I have some oil, please?

请给我加些油。

qǐng gěi wǒ jiā xiē yóu.

More bread, please.

请再给些面包。

qǐng zài gěi xiē miàn bāo.

I am lactose intolerant.

我不吃含乳糖的食物。

wǒ bù chī hán rǔ táng de shí wù.

Would you recommend something without milk?

您能给我推荐不含奶的食品吗?

nín néng gěi wǒ tuī jiàn bù hán nǎi de shí pǐn ma?

I am allergic to ____

我对____过敏。

wǒ duì ____ guò mǐn.

seafood.

海鲜

hǎi xiān

shellfish.

贝类

bèi lèi

nuts.	坚果 *jiān guǒ*
peanuts.	花生 *huā shēng*
Water _____, please.	请上_____水。 *qǐng shàng _____ shuǐ。*
with ice	加冰 *jiā bīng*
without ice	不加冰 *bù jiā bīng*
I'm sorry, I don't think this is what I ordered.	对不起，我想这不是我点的菜。 *duì bù qǐ, wǒ xiǎng zhè bù shì wǒ diǎn de cài。*
My meat is a little over / under cooked.	这盘肉烧得有点过久 / 火候不够。 *zhè pán ròu shāo dé yǒu diǎn guò jiǔ / huǒ hou bù gòu。*
My vegetables are a little over / under cooked.	这道蔬菜有一点熟过头 / 生。 *zhè dào shū cài yǒu yì diǎn shú guò tóu / shēng。*
There's a bug in my food!	我看见食物里有虫子！ *wǒ kàn jiàn shí wù lǐ yǒu chóng zi!*
May I have a refill?	我可以再加一些吗？ *wǒ kě yǐ zài jiā yī xiē ma?*
A dessert menu, please.	请给我甜点单。 *qǐng gěi wǒ tián diǎn dān。*

DRINKS

alcoholic	含酒精饮料 *hán jiǔ jīng yǐn liào*
neat / straight	不掺水的 / 纯酒的 *bù chān shuǐ de / chún jiǔ de*
on the rocks	加冰 *jiā bīng*
with (seltzer or soda) water	加（矿泉或苏打）水 *jiā (kuàng quán huò sū dǎ) shuǐ*

DINING

beer	啤酒
	pí jiǔ
white wine	干白葡萄酒
	gān bái pú tao jiǔ
red wine	红葡萄酒
	hóng pú tao jiǔ
liqueur	利口酒
	lì kǒu jiǔ
brandy	白兰地
	bái lán dì
cognac	干邑酒
	gān yì jiǔ
gin	杜松子酒
	dù sōng zǐ jiǔ
vodka	伏特加
	fú tè jiā
rum	朗姆酒
	lǎng mǔ jiǔ
rice wine	米酒
	mǐ jiǔ
Scotch	苏格兰
	sū gé lán
Whiskey	威士忌
	wēi shì jì
nonalcoholic	非酒精饮料
	fēi jiǔ jīng yǐn liào
hot chocolate	热巧克力
	rè qiǎo kè lì
lemonade	柠檬水
	níng méng shuǐ
milkshake	奶昔
	nǎi xī
milk	牛奶
	niú nǎi

green tea	红茶
	hóngchá
black tea	绿茶
	lǜchá
coffee	咖啡
	kā fēi
iced coffee	冰咖啡
	bīng kā fēi
mineral water	矿泉水
	kuàng quán shuǐ
fruit juice	果汁
	guǒ zhī

For a full list of fruits, see p97.

SETTLING UP

I'm stuffed.	我吃饱了。
	wǒ chī bǎo le。
The meal was excellent.	饭菜好极了。
	fàn cài hǎo jí le。
There's a problem with my bill.	我的帐单不太对。
	wǒ de zhàng dān bù tài duì。
Is the tip included?	包括小费吗?
	bāo kuò xiǎo fèi ma?
Check, please.	请给我帐单。
	qǐng gěi wǒ zhàng dān。

MENU READER

Chinese cuisine varies greatly from region to region, but we've tried to make our list of classic dishes as encompassing as possible.

APPETIZERS

barbecued pork	叉烧肉
	chā shāo ròu
braised bamboo shoots	油焖笋
	yóu mèn sǔn
cold platter	冷盘
	lěng pán

dried bean curd	豆腐干 *dòu fǔ gān*
hot pickled cabbage	辣白菜 *là bái cài*
jellyfish	海蜇皮 *hǎi zhē pí*
marinated beef	酱牛肉 *jiàng niú ròu*
pan-fried pork dumplings	锅贴 *guō tiē*
peanuts	花生米 *huā shēng mǐ*
pickled cucumber	腌黄瓜 *yān huáng gua*
pickled vegetables	泡菜 *pào cài*
sesame chicken	芝麻鸡 *zhī ma jī*
smoked chicken	熏鸡 *xūn jī*
spring roll	春卷 *chūn juàn*

SOUPS

egg drop soup	蛋花汤 *dàn huā tāng*
hot and sour soup	酸辣汤 *suān là tāng*
shark's fin soup	鱼翅汤 *yú chì tāng*
wonton soup	馄饨汤 *hún tun tāng*

STARCH DISHES

steamed rice	蒸饭 *zhēng fàn*

fried rice	炒饭
	chǎo fàn
steamed bread	馒头
	mán tóu
pork dumplings	猪肉饺
	zhū ròu jiǎo
vegetarian dumplings	素菜饺
	sù cài jiǎo
noodles	面条
	miàn tiáo
steamed rolls	花卷
	huā juǎn

SEAFOOD DISHES

braised fish	红烧鱼
	hóng shāo yú
clams	蛤蜊
	há li
crabs	螃蟹
	páng xiè
deep-fried shrimp balls	炸虾球
	zhà xiā qiú
jellyfish	海蜇皮
	hǎi zhē pí
lobster	龙虾
	lóng xiā
oysters	蚝
	háo
sautéed prawns	炒明虾
	chǎo míng xiā
scallops	鲜贝
	xiān bèi
sea cucumber (sea slugs)	海参
	hǎi shēn
shrimp with egg white	芙蓉虾仁
	fú róng xiā rén

DINING

steamed whole fish 清蒸全鱼
qīng zhēng quán yú

MEAT DISHES
beef 牛肉
niú ròu

pork 猪肉
zhū ròu

lamb 羊肉
yáng ròu

sweet and sour spareribs 糖醋排骨
táng cù pái gǔ

beef with oyster sauce 蚝油牛肉
háo yóu niú ròu

Mongolian barbecue 蒙古烤肉
měng gǔ kǎo ròu

sliced beef with Chinese 芥兰牛肉
broccoli *jiè lán niú ròu*

lamb shishkabob 羊肉串
yáng ròu chuàn

POULTRY DISHES
chicken 鸡
jī

duck 鸭
yā

goose 鹅
é

pigeon 鸽子
gē zi

diced chicken with 腰果鸡丁
cashew nuts *yāo guǒ jī dīng*

lemon chicken 柠檬鸡
níng méng jī

Peking duck 北京烤鸭
běi jīng kǎo yā

VEGETARIAN DISHES

braised bean curd in soy
sauce

红烧豆腐
hóng shāo dòu fǔ

family-style bean curd

家常豆腐
jiā cháng dòu fǔ

Chinese cabbage in cream
sauce

奶油白菜
nǎi yóu bái cài

sautéed string beans

干煸四季豆
gān biān sì jì dòu

spicy eggplant with garlic

鱼香茄子
yú xiāng qié zi

DIM SUM

egg tarts

蛋挞
dàn tà

fried pork dumplings

锅贴
guō tiē

shrimp balls

虾丸
xiā wán

shrimp dumplings

虾饺
xiā jiǎo

small steamed pork buns

小笼包
xiǎo lóng bāo

deep fried taro root

炸芋饺
zhà yù jiǎo

stuffed bean curd

酿豆腐
niàng dòu fǔ

stuffed peppers

酿青椒
niàng qīng jiāo

sweet bean buns

豆沙包
dòu shā bāo

radish cake

萝卜糕
luó bo gāo

sweet rice with meat
stuffed in lotus leaves

肉粽
ròu zòng

DESSERTS

almond gelatin	杏仁豆腐
	xìng rén dòu fǔ
sweet bean buns	豆沙包
	dòu shā bāo
cake	蛋糕
	dàn gāo
fresh fruit	新鲜水果
	xīn xiān shuǐ guǒ
ice cream	冰淇淋
	bīng qí lín
red bean soup	红豆汤
	hóng dòu tāng
eight treasures glutinous rice pudding	八宝饭
	bā bǎo fàn

BUYING GROCERIES

In China, groceries can be bought at open-air farmers' markets, neighborhood stores or large supermarkets.

AT THE SUPERMARKET

Which aisle has ____	哪一排卖____
	nǎ yī pái mài ____
spices?	调味料?
	tiáo wèi liào?
soaps and detergents?	肥皂与清洁剂?
	féi zào yǔ qīng jié jì?
canned goods?	罐装食品?
	guàn zhuāng shí pǐn?
snack food?	小吃类食品?
	xiǎo chī lèi shí pǐn?
water?	水?
	shuǐ?
juice?	果汁?
	guǒ zhī?
bread?	面包?
	miàn bāo?

fruit?	水果? *shuǐ guǒ?*
frozen foods?	冷冻食品? *lěng dòng shí pǐn?*

AT THE BUTCHER SHOP

Is the meat fresh?	肉是新鲜的吗? *ròu shì xīn xiān de ma?*
Do you sell fresh ____	你们卖不卖新鲜的_____ *nǐ mén mài bù mài xīn xiān de* ____
beef?	牛肉? *niú ròu?*
pork?	猪肉? *zhū ròu?*
lamb?	羊肉? *yáng ròu?*
I would like a cut of ____	我想买一块_____ *wǒ xiǎng mǎi yī kuài* ____
tenderloin.	里脊肉。 *lǐ jǐ ròu。*
T-bone.	**T**-骨牛排。 *T-gǔ niú pái。*
brisket.	胸肉。 *xiōng ròu。*
rump roast.	大腿肉。 *dà tuǐ ròu。*
chops.	排骨。 *pái gǔ。*
filet.	肉片。 *ròu piàn。*
Thick / Thin cuts please.	请切厚 / 薄片。 *qǐng qiē hòu / báo piàn。*
Please trim the fat.	请割去肥肉。 *qǐng gē qù féi ròu。*

Is the ____ fresh?	____是新鲜的吗?
	____ shì xīn xiān de ma?
fish	鱼
	yú
seafood	海鲜
	hǎi xiān
shrimp	虾
	xiā
octopus	章鱼
	zhāng yú
squid	鱿鱼
	yóu yú
sea bass	鲈鱼
	lú yú
flounder	比目鱼
	bǐ mù yú
clams	蛤肉
	há ròu
oysters	牡蛎
	mǔ lì
shark	鲨鱼肉
	shā yú ròu
turtle	海龟肉
	hǎi guī ròu
May I smell it?	我能闻一下吗?
	wǒ néng wén yī xià ma?
Would you please ____	您能____
	nín néng ____
filet it?	切片吗?
	qiē piàn ma?
debone it?	去骨吗?
	qù gǔ ma?
remove the head and tail?	去头去尾吗?
	qù tóu qù wěi ma?

AT THE PRODUCE STAND / MARKET
Fruits

banana	香蕉 *xiāng jiāo*
apple	苹果 *píng guǒ*
grapes (green, red)	葡萄 *pú tao*
lichee	荔枝 *lì zhī*
orange	桔子 *jú zi*
papaya	木瓜 *mù guā*
peach	桃子 *táo zi*
pear	梨子 *lí zi*
persimmon	柿子 *shì zi*
watermelon	西瓜 *xī guā*

Vegetables

bamboo shoots	竹笋 *zhú sǔn*
beancurd	豆腐 *dòu fǔ*
broccoli	西兰花 *xī lán huā*
cabbage	卷心菜 *juǎn xīn cài*
carrots	胡萝卜 *hú luó bo*
cauliflower	菜花 *cài huā*

corn	玉米
	yù mǐ
lotus root	莲藕
	lián ǒu
straw mushroom	草菇
	cǎo gū
snow pea	雪豆
	xuě dòu
soybean	大豆
	dà dòu
spinach	菠菜
	bō cài
water chestnut	荸荠
	bí qi

Fresh herbs and spices

garlic	大蒜
	dà suàn
ginger	姜
	jiāng
hot pepper	辣椒
	là jiāo
mustard	芥末
	jiè mò
pepper	胡椒
	hú jiāo
salt	盐
	yán
sesame oil	香油
	xiāng yóu

CHINESE DINING ETIQUETTE

Practice using chopsticks before you attend any business banquet or meal in someone's home. Never position chopsticks in your rice bowl upright, since this gesture symbolizes death.

Whenever someone tries to serve you from a communal plate, tell them you'll do it yourself. They will insist on serving you anyway, and after several short protests let them. Do not take even a sip of a drink before saying "Gan Bei!" to your host. Then take only a short sip, and raise the glass slightly again, as if to make another toast.

Table Manners

These differ from one culture to another. The Chinese have no problem slurping their soup rather loudly or belching during or after a meal. Don't be surprised if you witness both even at a formal gathering. To remain polite and in everyone's good graces, you should always make an attempt to serve someone else before you serve yourself, otherwise you will appear rude and self-centered. Don't finish all the food on your plate. Your host will just insist on filling it up again.

Paying the Bill

Most Westerners are surprised to discover chaotic, noisy scenes at the end of any meal in a Chinese restaurant, as everyone fights to pay the bill. The Chinese consider it good manners to vociferously attempt to wrest the bill out of the hands of whoever has it. The gesture of being eager and willing to pay is always appreciated. Only tip restaurant servers if you feel you received a very special service.

CHINESE REGIONAL CUISINES

Different regions of China specialize in different types of cuisine. Each province has its own specialties, cooking style and favorite ingredients. Some corner the market on spicy food and others showcase foods that may seem bland to the Western palate. No matter where you go in China, though, you're sure to discover a new taste or two along the way.

Northern Chinese Cuisine

Found in places like Beijing, this cuisine is famous for a wide variety of meat dishes, especially beef, lamb and duck (lest we forget Peking Duck). Copious amounts of garlic and scallions are added to garnish the meat. Northern cooking tends to be bland because of the lack of excessive condiments, so don't expect anything overtly salty, sweet or spicy.

Shanghai Cuisine

Included in this category are the cuisines of neighboring Jiangsu and Zhejiang provinces, all representing what can be termed Eastern Chinese cuisine. Since this area is close to the sea and has many lakes, there is an infinite variety of seafood. Fresh vegetables, different kinds of bamboo, and plenty of soy sauce and sugar are also hallmarks of this region's cuisine.

Western Chinese Cuisine

This cuisine consists of food from Sichuan and Hunan provinces, well known to Westerners who enjoy spicy Chinese food in the United States. Since this part of China is hot and humid, hot peppers and salt are common ingredients.

Southern Chinese Cuisine

This type of food hails from Guangdong (formerly known as Canton), as well as from Fujian and Taiwan. Similar to Shanghai cuisine, it offers plentiful amounts of seafood, fresh fruits, and vegetables. One of the most famous types of food from Guangdong that you've no doubt heard of is dim sum, which consists of bite-sized portions of all manner of Chinese cuisine from the south.

DIM SUM

Dim sum is incredibly popular with the people in Guangdong Province and Hong Kong. In Hong Kong, you can find it served for breakfast, lunch and dinner. Vendors even sell dim sum snacks in subway stations. Dim sum's main claim to fame is that it comes in mini portions, and is often served with tea to help cut through the oil and grease. You must signal the waiters when you want a dish on the dim sum cart as it's pushed through the restaurant; otherwise, they will keep strolling past you. Dim sum restaurants are traditionally crowded and boisterous, only adding to the fun. Since the portions are so small, waiters often tally the total simply by adding the number of plates left on your table.

CHINESE NEW YEAR FOOD

On the eve of the Chinese lunar New Year, known as "chu xi" (pronounced "choo she"), the Chinese eat a big dinner known as "nianyefan" (pronounced "nyan yeh fahn"). This always includes a whole cooked fish (the Chinese word for fish rhymes with the word for abundance, even though the written characters for the two words look quite different).

In some of the less well-off parts of northern China people often eat dumplings (known as "jiaozi," and pronounced "jyow dzuh") instead of fish because their shape resembles traditional gold ingots used in earlier times by people of means. The hope is that some of this prosperity will rub off on them.

Southerners often eat a kind of stringy black vegetable called "fa cai" (pronounced "fah tsye"), a word that rhymes with the words that mean "to get wealthy" and "prosper" (although spoken in different tones). The most common greeting on New Year's Day is "gongxi fa cai!" (pronounced "goong she fah tsye"), meaning "Congratulations and may you prosper!"

CHINESE TEA

Tea is always offered to guests the minute they enter a Chinese home. The hosts aren't just being polite. The offering of tea shows respect to the guest and is a concrete way of sharing something that everyone can enjoy. It is considered rude not to take at least a sip.

There are about as many different kinds of tea in China as there are dialects: Hundreds. To make ordering or purchasing this beverage easier, however, you need only know the most common kinds of tea:

Green Tea   Pronounced "lyew chah" in Chinese, this is the oldest of all the teas in China, with many unfermented sub-varieties. The most famous green tea is Dragon Well tea (pronounced "long jeeng chah"), found near the famous West Lake region in Hangzhou. People in the south generally prefer this type of tea as well.

Black Tea   Pronounced "hoong chah," which literally means "red tea," black teas are fermented and enjoyed primarily by people in Fujian province, close to Taiwan.

Black Dragon Tea   Pronounced "oo long chah," this kind of tea is semi-fermented and a favorite in Guangdong and Fujian provinces, as well as in Taiwan.

Jasmine Tea   Pronounced "maw lee hwah chah," Jasmine tea is made up of a combination of black, green and Black Dragon teas, in addition to some fragrant flowers like jasmine or magnolia thrown in for good measure. Most northerners are partial to jasmine tea, perhaps because the north is cold and this type of tea raises the body's temperature.

CHAPTER FIVE

SOCIALIZING

Whether you're meeting people in a bar or a park, you'll find the language in this chapter to help you make new friends.

GREETINGS

Hello.	您好。 *nín hǎo。*
How are you?	您好吗? *nín hǎo ma?*
Fine, thanks.	很好，谢谢。 *hěn hǎo, xiè xiè。*
And you?	您呢? *nín ne?*
I'm exhausted from the trip.	我旅行归来很疲惫。 *wǒ lǚ xíng guī lái hěn pí bèi。*
I have a headache.	我头痛。 *wǒ tóu tòng。*
I'm terrible.	我感觉很槽糕。 *wǒ gǎn jué hěn zāo gāo。*
I have a cold.	我感冒了。 *wǒ gǎn mào le。*
Good morning.	早晨好。 *zǎo chén hǎo。*
Good evening.	晚上好。 *wǎn shàng hǎo。*
Good afternoon.	下午好。 *xià wǔ hǎo。*
Good night.	晚安。 *wǎn ān。*

Listen Up: Common Greetings

很荣幸。 *hěn róng xìng。*	It's a pleasure.
我心欢喜。 *wǒ xīn huān xǐ。*	Delighted.
乐意为您效劳。/ 如您所愿。 *lè yì wéi nín xiào láo。 /* *rú nín suǒ yuàn。*	At your service. / As you wish.
幸会。 *xìng huì。*	Charmed.
一天愉快。 *yī tiān yú kuài。*	Good day.
您好。 *nín hǎo。*	Hello.
最近忙什么? *zuì jìn máng shén me?*	How's it going?
最近怎么样? *zuì jìn zěn me yàng?*	What's up?
拜拜! *bài bài!*	Bye!
再见。 *zài jiàn。*	Goodbye.
回见。 *huí jiàn。*	See you later.

THE LANGUAGE BARRIER

I don't understand.	我不懂。 *wǒ bù dǒng。*
Please speak more slowly.	请您再说慢点儿。 *qǐng nín zài shuō màn diǎn ér。*
Please speak louder.	请大点声说。 *qǐng dà diǎn shēng shuō。*
Do you speak English?	您说英语吗? *nín shuō yīng yǔ ma?*

I speak ____ better than Chinese.	我的____语说得比汉语好。
	wǒ de ____yǔ shuō dé bǐ hàn yǔ hǎo。
Please spell that.	请问它怎么写。
	qǐng wèn tā zěn me xiě。
Please repeat that.	请再说一遍。
	qǐng zài shuō yī biàn。
How do you say ____?	您如何说____?
	nín rú hé shuō ____?
Would you show me that [word] in this dictionary?	您能在这本字典里把它指给我看吗?
	nín néng zài zhè běn zì diǎn lǐ bǎ tā zhǐ gěi wǒ kàn ma?

Curse Words

Here are some common curse words, used across mainland China.

狗屎	shit
gǒu shǐ	
笨蛋	jerk
bèn dàn	
该死	damn
gāi sǐ	
傻瓜	ass
shǎ guā	
晕	screwed up
yūn	
私生子	bastard
sī shēng zǐ	
靠	fucked up
kào	
他妈的	to fuck
tā mā de	

GETTING PERSONAL

People in China and Taiwan are quite friendly, but more mindful of age and status hierarchies than Americans or Europeans. Remember to use the *nín* form of address for elders and those in higher positions, rather than the informal *ní*.

INTRODUCTIONS

What is your name?	您叫什么名字？
	nín jiào shén me míng zi?
My name is ____.	我叫＿＿＿。
	wǒ jiào ＿＿＿。
I'm very pleased to meet you.	很高兴见到您。
	hěn gāo xìng jiàn dào nín。
May I introduce my ____	我可以介绍我的＿＿＿吗？
	wǒ kě yǐ jiè shào wǒ de ＿＿＿ma?
How is your ____	您的＿＿＿好吗？
	nín de ＿＿＿hǎo ma?

wife?	妻子
	qī zǐ
husband?	丈夫
	zhàng fū
child?	孩子
	hái zi
friends?	朋友
	péng yǒu
boyfriend / girlfriend?	男朋友 / 女朋友
	nán péng yǒu / nǚ péng yǒu
family?	家人
	jiā rén
mother?	母亲
	mǔ qīn
father?	父亲
	fù qīn
brother / sister?	兄弟 / 姐妹
	xiōng dì / jiě mèi

friend?	朋友
	péng yǒu
neighbor?	邻居
	lín jū
boss?	老板
	lǎo bǎn
cousin?	表哥 / 表弟 / 表姐 / 表妹
	biǎo gē* / biǎo dì* / biǎo jiě* / biǎo mèi*
aunt / uncle?	姑姑 / 阿姨 / 叔叔 / 舅舅
	gū gū / ā yí / shū shū / jiù jiù
fiancée / fiancé?	未婚妻 / 未婚夫
	wèi hūn qī / wèi hūn fū

Gender & Age Distinctions

Gender and age hierarchies are clearly distinguished in Chinese terms for relatives. In English, a cousin is just a cousin. Chinese has separate terms, however, for older, younger, female, or male cousins. Similarly, relatives on the mother's side of the family often have the word "wai" — meaning "outside" the paternal family unit — before the actual term for aunt, uncle, grandparents, etc., while those on the father's side of the family will often have the word "zu" (referring to "lineage") preceding such terms.

Cousins

* biǎo gē = older male cousin
* biǎo dì = younger male cousin
* biǎo jiě = older female cousin
* biǎo mèi = younger female cousin

Note

Gu mu = father's sister (married)
Yi mu = maternal aunt
Yi ma = maternal aunt (married)
Bo mu = wife of father's elder brother
Shu mu = wife of father's younger brother
Bo bo = father's eldest brother
Bo fu = father's elder brother
Shu zu = paternal grandfather's younger brother
Shu zu mu = wife of paternal grandfather's younger brother

partner?	伴侣 *bàn lǚ*
niece / nephew?	侄女 / 侄子 *zhí nǚ / zhí zi*
parents?	父母 *fù mǔ*
grandparents?	祖父母 *zǔ fù mǔ*
Are you married / single?	您结婚了 / 单身吗? *nín jié hūn le / dān shēn ma?*
I'm married.	我结婚了。 *wǒ jié hūn le。*
I'm single.	我单身。 *wǒ dān shēn。*
I'm divorced.	我离婚了。 *wǒ lí hūn le。*
I'm a widow / widower.	我丈夫 / 妻子已经去世了。 *wǒ zhàng fū / qī zǐ yǐ jīng qù shì le。*
We're separated.	我们已分居。 *wǒ mén yǐ fēn jū。*
I live with my boyfriend / girlfriend.	我与我的男朋友 / 女朋友一起生活。 *wǒ yǔ wǒ de nán péng yǒu / nǚ péng yǒu yī qǐ shēng huó。*

How old are you?	您多大了？ *nín duō dà le?*
How old are your children?	您的孩子几岁？ *nín de hái zǐ jǐ suì?*
Wow! That's very young.	哇！很年轻。 *wa! hěn nián qīng.*
No you're not! You're much younger.	怎么会！你看起来一点都不像。 *zěn me huì! nǐ kàn qǐ lái yī diǎn dōu bù xiàng.*
Your wife / daughter is beautiful.	您妻子 / 女儿很漂亮。 *nín qī zǐ / nǚ ér hěn piào liang.*
Your husband / son is handsome.	您丈夫 / 儿子很英俊。 *nín zhàng fū / ér zǐ hěn yīng jùn.*
What a beautiful baby!	多漂亮的宝宝啊！ *duō piào liang de bǎo bǎo ā!*
Are you here on business?	您是到这出差吗？ *nín shì dào zhè chū chāi ma?*
I am vacationing.	我正在度假。 *wǒ zhèng zài dù jià.*
I'm attending a conference.	我在参加一个会议。 *wǒ zài cān jiā yī gè huì yì.*
How long are you staying?	您将停留多长时间？ *nín jiāng tíng liú duō cháng shí jiān?*
What are you studying?	您在学什么？ *nín zài xué shén me?*
I'm a student.	我是一名学生。 *wǒ shì yī míng xué shēng.*
Where are you from?	你从哪里来？ *nǐ cóng nǎ lǐ lái?*

PERSONAL DESCRIPTIONS

blond(e)	金发的 *jīn fā de*
brunette	黑发的 *hēi fā de*
redhead	红发的 *hóng fā de*

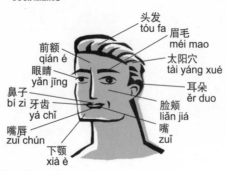

straight hair	直发
	zhí fā
curly hair	卷发
	juàn fā
kinky hair	卷缩发
	juàn suō fā
long hair	长发
	cháng fā
short hair	短发
	duǎn fā
tanned	茶色
	chá sè
pale	苍白的
	cāng bái de
mocha-skinned	咖啡色皮肤的
	kā fēi sè pí fū de
black	黑色的
	hēi sè de
white	白色的
	bái sè de
Asian	亚洲人
	yà zhōu rén

African-American	非裔美洲人
	fēi yì měi zhōu rén
Caucasian	白种人
	bái zhǒng rén
biracial	混杂种族人
	hùn zá zhǒng zú rén
tall	高
	gāo
short	矮
	ǎi
thin	瘦
	shòu
fat	胖
	pàng
blue eyes	蓝眼睛
	lán yǎn jīng
brown eyes	棕色眼睛
	zōng sè yǎn jīng
green eyes	绿眼睛
	lǜ yǎn jīng
hazel eyes	淡褐色眼睛
	dàn hè sè yǎn jīng
eyebrows	眉毛
	méi mao
eyelashes	眼睫毛
	yǎn jié máo
freckles	斑
	bān
moles	痣
	zhì
face	脸
	liǎn

Listen Up: Ethnic Backgrounds

我是中国台湾人。 *wǒ shì zhōng guó tái wān rén。*	I'm Taiwanese.
我是中国西藏人。 *wǒ shì zhōng guó xī cáng rén。*	I'm Tibetan.
我是韩国人。 *wǒ shì hán guó rén。*	I'm Korean.
我是菲律宾人。 *wǒ shì fēi lǜ bīn rén。*	I'm Phillipino.
我是中国人。 *wǒ shì zhōng guó rén。*	I'm Chinese.
我是中国澳门人。 *wǒ shì zhōng guó ào mén rén。*	I'm Macanese.
我是泰国人。 *wǒ shì tài guó rén。*	I'm Thai.
我是马来西亚人。 *wǒ shì mǎ lái xī yà rén。*	I'm Malaysian.
我是越南人。 *wǒ shì yuè nán rén。*	I'm Vietnamese.
我是尼泊尔人。 *wǒ shì ní bó ěr rén。*	I'm Nepalese.
我是老挝人。 *wǒ shì lǎowō rén。*	I'm Laotian.
我是印度人。 *wǒ shì yìn dù rén。*	I'm Indian.
我是缅甸人。 *wǒ shì miǎn diàn rén*	I'm Burmese.
我是俄国人。 *wǒ shì é guó rén。*	I'm Russian
我是日本人。 *wǒ shì rì běn rén。*	I'm Japanese.

For a full list of nationalities, see English / Chinese dictionary.

DISPOSITIONS AND MOODS

sad	伤心 *shāng xīn*
happy	高兴 *gāo xìng*
angry	生气 *shēng qì*
tired	累 *lèi*
depressed	沮丧 *jǔ sàng*
stressed	有压力的 *yǒu yā lì de*
anxious	焦虑的 *jiāo lǜ de*
confused	困惑的 *kùn huò de*
enthusiastic	热情的 *rè qíng de*

PROFESSIONS

What do you do for a living?	您是做什么工作的? *nín shì zuò shén me gōng zuò de?*
Here is my business card.	这是我的名片。 *zhè shì wǒ de míng piàn。*
I am _____	我是_____ *wǒ shì _____*
a doctor.	医生。 *yī shēng。*
an engineer.	工程师。 *gōng chéng shī。*
a lawyer.	律师。 *lǜ shī。*

a salesperson.	销售。
	xiāo shòu.
a writer.	作家。
	zuò jiā.
an editor.	编辑。
	biān jí.
a designer.	设计师。
	shè jì shī.
an educator.	教育工作者。
	jiào yù gōng zuò zhě.
an artist.	搞艺术的。
	gǎo yì shù de.
a craftsperson.	手艺人。
	shǒu yì rén.
a homemaker.	家庭主妇。
	jiā tíng zhǔ fù.
an accountant.	会计。
	kuài jì.
a nurse.	护士。
	hù shì.
a musician.	搞音乐的。
	gǎo yīnyuè de.
a military professional.	军事专家。
	jūn shì zhuān jiā.
a government employee.	公务员。
	gōng wù yuán.

DOING BUSINESS

I'd like an appointment.	我要安排一次约会。
	wǒ yào ān pái yī cì yuē huì.
I'm here to see ____.	我到这里看_____。
	wǒ dào zhè lǐ kàn _____.
May I photocopy this?	我可以影印这份材料吗?
	wǒ kě yǐ yǐng yìn zhè fèn cái liào ma?

May I use a computer here?	我可以使用这里的计算机吗？
	wǒ kě yǐ shǐ yòng zhè lǐ de jì suàn jī ma?
What's the password?	密码是什么？
	mì mǎ shì shén me?
May I access the Internet?	我可以上网吗？
	wǒ kě yǐ shàng wǎng ma?
May I send a fax?	我可以发份传真吗？
	wǒ kě yǐ fā fèn chuán zhēn ma?
May I use the phone?	我可以使用电话吗？
	wǒ kě yǐ shǐ yòng diàn huà ma?

PARTING WAYS

Keep in touch.	保持联络。
	bǎo chí lián luò。
Please write or email.	请写信或发送电子邮件。
	qǐng xiě xìn huò fā sòng diàn zǐ yóu jiàn。
Here's my phone number. Call me.	这是我的电话号码。 打电话给我。
	zhè shì wǒ de diàn huà hào mǎ。
	dǎ diàn huà gěi wǒ。
May I have your phone number / e-mail please?	请给我您的电话号码／电子邮件好吗？
	qǐng gěi wǒ nín de diàn huà hào mǎ / diàn zǐ yóu jiàn hǎo ma?
May I have your card?	可以给我您的名片吗？
	kě yǐ gěi wǒ nín de míng piàn ma?
Give me your address and I'll write you.	给我您的地址，我会写信给你。
	gěi wǒ nín de dì zhǐ, wǒ huì xiě xìn gěi nǐ。

TOPICS OF CONVERSATION

As in the United States or Europe, the weather and current affairs are common conversation topics.

THE WEATHER

It's so _____	今天天气_____
	jīn tiān tiān qì _____
Is it always so _____ ?	天气总是这样_____?
	tiān qì zǒng shì zhè yàng _____?
sunny.	晴朗吗
	qíng lǎng ma
rainy.	多雨吗
	duō yǔ ma
cloudy.	多云吗
	duō yún ma
humid.	潮湿吗
	cháo shī ma
warm.	暖和吗
	nuǎn huó ma
cool.	凉爽吗
	liáng shuǎng ma
windy.	有风吗
	yǒu fēng ma
Do you know the weather forecast for tomorrow?	您知道明天的天气预报吗?
	nín zhī dào míng tiān de tiān qì yù bào ma?

THE ISSUES

What do you think about _____	您怎样看待_____
	nín zěn yàng kàn dài _____
democracy?	民主主义?
	mín zhǔ zhǔyi?
socialism?	社会主义?
	shè huì zhǔ yì?
American Democrats?	美国民主党?
	měi guó mín zhǔ dǎng?

American Republicans?	美国共和党?
	měi guó gòng hé dǎng?
the environment?	环境问题?
	huán jìng wèn tí?
monarchy?	君主政体?
	jūn zhǔ zhèng tǐ?
climate change?	气候变化?
	qì hòu biàn huà?
the economy?	经济形势?
	jīng jì xíng shì?
What political party do you belong to?	您属于什么党派?
	nín shǔ yú shén me dǎng pài?
What did you think of the election in ____?	你对---- 的大选怎么看?
	nǐ duì ____ de dà xuǎn zěn me kàn?
What do you think of the war in ____?	您怎样看待____战争?
	nín zěn yàng kàn dài _____ zhàn zhēng?

RELIGION

Do you go to church / temple / mosque?	您上教堂 / 寺庙 / 清真寺吗?
	nín shàng jiào táng / sì miào / qīng zhēn sì ma?
Are you religious?	您信仰宗教吗?
	nín xìn yǎng zōng jiào ma?
I'm ____ / I was raised ____	我信仰_____ / 我受教于_____
	wǒ xìn yǎng _____ / wǒ shòu jiào yú _____
Protestant.	新教。
	xīn jiào。
Catholic.	天主教。
	tiān zhǔ jiào。
Jewish.	犹太教。
	yóu tài jiào。
Muslim.	穆斯林教 / 伊斯兰教。
	mù sī lín jiào / ī sī lán jiào。

Buddhist.	佛教。 *fó jiào。*
Greek Orthodox.	希腊正教。 *xī là zhèng jiào。*
Hindu.	印度教。 *yìn dù jiào。*
agnostic.	不可知论。 *bù kě zhī lùn。*
atheist.	无神论。 *wú shén lùn。*
I'm spiritual but I don't attend services.	我精神上信仰但不参加活动。 *wǒ jīng shen shàng xìn yǎng dàn bù cān jiā huó dòng。*
I don't believe in that.	我不信仰宗教。 *wǒ bù xìn yǎng zōng jiào。*
That's against my beliefs.	这违背我的信仰。 *zhè wéi bèi wǒ de xìn yǎng。*
I'd rather not talk about it.	我不想谈这个问题。 *wǒ bù xiǎng tán zhè gè wèn tí。*

GETTING TO KNOW SOMEONE

Following are some conversation starters.

MUSICAL TASTES

What kind of music do you like?	您喜欢哪种音乐? *nín xǐ huān nǎ zhǒng yīn yuè?*
I like _____	我喜欢_____ *wǒ xǐ huān _____*
rock 'n' roll.	摇滚乐。 *yáo gǔn yuè。*
hip hop.	街舞。 *jiē wǔ。*
techno.	电子音乐。 *diàn zǐ yīn yuè。*
soul.	灵魂音乐 *líng hún yīn yuè。*

classical.	古典音乐。
	gǔ diǎn yīn yuè.
jazz.	爵士乐。
	jué shì yuè.
country and western.	乡村和西部音乐。
	xiāng cūn hé xī bù yīn yuè.
reggae.	瑞格舞。
	ruì gé wǔ.
opera.	歌剧。
	gē jù.
show-tunes / musicals.	歌剧音乐 / 音乐剧。
	gē jù yīn yuè / yīn yuè jù.
New Age.	新世纪音乐。
	xīn shì jì yīn yuè.
pop.	流行音乐。
	liú xíng yīn yuè.

HOBBIES

What do you like to do in your spare time?	您业余时间喜欢做什么？
	nín yè yú shí jiān xǐ huān zuò shén me?
I like _____	我喜欢_____
	wǒ xǐ huān _____
playing guitar.	弹吉他。
	tán jí tā.
piano.	弹钢琴。
	tán gāng qín.

For other instruments, see the English / Chinese dictionary.

painting / drawing.	画画。
	huà huà.
dancing.	跳舞。
	tiào wǔ.
reading.	阅读。
	yuè dú.
watching TV.	看电视。
	kàn diàn shì.
shopping.	购物。
	gòu wù.

going to the movies.	看电影。 *kàn diàn yǐng。*
hiking.	徒步旅行。 *tú bù lǚ xíng。*
camping.	露营。 *lù yíng。*
hanging out.	闲逛。 *xián guàng。*
traveling.	旅行。 *lǚ xíng。*
eating out.	到外面吃。 *dào wài miàn chī。*
cooking.	烹饪。 *pēng rèn。*
sewing.	做缝纫。 *zuò féng rèn。*
sports.	做运动。 *zuò yùn dòng。*
Do you like to dance?	您喜欢跳舞吗？ *nín xǐ huān tiào wǔ ma?*
Would you like to go out?	您喜欢外出吗？ *nín xǐ huān wài chū ma?*
May I buy you dinner sometime?	我什么时候能请您吃饭吗？ *wǒ shén me shí hòu néng qǐng nín chī fàn ma?*
What kind of food do you like?	您喜欢哪种食物？ *nín xǐ huān nǎ zhǒng shí wù?*

For a full list of food types, see Dining in Chapter 4.

Would you like to go _____	您想去_____ *nín xiǎng qù_____*
to a movie?	看电影吗？ *kàn diàn yǐng ma?*
to a concert?	听音乐会吗？ *tīng yīn yuè huì ma?*
to the zoo?	动物园吗？ *dòng wù yuán ma?*

to the beach?	海滩吗？
	hǎi tān ma?
to a museum?	博物馆吗？
	bó wù guǎn ma?
for a walk in the park?	公园散步吗？
	gōng yuán sàn bù ma?
dancing?	跳舞吗？
	tiào wǔ ma?
Would you like to ____	您想_____
	nín xiǎng _____
have lunch?	吃午餐吗？
	chī wǔ cān ma?
have coffee?	喝咖啡吗？
	hē kā fēi ma?
have dinner?	吃晚餐吗？
	chī wǎn cān ma?
What kind of books do you like to read?	您喜欢读哪种类型的书？
	nín xǐ huān dú nǎ zhǒng lèi xíng de shū?
I like ____	我喜欢_____
	wǒ xǐ huān _____
mysteries.	神话故事。
	shén huà gù shì.
Westerns.	西部题材。
	xī bù tí cái.
dramas.	戏剧。
	xì jù.
novels.	小说。
	xiǎo shuō.
biographies.	传记。
	zhuàn jì.
auto-biographies.	自传。
	zì zhuàn.
romance.	浪漫爱情故事。
	làng màn ài qíng gù shì.
history.	历史。
	lì shǐ.

For dating terms, see Nightlife in Chapter 10.

SOCIALIZING BASICS

Expressing political or religious opinions or your views on sex or sexual orientation (at least in public) is not generally done, so avoid these topics when in groups or you may be putting your hosts and potential friends on the spot (and possibly even in danger). On the other hand, be prepared for questions that might take you aback. These can include direct queries about your age, salary or the cost of your clothing, as well as your marital status, whether or not you have children, and if not, why.

Caveats for Socializing

There are cultural sensitivities particular to the Chinese that should be borne in mind in any social setting. The following are some of the most important to remember:

Never Accept a Compliment Graciously   You may find yourself at a loss for words when you compliment a Chinese host on the wonderful meal, and he responds, "No, no the food was really horrible." Your host is merely being humble and polite. Foreigners would do well to practice feigning humility.

Never Publicly Humiliate Someone   This is perhaps the worst thing you can manage to do to a Chinese acquaintance. Never publicly embarrass someone by pointing out mistakes or yelling at him or her. On the other hand, it is greatly appreciated if you compliment someone in public and give credit where and when credit is due.

Never Get Angry in Public   The Chinese place a premium on group harmony, so foreigners should try to be polite and cope with frustrations privately. Negative feelings such as jealousy, anger, disappointment or unhappiness are considered private matters. If you can mask these emotions, the Chinese will respect you and you'll increase the likelihood of achieving your goals.

Never Address People By Their First Names   Chinese people should be addressed by their last name first, followed by their given name. Only family members and a few close friends ever refer to others by their given name alone, often with the prefix for "old" or "young" before it.

Never Accept Food, Drinks or Gifts Without Refusing First   If someone offers you something in their home, no matter how eager you are to receive it, proper Chinese etiquette dictates that you not appear too greedy or eager. Politely refuse several times before grudgingly accepting.

Never Take the First "No Thank You" Literally   Chinese people will automatically refuse food or drinks several times, even if they're very hungry or thirsty. Never take the first "no, thank you" literally. Offer it again. A good guest is expected to refuse at least once, and a good host is supposed to make the offer at least twice.

MEET THE CHINESE

The following locations are well-known for hanging out, people-watching, and striking up conversations with others:

Beijing

Walking Along the Great Wall   The three most popular sections of the Great Wall (Badaling, Mutianyu and Simatai), located in beautiful mountain forests outside Beijing, are ideal for spectacular treks and photo opportunities. They provide a dramatic background for meeting others equally enthralled by the beauty and wonder of China's most well-known landmark and its incredible history.

Picnicking at the Old Summer Palace   Left in haunting ruins by Western armies in the 1860s, the Old Summer Palace is the perfect place for a picnic and a hike. The lakes, arched bridges, and crumbling pavilions recall the days of imperial majesty, when this park was reserved for emperors and their courts.

Burning Incense in the Temples   The Lama Temple in Beijing is popular among visitors and foreign residents alike, and has all the hallmarks of a typical large and active Buddhist temple. A lively shrine more frequented by locals is the White Cloud Temple, where ancient beliefs and superstitions are alive and flourishing, the incense is always burning, and hundreds of Beijingers converge to make wishes and pray that they come true.

Window Shopping on Wangfujing Street   Beijing's top shopping street in the heart of the capital now offers everything from art galleries and scroll shops to wedding stores and chic boutiques. Aging department stores compete with state-of-the-art shopping plazas. The best native fast food is served from stalls in the night market off Wangfujing (Donghuamen Yeshi).

Lingering in the Teahouses   The teahouse tradition has staged a comeback in Beijing, with tea and snacks served in old teahouses to the accompaniment of singing, dancing, comedy, acrobatics, and magic. The best place to soak up the Qing Dynasty (1644-1911) atmosphere is the **Tianqiao Happy Teahouse** (✆ **010/6304-0616**), where your tea cup is always full and the intimate stage is filled with opera singers and acrobats.

Shanghai

Strolling the Bund   You'll want to stroll along the most widely known street in Asia, with its gorgeous colonial buildings that were the banks, hotels, trading firms and private clubs of foreign taipans (bosses of old Shanghai's trading firms) in an earlier era. Some architectural gems to look for are the **Peace Hotel**, the **Customs House**, and the former **Hong Kong and Shanghai Bank**. The **Bund Promenade** is where the masses mingle amid the splendor and grandeur of old Shanghai. At night it's truly romantic. Tai chi, performed by thousands of Chinese along the Bund early in the morning, is always fascinating to watch.

Cruising the Huangpu River   A 17-mile pleasure cruise from the Bund to the mouth of the Yangzi River, past endless wharves, factories and tankers at anchor, gives substance to Shanghai's claim as China's largest port. Nearly half of China's trade with the outside world travels these waters. The cruise lasts more than an hour and offers you an opportunity to get to know fellow tourists and Chinese alike.

Visiting Nanjing Lu, China's #1 Shopping Street   This is a requisite for any visit to Shanghai, if only for a chance to marvel at the sheer numbers of people everywhere. A pedestrian mall makes strolling and browsing that much easier as well as that much more crowded. While it may not be the most leisurely experience, it will be a memorable one.

Listening to the Peace Hotel Jazz Band   Nightly performances of New Orleans-style jazz, where some members of the band have been playing since before the Revolution of 1949, offer the ultimate in colonial nostalgia. Don't miss it.

Hanging out at Xin Tiandi   "New Heaven on Earth," known as "Xin Tiandi" in Chinese (pronounced "shin tyan dee") is a trendy pedestrian mall comprised of restaurants, bars and boutiques in restored "shikumen" (stone gate) houses designed by Ben Wood, a Boston architect, in the 1990s. Here you can see how today's hip young Shanghainese like to spend their free time (and hard earned money). The capitalistic lifestyle here is particularly ironic given that the development is anchored in the south, by the site of the First National Congress of the Communist Party, established in 1921.

CHAPTER SIX

MONEY & COMMUNICATIONS

This chapter covers money, the mail, phone, Internet service, and other tools you need to connect with the outside world.

MONEY

Do you accept ____	可以_____ *kě yǐ* _____
Visa / MasterCard / Discover / American Express / Diners' Club? credit cards?	用 Visa 卡 / MasterCard 卡 / Discover 卡 / American Express 卡 / Diners' Club 卡吗？ 用信用卡吗？ *yòng Visa kǎ / MasterCard kǎ / Discover kǎ / American Express kǎ / Diners' Club kǎ ma?* *yòng xìn yòng kǎ ma?*
bills?	用纸币吗？ *yòng zhǐ bì ma?*
coins?	用硬币吗？ *yòng yìng bì ma?*
checks?	用支票吗？ *yòng zhī piào ma?*
travelers checks?	用旅行支票吗？ *yòng lǚ xíng zhī piào ma?*
money transfer?	转帐吗？ *zhuǎn zhàng ma?*
May I wire transfer funds here?	可以在这里办电汇吗？ *kě yǐ zài zhè lǐ bàn diàn huì ma?*
Would you please tell me where to find ____	您能告诉我哪里有_____吗？ *nín néng gào sù wǒ nǎ lǐ yǒu* _____*ma?*
a bank?	银行 *yín háng*

a credit bureau?	信用局 *xìn yòng jú*
an ATM?	自动取款机 *zì dòng qǔ kuǎn jī*
a currency exchange?	货币兑换处 *huò bì duì huàn chù*
A receipt, please.	请给我一份收据。 *qǐng gěi wǒ yī fèn shōu jù。*
Would you tell me ____	您能告诉我_____ *nín néng gào sù wǒ _____*
the exchange rate for dollars to ____?	美元对_____的汇率吗? *měi yuán duì _____ de huì lǜ ma?*
the exchange rate for pounds to ____?	英镑对_____的汇率吗? *yīng bàng duì _____ de huìlǜ ma?*
Is there a service charge?	有服务费吗? *yǒu fú wù fèi ma?*
May I have a cash advance on my credit card?	我可以在我的信用卡上预提现金吗? *wǒ kě yǐ zài wǒ de xìn yòng kǎ shàng yù tí xiàn jīn ma?*
Will you accept a credit card?	可以用信用卡吗? *kě yǐ yòng xìn yòng kǎ ma?*

Listen Up: Bank Lingo

请在这里签字。 *qǐng zài zhè lǐ qiān zì。*	Please sign here.
这是您的收据。 *zhè shì nín de shōu jù。*	Here is your receipt.
请出示一下您的身份证，好吗? *qǐng chū shì yī xià nín de shēn fèn zhèng, hǎo ma?*	May I see your ID, please?
我们接受旅行支票。 *wǒ mén jiē shòu lǚ xíng zhī piào。*	We accept travelers checks.
只收现金。 *zhǐ jǐn shōu xiàn jīn。*	Cash only.

May I have smaller bills, please.	我能要些面额小点的钞票吗？
	wǒ néng yào xiē miàn é xiǎo diǎn de chāo piào ma?
Can you make change?	可以换零钱吗？
	kě yǐ huàn líng qián ma?
I only have bills.	我只有纸币。
	wǒ zhǐ yǒu zhǐ bì。
Some coins, please.	请给我一些硬币。
	qǐng gěi wǒ yī xiē yìng bì。

ATM Machine

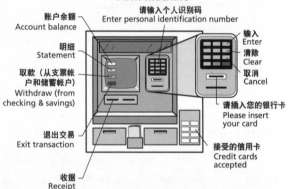

账户余额
Account balance

请输入个人识别码
Enter personal identification number

输入
Enter

明细
Statement

清除
Clear

取款（从支票帐户和储蓄帐户）
Withdraw (from checking & savings)

取消
Cancel

退出交易
Exit transaction

请插入您的银行卡
Please insert your card

收据
Receipt

接受的信用卡
Credit cards accepted

PHONE SERVICE

Where can I buy or rent a cell phone?	在哪里可以买到或租到移动电话？
	zài nǎ lǐ kě yǐ mǎi dào huò zū dào yí dòng diàn huà?
What rate plans do you have?	请问是怎么收费的？
	qǐng wèn shì zěn me shōu fèi de?
Is this good throughout the country?	这在全国通用吗？
	zhè zài quán guó tōng yòng ma?

May I have a prepaid phone?

给我一部预付费电话好吗?

gěi wǒ yī bù yù fù fèi diàn huà hǎo ma?

Where can I buy a phone card?

在哪里能买到电话卡?

zài nǎ lǐ néng mǎi dào diàn huà kǎ?

May I add more minutes to my phone card?

电话卡里还能添加更多分钟吗?

diàn huà kǎ lǐ hái néng tiān jiā gèng duō fēn zhōng ma?

MAKING A CALL

May I dial direct?

可以直接拨号吗?

kě yǐ zhí jiē bō hào ma?

Operator please.

请找接线员。

qǐng zhǎo jiē xiàn yuán。

I'd like to make an international call.

我想打一个国际电话。

wǒ xiǎng dǎ yī gè guó jì diàn huà。

Listen Up: Telephone Lingo

您好?
Nín hǎo?

Hello?

号码是多少?
Hào mǎ shì duō shǎo?

What number?

对不起, 您拨的电话正忙。
duì bù qǐ, nín bō de diàn huà zhèng máng。

I'm sorry, the line is busy.

请挂掉再重拨。
qǐng guà diào zài chóng bō。

Please, hang up and redial.

对不起, 您拨的电话无人接听。
duì bù qǐ, nín bō de diàn huà wú rén jiē tīng。

I'm sorry, nobody is answering.

您的电话卡还可用十分钟。
nín de diàn huà kǎ hái kě yòng shí fēn zhōng。

Your card has ten minutes left.

I'd like to make a collect call.

我想打一个对方付费电话。

wǒ xiǎng dǎ yī gè duì fāng fù fèi diàn huà。

I'd like to use a calling card.

我想用电话卡。

wǒ xiǎng yòng diàn huà kǎ。

Bill my credit card.

用我的信用卡付款。

yòng wǒ de xìn yòng kǎ fù kuǎn。

May I bill the charges to my room?

可以把费用转到我的房费上吗?

kě yǐ bǎ fèi yòng zhuǎn dào wǒ de fáng fèi shàng ma?

May I bill the charges to my home phone?

可以把费用转到我的家庭电话上吗?

kě yǐ bǎ fèi yòng zhuǎn dào wǒ de jiā tíng diàn huà shàng ma?

Information desk, may I help you?

请讲。

qǐng jiǎng。

I'd like the number for ____.

我想要_____号码。

wǒ xiǎng yào _____ hào mǎ。

I just got disconnected.

我的电话刚刚断了。

wǒ de diàn huà gāng gāng duàn le。

The line is busy.

线路正忙。

xiàn lù zhèng máng。

I lost the connection.

我断线了。

wǒ duàn xiàn le。

INTERNET ACCESS

Where is an Internet café?	哪里有网吧？
	nǎ lǐ yǒu wǎng bā?
Is there a wireless hub nearby?	附近有无线通讯中枢吗？
	fù jìn yǒu wú xiàn tōng xùn zhōng shū ma?
How much do you charge per minute / hour?	每分钟 / 小时收费是多少？
	měi fēn zhōng / xiǎo shí shōu fèi shì duō shǎo?
Can I print here?	这里能打印吗？
	zhè lǐ néng dǎ yìn ma?
Can I burn a CD?	我能刻张 CD 吗？
	wǒ néng kè zhāng CD ma?
Would you please help me change the language preference to English?	请帮我把首选语言改成英语好吗？
	qǐng bāng wǒ bǎ shǒu xuǎn yǔ yán gǎi chéng yīng yǔ hǎo ma?
May I scan something?	我能扫描一些资料吗？
	wǒ néng sǎo miáo yī xiē zī liào ma?
Can I upload photos?	我能上传照片吗？
	wǒ néng shàng chuán zhào piàn ma?
Do you have a USB port so I can download music?	有 USB 接口吗？我想下载音乐。
	yǒu USB jiē kǒu ma? wǒ xiǎng xià zǎi yīn yuè.

Do you have a machine compatible with iTunes?

有能兼容 iTunes 的机器吗?

yǒu néng jiān róng iTunes de jī qì ma?

Do you have a Mac?

有苹果机吗?

yǒu píng guǒ jī ma?

Do you have a PC?

有个人计算机吗?

yǒu gè rén jì suàn jī ma?

Do you have a newer version of this software?

这个软件有更新的版本吗?

zhè gè ruǎn jiàn yǒu gēng xīn de bǎn běn ma?

Do you have broadband?

有宽带吗?

yǒu kuān dài ma?

How fast is your connection speed here?

这里的连接速度有多快?

zhè lǐ de lián jiē sù dù yǒu duō kuài?

GETTING MAIL

Where is the post office?

邮局在哪里?

yóu jú zài nǎ lǐ?

May I send an international package?

我可以寄一个国际包裹吗?

wǒ kě yǐ jì yī gè guó jì bāo guǒ ma?

Do I need a customs form?

我需要填写海关表格吗?

wǒ xū yào tián xiě hǎi guān biǎo gé ma?

Do you sell insurance for packages?

可以为包裹购买保险吗?

kě yǐ wéi bāo guǒ gòu mǎi bǎo xiǎn ma?

Please, mark it fragile.

请标明易碎物品。

qǐng biāo míng yì suì wù pǐn。

Please, handle with care.

请小心轻放。

qǐng xiǎo xīn qīng fàng。

Do you have twine?

有细绳吗?

yǒu xì shéng ma?

Listen Up: Postal Lingo

下一个！ *xià yī gè!*	Next!
请放在这里。 *qǐng fàng zài zhè lǐ.*	Please, set it here.
哪一类？ *nǎ yī lèi?*	Which class?
您想要哪种服务？ *nín xiǎng yào nǎ zhǒng fú wù?*	What kind of service would you like?
可以为您做些什么？ *kě yǐ wéi nín zuò xiē shén me?*	How can I help you?
邮件投入窗口 *yóu jiàn tóu rù chuāng kǒu*	dropoff window
领取窗口 *lǐng qǔ chuāng kǒu*	pickup window

COMMUNICATIONS

Where is a DHL office?	哪里有 **DHL** 营业所？ *nǎ lǐ yǒu DHL yíng yè suǒ?*
Do you sell stamps?	卖邮票吗？ *mài yóu piào ma?*
Do you sell postcards?	卖明信片吗？ *mài míng xìn piàn ma?*
May I send that first class?	我可以按第一类邮件邮寄吗？ *wǒ kě yǐ àn dì yī lèi yóu jiàn yóu jì ma?*
How much to send that express / air mail?	特快专递／空邮要多少钱？ *tè kuài zhuān dì / kōng yóu yào duō shǎo qián?*
Do you offer overnight delivery?	提供隔夜交付服务吗？ *tí gōng gé yè jiāo fù fú wù ma?*

How long will it take to reach the United States?	寄到美国需要多长时间？ *jì dào měi guó xū yào duō cháng shí jiān?*
I'd like to buy an envelope.	我想买一张信封。 *wǒ xiǎng mǎi yī zhāng xìn fēng.*
May I send it airmail?	我可以寄航空邮件吗？ *wǒ kě yǐ jì háng kōng yóu jiàn ma?*
I'd like to send it certified / registered mail.	我想寄挂号邮件。 *wǒ xiǎng jì guà hào yóu jiàn.*

MONEY

Payment for goods and services in China must be done with the Chinese yuán (¥). It's generally a good idea to change at least some money before you head overseas, but Chinese yuán are not readily available in the U.S. and Canada, and the exchange rate is likely to be highly unfavorable. Currency exchange is legal in China if conducted at hotels, banks and stores, at the official rate set by the central government through the Bank of China; the rate is the same at all nationwide outlets. Don't change money with private individuals or shops, at rates different from the official rate. It is not only illegal, but you may end up with phony bills. Any kind of currency exchange will require you to show your passport, so be sure to carry it with you at all times. Keep all receipts when you change money since you will need them if you wish to reconvert any excess yuán into your home currency on your return.

Yuán Notes & Exchange Rates

Chinese currency is known as **renminbi** (RMB) (pronounced "run mean be," which literally means "the people's money") or **yuán**. It's most commonly referred to as "**kuai qian**" (pronounced "kwye chyan"), which means "pieces of money."

Bills come in denominations of ¥100, ¥50, ¥20, ¥10, ¥5, ¥2 and ¥1, which also appears as a coin. The next smallest unit is the **jiao** (pronounced "jyow"), also referred to as **mao** (pronounced "maow"), which is equal to ¥.10. There are notes and coins for ¥.50, ¥.20, and ¥.10. The smallest and almost worthless unit is the **fen** (pronounced "fun") or cent and, unbelievably, when you change money you may be given tiny notes or lightweight coins for ¥.05, ¥.02, and ¥.01, but this is the only time you'll see them except in the bowls of beggars or donation boxes in temples. The most useful note is the ¥10, so keep a good stock.

ATMs

China has many ATMs, but only a few accept foreign issued cards. Check the back of your ATM card to see which network your bank belongs to: **Cirrus** (www.mastercard.com), **PLUS** (www.visa.com), or **AEON** (www.americanexpress.com). Before you leave home, contact your network to locate a list of working ATMs in China. Be sure you know your **personal identification number** (PIN) and **daily withdrawal limit** before you depart. In general, ATMs at major branches of the **Bank of China** will accept your card. Bank of China currently allows a maximum withdrawal of ¥2,500 per transaction, but you're permitted to make other withdrawals the same day for a maximum daily withdrawal of ¥20,000. Remember that fees are usually higher for international transactions than they are at home. In addition, the bank from which you withdraw cash may charge its own fee.

Credit Cards

Credit cards are a safe way to carry money while in China, although they are usually accepted only at top international hotels, and at restaurants and shops catering to foreigners. You can obtain cash advances (in yuán) against your American Express, Visa, MasterCard, and Diners Club card at major branches of the Bank of China, but there is usually a minimum withdrawal of $150, and you will have to pay a commission plus whatever your card issuer charges you, so this should only be a last resort. If you plan to use your credit cards in China, notify your issuer beforehand, as many of them put a hold on cards that suddenly start registering foreign charges.

Traveler's Checks

These are still a popular way to bring money into China, but they are only accepted at major branches of the Bank of China, at foreign exchange desks in hotels, and occasionally at major department stores and shops targeting foreign tourists. The exchange rate for traveler's checks is fractionally better than for cash, though the commission charged on checks (0.75%) usually offsets any gains. Most Chinese banks will change U.S. dollars into yuán, so it's a good idea to have some U.S. dollar notes on hand in case of emergencies. If you carry traveler's checks, be sure to keep a separate record of their serial numbers to expedite your refund, should they get lost or stolen.

STAYING CONNECTED

Telephones

To call within China For calls within the same city, omit the city code, which always begins with a zero when used (010 for Beijing, 020 for Guangzhou, and so on).

To make international calls from mainland China or Macau First dial 00 and then the country code (U.S. or Canada 1, U.K. 44, Ireland 353, Australia 61, New Zealand 64). Next, dial the area or city code, omitting any leading zero, and then the number. For example, if you want to call the British Embassy in Washington, D.C., you would dial © 00-1-202/588-7800.

For directory assistance In mainland China dial © 114. No English is spoken, and only local numbers are available. If you want other cities, dial the city code followed by 114—a long-distance call. In Hong Kong dial 1081 for a local number, and 10013 for international ones. In Macau dial 181 for domestic numbers, and 101 for international ones.

For operator assistance In mainland China, if you need operator assistance in making a call, just ask for help at your hotel. In Hong Kong dial 10010 for domestic assistance, 10013 for international assistance.

Cellphones in China Make sure your cell phone is at least a tri-band (900 Mhz/1800 Mhz/1900 Mhz) phone that has been "unlocked" to receive service in China. Call your wireless operator at home and ask for "international roaming" to be activated on your account. These charges can be exorbitant, so you may want to consider buying a prepaid SIM card, (they cost about ¥100 in China), which you can install in your phone. Recharge cards are available at post offices and mobile phone stores. It is also easy to rent a phone in Beijing and Shanghai (consult www.china-mobile-phones.com for more information). Rental costs range from $2 to $9 a day before airtime and long-distance charges.

Internet

Despite highly publicized clamp-downs on Internet cafes, monitoring of traffic, and blocking of websites, China remains one of the easiest countries in the world in which to get online.

Without your Own Computer   Almost any hotel with a business center, right down to Chinese government–rated two-star level, offers expensive Internet access, and almost every town has a few Internet cafes (wangba), with rates typically ¥2 to ¥3 per hour, many open 24 hours a day.

With your Own Computer   It's just possible that your ISP has a low-cost local access number in China, but that's unlikely. Never mind, because there's free, anonymous dial-up access across most of China. You can connect directly by dialing the city number and making that the account number and password. It costs a bit more than a local call. A list of city numbers for China can be found at: www.justphonecards.com/country-code-city-code/cn.html.

CHAPTER SEVEN

CULTURE

CINEMA

Is there a movie theater nearby?
附近有电影院吗?
fù jìn yǒu diàn yǐng yuàn ma?

What's playing tonight?
今晚放什么片子?
jīn wǎn fàng shén me piān zi?

Is that in English or Chinese?
是英语的还是汉语的?
shì yīng yǔ de hái shì hàn yǔ de?

Are there English subtitles?
有英文字幕吗?
yǒu yīng wén zì mù ma?

Is the theater air conditioned?
电影院有空调吗?
diàn yǐng yuàn yǒu kōng tiáo ma?

How much is a ticket?
一张票多少钱?
yī zhāng piào duō shǎo qián?

Do you have a ____ discount?
有_____折扣吗?
yǒu _____ zhé kòu ma?

  senior
  老年人
  lǎo nián rén

  student
  学生
  xué shēng

  children's
  儿童
  ér tóng

What time is the movie showing?
电影几点放映?
diàn yǐng jǐ diǎn fàng yìng?

How long is the movie?
电影片长是多久?
diàn yǐng piàn cháng shì duō jiǔ?

May I buy tickets in advance?
我可以提前买票吗?
wǒ kě yǐ tí qián mǎi piào ma?

Is it sold out?
票售完了吗?
piào shòu wán le ma?

When does it begin?
什么时候开始?
shén me shí hòu kāi shǐ?

PERFORMANCES

Do you have ballroom dancing?	有交际舞吗？ *yǒu jiāo jì wǔ ma?*
Are there any plays showing right now?	现在有什么片子正在放映吗？ *xiàn zài yǒu shén me piān zi zhèng zài fàng yìng ma?*
Is there a dinner theater?	有晚餐剧场吗？ *yǒu wǎn cān jù chǎng ma?*
Where can I buy tickets?	在哪里能买到票？ *zài nǎ lǐ néng mǎi dào piào?*
Are there student discounts?	有学生折扣吗？ *yǒu xué shēng zhé kòu ma?*
I need ____ seats.	我需要＿＿＿＿座位。 *wǒ xū yào ＿＿＿＿ zuò wèi.*

For a full list of numbers, see p7.

An aisle seat.	靠过道的座位。 *kào guò dào de zuò wèi.*
Orchestra seat, please.	请给我前排座位。 *qǐng gěi wǒ qián pái zuò wèi.*

Listen Up: Box Office Lingo

您想看什么片子？ *nín xiǎng kàn shén me piān zi?*	What would you like to see?
几张？ *jǐ zhāng?*	How many?
两个成年人吗？ *liǎng gè chéng nián rén ma?*	For two adults?
要爆米花吗？ *yào bào mǐ huā ma?*	Would you like some popcorn?
还需要其他的吗？ *hái xū yào qí tā de ma?*	Would you like anything else?

What time does the play start?	演出什么时候开始？
	yǎn chū shén me shí hòu kāi shǐ?
Is there an intermission?	有幕间休息吗？
	yǒu mù jiān xiū xi ma?
Do you have an opera house?	有歌剧院吗？
	yǒu gē jù yuàn ma?
Is there a local symphony?	有本地交响乐团吗？
	yǒu běn dì jiāo xiǎng yuè tuán ma?
May I purchase tickets over the phone?	可以电话购票吗？
	kě yǐ diàn huà gòu piào ma?
What time is the box office open?	售票处什么时候开始售票？
	shòu piào chù shén me shí hòu kāi shǐ shòu piào?
I need space for a wheelchair, please.	麻烦您，我需要方便坐轮椅的人观看的位置。
	má fan nín, wǒ xū yào fāng biàn zuò lún yǐ de rén guān kàn de wèi zhì.
Do you have private boxes available?	有独立包厢吗？
	yǒu dú lì bāo xiāng ma?
Is there a church concert?	有教堂音乐会吗？
	yǒu jiào táng yīn yuè huì ma?
A program, please.	请给我一张节目单。
	qǐng gěi wǒ yī zhāng jié mù dān.
Please show us to our seats.	请帮我们带位。
	qǐng bāng wǒ mén dài wèi.

MUSEUMS, GALLERIES, & SIGHTS

Do you have a museum guide?

有博物馆指南吗？

yǒu bó wù guǎn zhǐ nán ma?

Do you have guided tours?

有配导游的旅游吗？

yǒu pèi dǎo yóu de lǚ yóu ma?

What are the museum hours?

博物馆什么时间开放？

bó wù guǎn shén me shí jiān kāi fàng?

Do I need an appointment?

我需要预约吗？

wǒ xū yào yù yuē ma?

What is the admission fee?

门票是多少钱？

mén piào shì duō shǎo qián?

Do you have ____

您有____吗？

nín yǒu ____ ma?

student discounts?

学生折扣

xué sheng zhé kòu

senior discounts?

老年人折扣

lǎo nián rén zhé kòu

Do you have services for the hearing impaired?

有为听障人士提供的服务吗？

yǒu wèi tīng zhàng rén shì tí gōng de fú wù ma?

Do you have audio tours in English?

有用英文解说的语音导览设备吗？

yǒu yòng yīng wén jiě shuō de yǔ yīn dǎo lǎn shè bèi ma?

CHINESE ETIQUETTE AND CUSTOMS

Greetings

A simple "Ni hao" ("hello," pronounced "nee how") is enough to acknowledge any Chinese you meet. Older people and those in positions of authority should be addressed as "nin" instead of "ni" for "you."

Never address anyone by their given name first. A person's surname (family name) comes first. Only family members and a few close friends ever refer to someone by their first names. Often the prefix "lao" (pronounced "laow" and meaning "old") or "xiao" (pronounced "shyeow" and meaning "small" or "young") is used to represent familiarity and closeness before the surname. In those cases, the given name is usually not used at all.

Most Chinese names consist of three characters. The one that appears first is the surname, and the remaining two are the given name. If a person has a title, such as Director (changzhang, pronounced "chahng jahng") or Chairman (zhuxi, pronounced "joo she"), it is good manners to address that person by using the family name followed by the title (such as "Mao Zhuxi" for Chairman Mao).

Gestures

Some gestures that we take for granted may not evoke the same response from a Chinese. Shrugging your shoulders as if to say, "I don't know," for example, won't be understood in China. On the other hand, giving the "thumbs up" sign is the same in both cultures, and nodding or shaking one's head for yes or no are also understood. Unlike the Japanese, who bow, the Chinese are accustomed to shaking hands as a form of greeting, albeit with a slight nod of the head as a mini bow of respect. Some gestures that differ between Americans and Chinese include the "come here" sign. The Chinese indicate this with a palm-down hand outstretched toward the listener, waving up and down. Fingers aren't used to motion toward themselves. When saying "I," the Chinese will point to their nose rather than to their heart.

Some postures and gestures are offensive to the Chinese, such as showing someone the bottoms of your feet or giving an enthusiastic bear hug or a slap on the back to a person you don't know well. Above all, do not come into physical contact with a Chinese of the opposite sex you don't know very well, since it will be misconstrued.

On the other hand, belching, spitting and passing gas in public are quite common, and smokers are ubiquitous. Staring is also accepted, as is pointing to people.

The concept of personal distance also differs between cultures. The Chinese will stand way too close for comfort to Americans. Often people of the same sex put their arms around each other, lean on each other, or even hold hands, although there is generally no sexual overtone to such same-sex touching in China.

Gift Giving

The Chinese are inveterate gift givers, so pack as many small, gender-non-specific gifts as possible before you go. You never know when someone will present a gift to you, and that will always necessitate a reciprocal gesture.

When you present the gift, do so with two hands and a slight bow or nod of the head. Protocol and appearances are very important in China. Do not try to compliment anything your hosts are wearing or possess, since it is customary for the Chinese to insist on giving those things to you. Don't be insulted if a Chinese person doesn't open your gift in your presence, as many will only do so when they're alone.

CHARMING CHINESE TOWNS & VILLAGES

China abounds with beautiful scenery, from lush, rice-terraced farmland in the south to haunting, rugged, mountainous terrain in the northwest. While villages in the countryside often come to mind first, several cities close to major metropolises are also worth your time.

Dali   This home of the Bai nationality, located in Yunnan province, is a backpacker's mecca and remains a retreat from the world. You can hike part of the impressive 19-peak Green Mountains to the west, sail on the cerulean Er Hai Lake to the east, and take a bike ride into any of the nearby Bai villages.

Hangzhou   Marco Polo proclaimed some seven centuries ago that Hangzhou, with its beautiful West Lake and surrounding tea plantations, was "the finest, most splendid city in the world." For visitors today, **West Lake**, surrounded by verdant hills, is the highlight. Its islets and temples, pavilions and gardens, causeways and arched bridges have stood as the supreme example of lakeside beauty in China ever since the Tang Dynasty, when Hangzhou came into its own with the completion of the Grand Canal in 609. The city served as China's capital during the Southern Song Dynasty (1127-1279). West of West Lake is the village of Longjing (pronounced "loong jeeng"), meaning "Dragon Well." This is the source of Hangzhou's famous **Longjing tea**, grown only on these hillsides and revered throughout China for its fine fragrance and smoothness. The best tea here is still picked and processed by hand.

Nanxun   Of all the many water villages in the upper reaches of the Yangzi River, the Song Dynasty town of Nanxun contains the most charming mix of traditional houses, flowing streams, ancient stone arched bridges, narrow cobblestone lanes, friendly residents, mansions and estates. Still relatively free of the usual tourist glitter, it can be visited on a long day trip from Shanghai or combined with a longer trip to Suzhou or Hangzhou.

Shaoxing   This city in Zhejiang province has gondolas with arched, black-painted woven bamboo awnings, whose boatmen cruise through areas of ancient housing, passing under Ming dynasty bridges.

CULTURE

Suzhou   Located to the northwest of Shanghai with its famous gardens and canals, which once earned it the moniker "the Venice of the Orient," Suzhou has an unparalleled collection of classic gardens as well as embroidery and silk factories that are the main surviving elements of a cultural center that dominated China's artistic scene for long periods during the Ming (1368-1644) and Qing (1644-1911) dynasties. Central Suzhou, surrounded by remnants of a moat and canals, has become a protected historical district. Of particular interest is the Master of the Nets Garden, the smallest but most perfect of Suzhou's gardens – a masterpiece of landscape compression. The lavish Hall for Keeping the Spring was the former owner's study. Furnished with lanterns and hanging scrolls, it was the model for the Astor Chinese Garden Court and the Ming Furniture Room in the Metropolitan Museum of Art in New York City.

Yangshuo   Located in Guangxi province, this small town on the Li River, nestled in a cluster of spiny pinnacles, has retained enough of its laid-back charm to be a delightful alternative to Guilin. Here the vast landscape is reduced to a garden scale, nature in microcosm, where hills, mountains, oceans, and rivers are reduced to rocks, karsts, streams and pools.

CHAPTER EIGHT

SHOPPING

This chapter covers the phrases you'll need to shop in a variety of settings, from the mall to the town square artisan market. We also threw in the terminology you'll need to visit the barber or hairdresser.

For coverage of food and grocery shopping, see p94.

GENERAL SHOPPING TERMS

Please tell me _____	请告诉我_____
	qǐng gào sù wǒ _____
how to get to a mall?	如何到购物中心？
	rú hé dào gòu wù zhōng xīn?
the best place for shopping?	最好的购物场所？
	zuì hǎo de gòu wù chǎng suǒ?
how to get downtown?	如何到市区？
	rú hé dào shì qū?
Where can I find a _____	哪里有_____？
	nǎ lǐ yǒu _____?
shoe store?	鞋店
	xié diàn
men's / women's / children's clothing store?	男式／女式／儿童服装店
	Nán shì / nǔ shì / ér tóng fú zhuāng diàn
designer fashion shop?	时装设计店
	shí zhuāng shè jì diàn
vintage clothing store?	古董服装店
	gǔ dǒng fú zhuāng diàn
jewelry store?	珠宝店
	zhū bǎo diàn
bookstore?	书店
	shū diàn

toy store?	玩具店
	wán jù diàn
stationery store?	文具店
	wén jù diàn
antique shop?	古董店
	gǔ dǒng diàn
cigar shop?	烟草商店
	yān cǎo shāng diàn
souvenir shop?	纪念品店
	jì niàn pǐn diàn
flea market?	跳蚤市场?
	tiào zǎo shì chǎng?

CLOTHES SHOPPING

I'd like to buy ____	我想买_____。
	wǒ xiǎng mǎi _____.
men's shirts.	男式衬衫
	nán shì chèn shān
women's shoes.	女式鞋
	nǚ shì xié
children's clothes.	儿童服装
	ér tóng fú zhuāng
toys.	玩具
	wán jù

For a full list of numbers, see p7.

I'm looking for a size ____	我要_____号。
	wǒ yào _____ hào。
small.	小
	xiǎo
medium.	中
	zhōng
large.	大
	dà
extra-large.	超大
	chāo dà

耳环
ěr huán

手表
shǒu biǎo

衣服
yī fu

衬衣
chèn yī

领带
lǐng dài

上衣
shàng yī

皮带
pí dài

裤子
kù zi

鞋
xié

I'm looking for ____	我要____
	wǒ yào ____
a silk blouse.	丝质宽松上衣。
	sī zhì kuān sōng shàng yī。
cotton pants.	棉质裤子。
	mián zhì kù zǐ。
a hat.	帽子。
	mào zǐ。
sunglasses.	太阳镜。
	tài yáng jìng。
underwear.	内衣。
	nèi yī。
cashmere.	羊绒衫。
	yáng róng shān。
socks.	短袜。
	duǎn wà。
sweaters.	毛衣。
	máo yī。

眼镜
yǎn jìng

T 恤
T xù

牛仔裤
niú zǎi kù

运动鞋
yùn dòng xié

a coat.	外套。
	wài tào。
a swimsuit.	泳衣。
	yǒng yī。
May I try it on?	我可以试穿吗?
	wǒ kě yǐ shì chuān ma?
Do you have fitting rooms?	有试衣间吗?
	yǒu shì yī jiān ma?
This is _____	这件_____
	zhè jiàn _____
too tight.	太紧。
	tài jǐn。
too loose.	太松。
	tài sōng。
too long.	太长。
	tài cháng。
too short.	太短。
	tài duǎn。
This fits great!	这件很合身!
	zhè jiàn hěn hé shēn!

Thanks, I'll take it.	谢谢，就买这件了。
	xiè xiè, jiù mǎi zhè jiàn le。
Do you have that in ____	那件衣服有_____
	nà jiàn yī fu yǒu _____
a smaller / larger size?	更小 / 更大的号吗？
	gèng xiǎo / gèng dà de hào ma?
a different color?	别的颜色吗？
	bié de yán sè ma?
How much is it?	这个多少钱？
	zhè gè duō shǎo qián?

ARTISAN MARKET SHOPPING

Is there a craft / artisan market?	有工艺品市场吗？
	yǒu gōng yì pǐn shì chǎng ma?
That's beautiful. May I look at it?	那个很漂亮。
	nà gè hěn piào liang。
	我可以看一下吗？
	wǒ kě yǐ kàn yī xià ma?
When is the farmers' market open?	农贸市场什么时间开放？
	nóng mào shì chǎng shén me shí jiān kāi fàng?
Is that open every day of the week?	一周的每一天都开放吗？
	yī zhōu de měi yī tiān dōu kāi fàng ma?
How much does that cost?	那需要多少钱？
	nà xū yào duō shǎo qián?
That's too expensive.	太贵了。
	tài guì le。
How much for two?	两个多少钱？
	liǎng gè duō shǎo qián?
Do I get a discount if I buy two or more?	如果我买两个或两个以上可以打折吗？
	rú guǒ wǒ mǎi liǎng gè huò liǎng gè yǐ shàng kě yǐ dǎ zhé ma?
Do I get a discount if I pay in cash?	如果我付现金可以打折吗？
	rú guǒ wǒ fù xiàn jīn kě yǐ dǎ zhé ma?

Listen Up: Market Lingo

要想细瞧商品，请先打个招呼。
*yào xiǎng xì qiáo shāng pǐn,
qǐng xiān dǎ gè zhāo hū。*

这是找您的零钱。
zhè shì zhǎo nín de líng qián。

两个共四十，先生。
*liǎng gè gòng sì shí, xiān
sheng。*

Please ask for help before
handling goods.

Here is your change.

Two for forty, sir.

No thanks, maybe I'll come back.	不，谢谢，可能我会回来的。 *bù, xiè xiè, kě néng wǒ huì huí lái de。*
Would you take $____?	_____ 美元怎么样？ *_____ měi yuán zěn me yàng?*

For a full list of numbers, see p7.

That's a deal!	就这么定了！ *jiù zhè me dìng le!*
Do you have a less expensive one?	有便宜点的吗？ *yǒu pián yi diǎn de ma?*
Is there tax?	有税吗？ *yǒu shuì ma?*

BOOKSTORE / NEWSSTAND SHOPPING

Is there a ____ nearby?	附近有_____吗？ *fù jìn yǒu _____ ma?*
a bookstore	书店 *shū diàn*
a newsstand	报亭 *bào tíng*
Do you have ____ in English?	您有英文的_____吗？ *nín yǒu yīng wén de _____ ma?*
books	书 *shū*

newspapers	报纸
	bào zhǐ
magazines	杂志
	zá zhì
books about local history	地方历史书籍
	dì fāng lì shǐ shū jí
picture books	图画书
	tú huà shū

SHOPPING FOR ELECTRONICS

Electricity used in China is 220 volts, so most devices from North America cannot be used without a transformer. Most outlets take the North American two-flat-pin plug, or the two-round-pin plugs common in Europe.

Can I play this in the United States?	在美国能玩这个吗？
	zài měi guó néng wán zhè gè ma?
Will this game work on my game console in the United States?	这款游戏可以在我的美国游戏机上运行吗？
	zhè kuǎn yóu xì kě yǐ zài wǒ de měi guó yóu xì jī shàng yùn xíng ma?
Do you have this in a U.S. market format?	您有这个产品的美国市场版本吗？
	nín yǒu zhè gè chǎn pǐn de měi guó shì chǎng bǎn běn ma?
Can you convert this to a U.S. market format?	您能把这个转换成美国市场版本吗？
	nín néng bǎ zhè gè zhuǎn huàn chéng měi guó shì chǎng bǎn běn ma?
Will this work with a 110 VAC adapter?	这个能使用 110 伏交流电适配器吗？
	zhè gè néng shǐ yòng 110 fú jiāo liú diàn shì pèi qì ma?
Do you have an adapter plug for 110 to 220?	您有用于 110 转 220 伏的适配器插头吗？
	nín yǒu yòng yú 110 zhuǎn 220 fú de shì pèi qì chā tóu ma?

Do you sell electronics adapters here?

这里卖电子适配器吗?

zhè lǐ mài diàn zǐ shì pèi qì ma?

Is it safe to use my laptop with this adapter?

我的笔记本电脑使用这个适配器安全吗?

wǒ de bǐ jì běn diàn nǎo shǐ yòng zhè gè shì pèi qì ān quán ma?

If it doesn't work, may I return it?

如果不能用,我可以退货吗?

rú guǒ bù néng yòng, wǒ kě yǐ tuì huò ma?

May I try it here in the store?

可以在店里试一下吗?

kě yǐ zài diàn lǐ shì yī xià ma?

AT THE BARBER / HAIRDRESSER

Do you have a style guide?

有发型样式介绍吗?

yǒu fà xíng yàng shì jiè shào ma?

A trim, please.

剪发。

jiǎn fà.

I'd like it bleached.

我想把头发漂白。

wǒ xiǎng bǎ tóu fà piāo bái.

Would you change the color _____

您能把颜色变得_____

nín néng bǎ yán sè biàn dé _____

 darker?

更深吗?

gèng shēn ma?

 lighter?

更浅吗?

gèng qiǎn ma?

Would you just touch it up a little?

稍稍剪高一点好吗?

shāo shāo jiǎn gāo yī diǎn hǎo ma?

I'd like it curled.

我想把头发弄卷。

wǒ xiǎng bǎ tóu fà nòng juàn.

Do I need an appointment?

我需要预约吗?

wǒ xū yào yù yuē ma?

Wash, dry, and set.	清洗、吹干并做个发型。
	qīng xǐ、chuī gān bìng zuò gè fà xíng。
Do you do permanents?	您做烫发吗？
	nín zuò tàng fà ma?
May I make an appointment?	我可以预约吗？
	wǒ kě yǐ yù yuē ma?
Please use low heat.	请使用低热。
	qǐng shǐ yòng dī rè。
Please don't blow dry it.	请不要吹干。
	qǐng bù yào chuī gān。
Please dry it curly / straight.	请弄卷 / 拉直后吹干。
	qǐng nòng juàn / lā zhí hòu chuī gàn。
Would you fix my braids?	您能修我的发辫吗？
	nín néng xiū wǒ de fà biàn ma?
Would you fix my highlights?	您能修我的挑染部分吗？
	nín néng xiū wǒ de tiāo rǎn bù fēn ma?
Do you wax?	您会去毛吗？
	nín huì qù máo ma?
Please wax my ____	请————
	*qǐng————
legs.	帮我去腿毛。
	bāng wǒ qù tuǐ máo。
bikini line.	去除我比基尼泳装所遮盖的三点部位线条的毛。
	qù chú wǒ bǐ jī ní yǒng zhuāng suǒ zhē gài de sān diǎn bù wèi xiàn tiáo de máo。
eyebrows.	帮我去眉毛。
	bāng wǒ qù méi máo。
under my nose.	去除我上唇上的毛。
	qù chú wǒ shàng chún shàng de máo。

Please trim my beard.	请修剪我的胡子。
	qǐng xiū jiǎn wǒ de hú zǐ.
A shave, please.	请帮我刮面。
	qǐng bāng wǒ guā miàn.
Use a fresh blade please.	请用新的刀片。
	qǐng yòng xīn de dāo piàn.
Sure, cut it all off.	当然，全剪掉。
	dāng rán, quán jiǎn diào.

BEST MARKETS

Beijing
Panjiayuan Jiuhuo Shichang   A vast outdoor market held on weekends, Panjiayuan teems with what is very likely the world's best selection of things Chinese: row upon row of everything from reproduction Ming furniture to the traditional clothing worn by China's many minorities to Mao memorabilia. Most of the antiques are fakes, although experts have made some surprising finds in the bedlam.

Guangzhou
Haizhu Square Wholesale Market   With so many markets to choose from in a city whose very raison d'être is commerce, it is difficult to know which one to choose first. This is one of the most colorful. If it was made in China then there is a very good chance that you will find it around here somewhere.

Hong Kong
Temple Street Night Market   Prices here are outrageous compared to those at China's other markets, but the scene at this night market is very entertaining, especially the fortune-tellers and street-side performers singing Chinese opera.

Kaifeng
Kaifeng Night Market   Visitors overnight in Kaifeng just so they can attend this famous and festive night market whose mainstay is the wide variety of delicious local snacks on offer, such as five-spice roasted bread, sesame soup, and spicy lamb kabob.

Kashgar
Kashgar Sunday Bazaar   Bearded Uighur men in traditional blue-and-white garb sharpen their knives and trim their sheep, small boys gorge themselves on Hami melons, Kyrgyz in dark fur hats pick up and drop dozens of lambs to test their weight and meatiness before settling deals with vigorous and protracted handshakes. Not to be missed.

SHOPPING

Khotan
Khotan Sunday Market   Here, jewelers pore over gemstones, blacksmiths busy themselves shoeing horses and repairing farm tools, blanket makers beat cotton balls, rat-poison sellers proudly demonstrate the efficacy of their products—the sights and smells are overwhelming. Don't miss the horse-riding enclosure toward the north side of the melee, where buyers test the road-worthiness of both beast and attached cart, with frequent spectacular tumbles.

Shanghai
Dongjiadu Fabric Market   Bales and bales of fabric (silk, cotton, linen, wool, and cashmere) are sold here at ridiculously low prices. Many stalls have their own in-house tailors who can stitch you a suit, or anything else you want, at rates that are less than half what you'd pay at retail outlets.

BEST BUYS

Bamboo   The ecologically minded will be impressed and amazed at the versatility of this wondrous plant. Apart from the usual carvings, look for bamboo fiber that has been made into everything from socks to bath towels and the delicious Anji Science Bamboo Beer.

Fake Name-Brand Clothing and Accessories   Adequate to near-perfect imitations of items by North Face, Louis Vuitton, Prada, and just about any other expensive label you can think of can be had for a song at several markets in China, especially at Beijing's Silk Street and Hongqiao markets, Shanghai's Xiangyang Lu market, and Shenzhen's Luo Hu Commercial City (although not quite as cheaply).

Khawachen Carpet and Wool Handicraft Co., Ltd. (Lhasa)   This U.S.-Tibetan factory's carpets have rich but tasteful shades woven into delightful traditional patterns. Carpets can also be made to order. You'll pay much less here than in New York or even Beijing.

Pottery   The city of Chen Lu in Shanxi province boasts 17 small factories which all turn out different styles of pottery, and their showrooms have starting prices so low you'll volunteer to pay more. You can also buy original works in the homes of individual artisans.

Tibetan Handicrafts   High-quality Tibetan handicrafts, including traditional Tibetan clothing, paper, incense, mandala *thangkas*, yak-hide boots, ceramic dolls, door hangings, bags and cowboy hats, are all made on-site at the **Jatson School** in Lhasa (*©* **0891/682-2130**).

Qipao   Tailors in Beijing and Shanghai will cut a custom-fit qipao, the tight-fitting traditional dress better known by its Cantonese name *cheongsam*, sometimes for hundreds of dollars less than in Hong Kong and the West. A quality tailored dress, lined with silk and finished with handmade buttons, typically costs between $100 and $200. Slightly less fancy versions go for as little as $50.

THE ART OF BARGAINING IN CHINA

It helps to know the going prices for items you're interested in. The **Friendship Store** in Beijing is worth scoping out with prices in mind because it marks the high-end price for most items. Hotel shops are also very expensive. The street markets usually have the lowest prices. Haggling is not common practice at government-run stores, most hotel stalls, and modern shops, but it is expected on the street and in small private stores. A good rule of thumb is to offer no more than a quarter of the quoted price and not to accept the first counteroffer. Try to reach a compromise (no more than half the quoted price). Walking away with a firm but polite "No" often brings about a more favorable price. Remember that locals are demon shoppers who scrutinize each potential purchase and exercise mountains of patience before making a buy.

SHOPPING

CLOTHING SIZES

Women's Clothing
Coats, dresses, suits, skirts, slacks

U.S.	4	6	8	10	12	14	16
Europe	36	38	40	42	44	46	48
China	32	34	36	38	40	42	44

Blouses/Sweaters

U.S.	32/6	34/8	36/10	38/12	40/14	42/16
Europe	38/2	40/3	42/4	44/5	46/6	48/7
China	34	36	38	40	42	44

Shoes

U.S.	4	4½-5	5½-6	6½-7	7½-8	8½-9	9½-10	11
Europe	35	35-36	36-37	37-38	38-39	39-40	40-41	42
China	34½	35-35½	36-36½	37-37½	38-38½	39-39½	40-40½	41

Men's Clothing
Suits/Coats

U.S.	34	36	38	40	42	44	46	48
Europe	44	46	48	50	52	54	56	58
China	44	46	48	50	52	54	56	58

Slacks

U.S.	30	31	32	33	34	35	36	37	38	39
Europe	38	39-40	41	42	43	44-45	46	47	48-49	50
China	38	39-40	41	42	43	44-45	46	47	48-49	50

Shirts

U.S.	14	14½	15	15½	16	16½	17	17½	18
Europe	36	37	38	39	40	41	42	43	44
China	35/36	37	38	39	40	41	42	43	44

Shoes

U.S.	7	7½	8	8½	9	9½	10	10½	11
Europe	39	40	41	42	43	43	44	44	45
China	39½	40	41	41½	42	42½	43	43½	44

CHAPTER NINE

SPORTS & FITNESS

GETTING FIT

Is there a gym nearby?
附近有体育馆吗?
fù jìn yǒu tǐ yù guǎn ma?

Do you have free weights?
有自由重量训练吗?
yǒu zì yóu zhòng liàng xùn liàn ma?

I'd like to go for a swim.
我想去游泳。
wǒ xiǎng qù yóu yǒng。

Do I have to be a member?
我必须是会员吗?
wǒ bì xū shì huì yuán ma?

May I come here for one day?
我可以来这里一天吗?
wǒ kě yǐ lái zhè lǐ yī tiān ma?

How much does a membership cost?
成为会员得花多少钱?
chéng wéi huì yuán děi huā duō shǎo qián?

I need to get a locker please.
麻烦您，我需要一个存物柜。
má fan nín, wǒ xū yào yī gè cún wù guì。

Do you have a lock?
有锁吗?
yǒu suǒ ma?

Do you have a treadmill?
有跑步机吗?
yǒu pǎo bù jī ma?

Do you have a stationary bike?

有健身车吗？

yǒu jiàn shēn chē ma?

Do you have handball / squash courts?

有手球 / 壁球场吗？

yǒu shǒu qiú / bì qiú chǎng ma?

Are they indoors?

是在室内吗？

shì zài shì nèi ma?

I'd like to play tennis.

我想打网球。

wǒ xiǎng dǎ wǎng qiú。

Would you like to play?

您想玩吗？

nín xiǎng wán ma?

I'd like to rent a racquet.

我想租一副球拍。

wǒ xiǎng zū yī fù qiú pāi。

I need to buy some ____

我需要买一些 _____

wǒ xū yào mǎi yī xiē _____

new balls.

新球。

xīn qiú。

safety glasses.

防护镜。

fáng hù jìng。

May I rent a court for tomorrow?

我可以租一个场地明天用吗？

wǒ kě yǐ zū yī gè chǎng dì míng tiān yòng ma?

May I have clean towels?

可以给我干净的毛巾吗？

kě yǐ gěi wǒ gān jìng de máo jīn ma?

Where are the showers / locker-rooms?

淋浴室 / 存物室在哪里？

lín yù shì / cún wù shì zài nǎ lǐ?

Do you have a workout room for women only?

有女性专用的健身房吗？

yǒu nǚ xìng zhuān yòng de jiàn shēn fáng ma?

Do you have aerobics classes?

有有氧运动课吗？

yǒu yǒu yǎng yùn dòng kè ma?

Do you have a women's pool?

有女士游泳池吗?

yǒu nǚ shì yóu yǒng chí ma?

Let's go for a jog.

我们去跑步吧。

wǒ mén qù pǎo bù bā。

That was a great workout.

这是很好的体育锻炼。

zhè shì hěn hǎo de tǐ yù duàn liàn。

CATCHING A GAME

Where is the stadium?

体育场在哪里?

tǐ yù chǎng zài nǎ lǐ?

Who is the best goalie?

最好的守门员是谁?

zuì hǎo de shǒu mén yuán shì sheí?

Are there any women's teams?

有女子队吗?

yǒu nǚ zǐ duì ma?

Do you have any amateur / professional teams?

有业余 / 专业队吗?

yǒu yè yú / zhuān yè duì ma?

Is there a game I could play in?

有我能参加的比赛吗?

yǒu wǒ néng cān jiā de bǐ sài ma?

Which is the best team?

哪一队是最好的?

nǎ yī duì shì zuì hǎo de?

Will the game be on television?

这比赛会上电视吗?

zhè bǐ sài huì shàng diàn shì ma?

Where can I buy tickets?	在哪里能买到票？ *zài nǎ lǐ néng mǎi dào piào?*
The best seats, please.	请给我最好的座位。 *qǐng gěi wǒ zuì hǎo de zuò wèi。*
The cheapest seats, please.	请给我最便宜的座位。 *qǐng gěi wǒ zuì pián yi de zuò wèi。*
How close are these seats?	这些座位离赛场有多远？ *zhè xiē zuò wèi lí sài chǎng yǒu duō yuǎn?*
May I have box seats?	可以给我包厢座位吗？ *kě yǐ gěi wǒ bāo xiāng zuò wèi ma?*
Wow! What a game!	哇！多精彩的比赛啊！ *wa! duō jīng cǎi de bǐ sài ā!*
Go Go Go!	加油加油加油！ *jiā yóu jiā yóu jiā yóu!*
Oh No!	噢，不！ *ō, bù!*
Give it to them!	传给他们！ *chuán gěi tā mén!*
Go for it!	全力以赴！ *quán lì yǐ fù!*
Score!	得分！ *dé fēn!*
What's the score?	得分是多少？ *dé fēn shì duō shǎo?*
Who's winning?	谁赢了？ *shéi yíng le?*

HIKING

Where can I find a guide to hiking trails?	哪里能找到徒步游向导？ *nǎ lǐ néng zhǎo dào tú bù yóu xiàng dǎo?*
Do we need to hire a guide?	我们需要雇一位导游吗？ *wǒ mén xū yào gù yī wèi dǎo yóu ma?*

Where can I rent equipment?
在哪里能租到装备?
zài nǎ lǐ néng zū dào zhuāng bèi?

Do they have rock climbing there?
那里有攀岩吗?
nà lǐ yǒu pān yán ma?

We need more ropes and carabiners.
我们需要更多的绳子和铁锁。
wǒ mén xū yào gèng duō de shéng zǐ hé tiě suǒ。

Where can we go mountain climbing?
我们在哪里能爬山?
wǒ mén zài nǎ lǐ néng pá shān?

Are the routes _____
路线_____
lù xiàn _____

  well marked?
  标志明确吗?
  biāo zhì míng què ma?

  in good condition?
  情形良好吗?
  qíng xíng liáng hǎo ma?

What is the altitude there?
那里海拔多高?
nà lǐ hǎi bá duō gāo?

How long will it take?
将用多长时间?
jiāng yòng duō cháng shí jiān?

Is it very difficult?	很困难吗？
	hěn kùn nán ma?
I'd like a challenging climb, but I don't want to take oxygen.	我喜欢富有挑战性的爬山，但我不想带氧气。
	wǒ xǐ huān fù yǒu tiǎo zhàn xìng de pá shān, dàn wǒ bù xiǎng dài yǎng qì。
I want to hire someone to carry my excess gear.	我想雇人携带我过多的装备。
	wǒ xiǎng gù rén xié dài wǒ guò duō de zhuāng bèi。
We don't have time for a long route.	我们没时间走长线路。
	wǒ mén méi shí jiān zǒu cháng xiàn lù。
I don't think it's safe to proceed.	我认为继续前进不安全。
	wǒ rèn wéi jì xù qián jìn bù ān quán。
Do we have a backup plan?	我们有备用计划吗？
	wǒ mén yǒu bèi yòng jì huà ma?
If we're not back by tomorrow, send a search party.	如果我们明天没有返回，请派出搜寻队。
	rú guǒ wǒ mén míng tiān méi yǒu fǎn huí, qǐng pài chū sōu xún duì。
Are the campsites marked?	露营地做标志了吗？
	lù yíng dì zuò biāo zhì le ma?
Can we camp off the trail?	我们能在线路外露营吗？
	wǒ mén néng zài xiàn lù wài lù yíng ma?
Is it okay to build fires here?	在这里点火没有问题吧？
	zài zhè lǐ diǎn huǒ méi yǒu wèn tí bā?
Do we need permits?	我们需要许可吗？
	wǒ mén xū yào xǔ kě ma?

For more camping terms, see p76.

BOATING OR FISHING

When do we sail?	我们什么时候启航？ *wǒ mén shén me shí hou qǐ háng?*
Where are the life preservers?	救生用具在哪里？ *jiù shēng yòng jù zài nǎ lǐ?*
Can I purchase bait?	我能买些饵吗？ *wǒ néng mǎi xiē ěr ma?*
Can I rent a pole?	我能租一根杆吗？ *wǒ néng zū yī gēn gǎn ma?*
How long is the voyage?	航程有多长？ *háng chéng yǒu duō cháng?*
Are we going up river or down?	我们在沿河上行还是下行？ *wǒ mén zài yán hé shàng xíng hái shì xià xíng?*
How far are we going?	我们走多远了？ *wǒ mén zǒu duō yuǎn le?*
How fast are we going?	我们走多快？ *wǒ mén zǒu duō kuài?*
How deep is the water here?	这里的水有多深？ *zhè lǐ de shuǐ yǒu duō shēn?*
I got one!	我钓到了！ *wǒ diào dào le!*
I can't swim.	我不会游泳。 *wǒ bù huì yóu yǒng。*
Can we go ashore?	我们能去岸上吗？ *wǒ mén néng qù àn shàng ma?*

For more boating terms, see p58.

DIVING

I'd like to go snorkeling.	我想去浮潜。
	wǒ xiǎng qù fú qián。
I'd like to go scuba diving.	我想去深潜。
	wǒ xiǎng qù shēn qián。
I have a NAUI / PADI certification.	我有 **NAUI / PADI** 证书。
	wǒ yǒu NAUI / PADI zhèng shū。
I need to rent gear.	我需要租装备。
	wǒ xū yào zū zhuāng bèi。
We'd like to see some shipwrecks if we can.	如果可以，我们希望能看到失事船只残骸。
	rú guǒ kě yǐ, wǒ mén xī wàng néng kàn dào shī shì chuán zhī cán hái。
Are there any good reef dives?	有好的跳水帆船吗？
	yǒu hǎo de tiào shuǐ fān chuán ma?
I'd like to see a lot of sea-life.	我想看许多海洋生物。
	wǒ xiǎng kàn xǔ duō hǎi yáng shēng wù。
Are the currents strong?	水流强吗？
	shuǐ liú qiáng ma?
How clear is the water?	水有多清澈？
	shuǐ yǒu duō qīng chè?
I want / don't want to go with a group.	我想 / 不想跟团去。
	wǒ xiǎng / bù xiǎng gēn tuán qù。
Can we charter our own boat?	我们能自己包艘小船吗？
	wǒ mén néng zì jǐ bāo sōu xiǎo chuán ma?

SURFING

I'd like to go surfing.	我想去冲浪。
	wǒ xiǎng qù chōng làng。
Are there any good beaches?	有好的海滩吗？
	yǒu hǎo de hǎi tān ma?

| Can I rent a board? | 我能租一艘船吗？ |
| | *wǒ néng zū yī sōu chuán ma?* |

| How are the currents? | 水流怎么样？ |
| | *shuǐ liú zěn me yàng?* |

| How high are the waves? | 波浪有多高？ |
| | *bō làng yǒu duō gāo?* |

| Is it usually crowded? | 经常那么拥挤吗？ |
| | *jīng cháng nà me yōng jǐ ma?* |

| Are there facilities on that beach? | 那个海滩上有设施吗？ |
| | *nà gè hǎi tān shàng yǒu shè shī ma?* |

| Is there wind surfing there also? | 那里也有滑浪风帆吗？ |
| | *nà lǐ yě yǒu huá làng fēng fān ma?* |

GOLFING

| I'd like to reserve a tee-time, please. | 麻烦您，我想预定开球时间。 |
| | *má fan nín, wǒ xiǎng yù dìng kāi qiú shí jiān。* |

| Do we need to be members to play? | 我们需要是会员才能玩吗？ |
| | *wǒ mén xū yào shì huì yuán cái néng wán ma?* |

| How many holes is your course? | 您的球场有多少洞？ |
| | *nín de qiú chǎng yǒu duō shǎo dòng?* |

| What is par for the course? | 球场的标准杆数是多少？ |
| | *qiú chǎng de biāo zhǔn gǎn shù shì duō shǎo?* |

| I need to rent clubs. | 我需要租球棒。 |
| | *wǒ xū yào zū qiú bàng。* |

I need to purchase a sleeve of balls.	我需要买一筒球。
	wǒ xū yào mǎi yī tǒng qiú。
I need a glove.	我需要一副手套。
	wǒ xū yào yī fù shǒu tào。
I need a new hat.	我需要一顶新帽子。
	wǒ xū yào yī dǐng xīn mào zǐ。
Do you require soft spikes?	您需要软道钉吗？
	nín xū yào ruǎn dào dìng ma?
Do you have carts?	您有高尔夫车吗？
	nín yǒu gāo ěr fū chē ma?
I'd like to hire a caddy.	我想雇一名球童。
	wǒ xiǎng gù yī míng qiú tóng。
Do you have a driving range?	有练习场吗？
	yǒu liàn xí chǎng ma?
How much are the greens fees?	果岭费是多少钱？
	guǒ lǐng fèi shì duō shǎo qián?
Can I book a lesson with the pro?	我能与职业高球手预订一节课吗？
	wǒ néng yǔ zhí yè gāo qiú shǒu yù dìng yī jié kè ma?
I need to have a club repaired.	我有一副球棒要修理。
	wǒ yǒu yī fù qiú bàng yào xiū lǐ。
Is the course dry	球场干吗？
	qiú chǎng gān ma?
Are there any wildlife hazards?	有野生物危险吗？
	yǒu yě shēng wù wēi xiǎn ma?
How many meters is the course?	球场有多少米？
	qiú chǎng yǒu duō shǎo mǐ?
Is it very hilly?	很陡吗？
	hěn dǒu ma?

TRADITIONAL SPORTS

Archery

Once archery was eliminated from the Imperial Military Examination in 1901 by the Emperor Guangxu, this traditional sport died out for the most part in China, although it had a revered history going back at least to the Tang dynasty. It played an important role in Chinese aristocratic life even before the Tang, and was mentioned in oracle bone inscriptions dating back almost 3,500 years to China's first dynasty, the Shang.

Inherent in archery as in virtually all Chinese martial arts forms, is the concept of face-to-face combat with the hands or weapons. Ritual archery, however, was singled out by Confucius as the only proper sport a "civilized man" could engage in, because it necessitated two competitors shooting at a common target. It was to instill decorum, elegance of movement and deference to one's peers, and was to be performed gracefully and with restraint.

Dragon Boat Racing

Dragon boat racing is a popular activity today, particularly south of the Yangzi River, where it is connected to an ancient legend. The poet Qu Yuan (c. 340-278 BC) of the Warring States period was drowned in the Miluo River in Hunan Province on the fifth day of the fifth lunar month before local people could rescue him by boat. Ever since then, dragon boat races have been held on that day each year to commemorate his death.

Shaolin Martial Arts

The Shaolin Monastery, built in 495 AD deep in the woods of a mountain near Dengfeng (Henan Province), is one of the best-known Buddhist temples in the world. It is considered the home of Chan (Zen) Buddhism because Bodhidharma, the father of Chan Buddhism in China, came here from India to teach Chan in 527. The Shaolin Monastery is where Buddhist monks would perfect the austere Zen practice of sitting for long periods of time cross-legged until they reached enlightenment.

To invigorate themselves, the monks would practice martial arts, so the Shaolin style is credited to Bodhidharma himself, who studied the movements of various animals and taught them to his students.

Taiji

The most visible form of exercise throughout China in the early morning hours is Taiji, especially along the Bund in Shanghai where literally thousands of people will be practicing this slow, rhythmic form of exercise around 5 a.m.

The term "taiji" (literally meaning "supreme ultimate" and commonly written "tai chi") refers to an expression from the Chinese Classic, the Book of Changes (Yi Jing). It is also the main concept of the philosophy of Daoism. The "supreme ultimate fist," or "Taiji quan," emerged as a martial art in China before the 16th century, inspired by the Daoist principles of yin and yang (the unity of opposites). Taiji is an ancient martial art focusing on smooth, slow movements that cultivate inner focus and the free flow of energy. Taiji is also thought of as moving meditation. Several different forms of Taiji exist, the most well-known of which are the Yang, the Wu and the Chen, all named for their founders.

CONTEMPORARY SPORTS

Climbing and Extreme Sports

Climbing can of course be done on any of China's sacred (or other) mountains in rural areas, but if you find yourself in a large city such as Shanghai, you should check out the **Masterhand Climbing Club** in the Hongkou District (© 021/5696-6657). Bungee jumping from the ceiling of the Shanghai Stadium is now an option at the **Extreme Sports Center** in the Xuhui District. There are **Go-cart** tracks where you can simulate a Formula One drive, at the **Shanghai Fushida Racing Car Club** (© 021/6531-6800) and the **SSC Karting Club** (© 021/6426-5116), in the Shanghai Stadium.

The ninth day of the ninth month on the Chinese lunar calendar is traditionally observed with a festival devoted to mountains and mountain climbing. In Shanghai, not generally noted for its peaks, the day was recently marked by a race to the top of the city's (and Asia's) highest skyscraper, the 88-story Jin Mao Tower. While some runners required oxygen infusions, the winner, **Hua Xiao**, made the 1,400-foot climb in under 15 minutes.

Equestrian Sports

Equestrian sports have enjoyed a steep rise in popularity lately in China. Currently there are more than 30 equestrian clubs in Beijing alone, including the **Beijing Green Equestrian Club** (✆ 010/6457-7166), and the **Equuleus International Riding Club** (✆ 010/6432-4947; www.equriding.com).

Fitness Centers

Many of China's luxury hotels offer state-of-the-art sports facilities. Even the older, state-run **Friendship Hotel** in Beijing (www.bjfriendshiphotel.com), located within a garden court, has indoor and outdoor pools, tennis courts, a golf range, snooker tables and a mini gym. First class indoor exercise facilities can be found at hotels such as the **Hilton** (www.hilton.com), the **Great Wall Sheraton** (✆ 010/6590-5566; www.sheraton.com/greatwall), **China World Hotel** (✆ 010/6505-2266; www.shangri-la.com/chinaworld), and the **Shangri-La Beijing Hotel** (✆ 010/6841-2211).

Golf

Golf is very much alive and well in China. In downtown Beijing, a 9-hole round can be played at the **Beijing Chaoyang Golf Club** (✆ 010/6501-8354). Other venues include the **Beijing International Golf Club** (✆ 010/6076-2288) and the more opulent **Pine Valley Golf Resort and Country Club** (✆ 010/8979-6868), about 35 miles west of Beijing, which includes an 18-hole Jack Nicklaus Signature Course. Excellent views of the mountains and glimpses of the Great Wall are part of the experience. There is also the **Beijing Country Golf Club** (✆ 010/6940-1111) near the Beijing Airport.

Jogging

The Chinese are very fitness minded, but the increasingly polluted air throughout China, particularly in the capital of Beijing, now hampers vigorous exercise. It is best to begin at dawn before the pollution is at its height. Try to find a college campus with tracks and fields a distance from major roads with heavy traffic. Other jogging venues in Beijing include the Western Hills, the Summer Palace, and Fragrant Hills.

Swimming

Since the Chinese are rather modest about showing their bodies in public, and because of their attempts to maintain a light complexion, swimming isn't exactly the most popular leisure activity in China. However, there are many public swimming pools in the cities and some great beaches along China's coast. Some popular places to sunbathe and swim are **Beidaihe**, a beach along the coast of Hebei Province, about 4 ½ hours from Beijing by train; **Qingdao**, along the coast of Shandong Province (well known for its beer, commonly spelled "Tsingtao"), and more recently the coast of **Hainan** Province, which is convenient for visitors from Hong Kong.

CHAPTER TEN

NIGHTLIFE

For coverage of movies and cultural events, see Chapter Seven, "Culture."

CLUB HOPPING

Where can I find _____	在哪里能找到_____
	zài nǎ lǐ néng zhǎo dào _____
a good nightclub?	好的夜总会？
	hǎo de yè zǒng huì?
a club with a live band?	有现场乐队演奏的俱乐部？
	yǒu xiàn chǎng yuè duì yǎn zòu de jù lè bù?
a reggae club?	瑞格舞俱乐部？
	ruì gé wǔ jù lè bù?
a hip hop club?	街舞俱乐部？
	jiē wǔ jù lè bù?
a techno club?	电子音乐俱乐部？
	diàn zǐ yīn yuè jù lè bù?
a jazz club?	爵士乐俱乐部？
	jué shì yuè jù lè bù?
a country-western club?	乡村音乐俱乐部？
	xiāng cūn yīn yuè jù lè bù?
a gay / lesbian club?	男同性恋 / 女同性恋俱乐部？
	nán tóng xìng liàn / nǚ tóng xìng liàn jù lè bù?
a club where I can dance?	可以跳舞的俱乐部？
	kě yǐ tiào wǔ de jù lè bù?
a club with Spanish / Mexican music?	有西班牙 / 墨西哥音乐的俱乐部？
	yǒu xī bān yá / mò xī gē yīn yuè de jù lè bù?
the most popular club in town?	本市最热门的俱乐部？
	běn shì zuì rè mén de jù lè bù?

a singles bar?	单身酒吧?
	dān shēn jiǔ bā?
a piano bar?	钢琴酒吧?
	gāng qín jiǔ bā?
the most upscale club?	最高级的俱乐部?
	zuì gāo jí de jù lè bù?
What's the hottest bar these days?	这些天最热闹的酒吧是哪个?
	zhè xiē tiān zuì rè nào de jiǔ bā shì nǎ gè?
What's the cover charge?	入场费是多少?
	rù chǎng fèi shì duō shǎo?
Do they have a dress code?	有着装规则吗?
	yǒu zhuó zhuāng guī zé ma?
Is it expensive?	贵吗?
	guì ma?
What's the best time to go?	什么时间去最好?
	shén me shí jiān qù zuì hǎo?
What kind of music do they play there?	那里放什么音乐?
	nà lǐ fàng shén me yīn yuè?
Is smoking allowed?	允许吸烟吗?
	yǔn xǔ xī yān ma?
Is it nonsmoking?	禁止吸烟吗?
	jìn zhǐ xī yān ma?
I'm looking for ____	我在找_____
	wǒ zài zhǎo _____
a good cigar shop.	好的雪茄店。
	hǎo de xuě jiā diàn。
a pack of cigarettes.	一包香烟。
	yī bāo xiāng yān。
I'd like ____	我想要_____
	wǒ xiǎng yào _____
a drink please.	一杯饮料。
	yī bēi yǐn liào。
a bottle of beer please.	一瓶啤酒。
	yī píng pí jiǔ。

Do You Mind If I Smoke?

您有香烟吗？　　　　　　　Do you have a cigarette?
nín yǒu xiāng yān ma?

您有打火机吗？　　　　　　Do you have a light?
nín yǒu dǎ huǒ jī ma?

我能帮您点火吗？　　　　　May I offer you a light?
wǒ néng bāng nín diǎn huǒ ma?

禁止吸烟。　　　　　　　　Smoking not permitted.
jìn zhǐ xī yān。

A beer on tap please.　　　请给我一杯扎啤。
　　　　　　　　　　　　qǐng gěi wǒ yī bēi zhā pí。

A shot of ＿＿ please.　　　请给我一口杯＿＿＿＿。
　　　　　　　　　　　　qǐng gěi wǒ yī kǒu bēi ＿＿＿＿。

For a full list of drinks, see p87.
Make it a double please!　请烈酒量加倍！
　　　　　　　　　　　　qǐng liè jiǔ liàng jiā bèi!

With ice, please.　　　　请加冰。
　　　　　　　　　　　　qǐng jiā bīng。

And one for the lady / the　给这位女士 / 先生一份！
gentleman!　　　　　　　*gěi zhè wèi nǚ shì / xiān sheng
　　　　　　　　　　　　yī fèn!*

How much for a bottle /　瓶 / 杯啤酒多少钱？
glass of beer?　　　　　*yī píng / bēi pí jiǔ duō shǎo qián?*
I'd like to buy a drink for　我想为那边那位女士/先生买份饮
that woman / man over　料。
there.　　　　　　　　　*wǒ xiǎng wéi nà biān nà wèi nǚ shì /
　　　　　　　　　　　　xiān sheng mǎi fèn yǐn liào。*

A pack of cigarettes, please.　请给我一包香烟。
　　　　　　　　　　　　qǐng gěi wǒ yī bāo xiāng yān。

Do you have a lighter or　有打火机或火柴吗？
matches?　　　　　　　　*yǒu dǎ huǒ jī huò huǒ chái ma?*

Do you smoke?

您吸烟吗？

nín xī yān ma?

Would you like a cigarette?

您想来支香烟吗？

nín xiǎng lái zhī xiāng yān ma?

May I run a tab?

可以记帐最后总付吗？

kě yǐ jì zhàng zuì hòu zǒng fù ma?

What's the cover?

入场费是多少？

rù chǎng fèi shì duō shǎo?

ACROSS A CROWDED ROOM

Excuse me; may I buy you a drink?

对不起；可以请您喝杯饮料吗？

duì bù qǐ; kě yǐ qǐng nín hē bēi yǐn liào ma?

You look amazing.

您看上去棒极了。

nín kàn shàng qù bàng jí le。

You look like the most interesting person in the room.

您看上去是这房间里最有趣的人。

nín kàn shàng qù shì zhè fáng jiān lǐ zuì yǒu qù de rén。

Would you like to dance?

您想跳舞吗？

nín xiǎng tiào wǔ ma?

Do you like to dance fast or slow?

您喜欢跳快舞还是慢舞？

nín xǐ huān tiào kuài wǔ hái shì màn wǔ?

Give me your hand.	把你的手给我。
	bǎ nǐ de shǒu gěi wǒ.
What would you like to drink?	您想喝点什么？
	nín xiǎng hē diǎn shén me?
You're a great dancer.	您舞跳得真棒。
	nín wǔ tiào dé zhēn bàng.
I don't know that dance!	我不会跳那种舞！
	wǒ bú huì tiào nà zhǒng wǔ!
Do you like this song?	你喜欢这首歌吗？
	nǐ xǐ huān zhè shǒu gē ma?
You have nice eyes!	你的眼睛真漂亮！
	nǐ de yǎn jīng zhēn piào liàng!

For a full list of features, see p110.

For a full list of features, see p110.

May I have your phone number?	可以把你的电话号码给我吗？
	kě yǐ bǎ nǐ de diàn huà hào mǎ gěi wǒ ma?

GETTING CLOSER

You're very attractive.	你很迷人。
	nǐ hěn mí rén.
I like being with you.	我喜欢和你在一起。
	wǒ xǐ huān hé nǐ zài yī qǐ.
I like you.	我喜欢你。
	wǒ xǐ huān nǐ.
I want to hold you.	我想抱抱你。
	wǒ xiǎng bào bào nǐ.

Kiss me. 吻我。
wěn wǒ.

May I give you _____ 我可以给你_____
wǒ kě yǐ gěi nǐ _____

a hug? 一个拥抱吗?
yī gè yōng bào ma?

a kiss? 一个吻吧?
yī gè wěn ba?

Would you like _____ 您想要_____
nín xiǎng yào _____

a back rub? 揉背吗?
róu bèi ma?

a massage? 按摩吗?
àn mó ma?

GETTING INTIMATE

Would you like to come 你想进来吗?
inside? *nǐ xiǎng jìn lái ma?*

May I come inside? 我可以进来吗?
wǒ kě yǐ jìn lái ma?

Let me help you out of that. 让我帮你。
ràng wǒ bāng nǐ.

Would you help me out 你能帮我吗?
of this? *nǐ néng bāng wǒ ma?*

You smell so good. 你闻起来好香。
nǐ wén qǐ lái hǎo xiāng.

You're beautiful / handsome. 你真漂亮 / 英俊。
nǐ zhēn piào liàng / yīng jùn.

May I? 我可以吗?
wǒ kě yǐ ma?

OK? 好了吗?
hǎo le ma?

Like this? 象这样吗?
xiàng zhè yàng ma?

How? 应该怎么做?
yīng gāi zěn me zuò?

HOLD ON A SECOND

Please don't do that.
请不要那样做。
qǐng bù yào nà yàng zuò.

Stop, please.
请停下来。
qǐng tíng xià lái.

Do you want me to stop?
您要我停下来吗？
nín yào wǒ tíng xià lái ma?

Let's just be friends.
让我们仅仅做个朋友。
ràng wǒ mén jǐn jǐn zuò gè péng you.

Do you have a condom?
您有避孕套吗？
nín yǒu bì yùn tào ma?

Are you on birth control?
您在避孕吗？
nín zài bì yùn ma?

I have a condom.
我有避孕套。
wǒ yǒu bì yùn tào.

Do you have anything
you should tell me first?
有什么要先告诉我的吗？
*yǒu shén me yào xiān gào sù wǒ
de ma?*

BACK TO IT

That's it.
就这样。
jiù zhè yàng.

That's not it.
不是这样。
bú shì zhè yàng.

Here.
这里。
zhè lǐ.

There.
那里。
nà lǐ.

For a full list of features, see p110.
For a full list of body parts, see p192.

More.
更多。
gèng duō.

Harder.
再猛烈些。
zài měng liè xiē.

Faster.
再快些。
zài kuài xiē.

Deeper.

再深些。

zài shēn xiē。

Slower.

再慢些。

zài màn xiē。

Easier.

再温和些。

zài wēn he xiē。

COOLDOWN

You're great.

您真棒。

nín zhēn bàng。

That was great.

太好了。

tài hǎo le。

Would you like _____

您想要_____

nín xiǎng yào _____

a drink?

一杯饮料吗?

yī bēi yǐn liào ma?

a snack?

一份小吃吗?

yī fèn xiǎo chī ma?

a shower?

淋浴吗?

lín yù ma?

May I stay here?

我可以待在这里吗?

wǒ kě yǐ dāi zài zhè lǐ ma?

Would you like to stay
here?

您想待在这里吗?

nín xiǎng dāi zài zhè lǐ ma?

I'm sorry. I have to go now.

我很抱歉。我现在必须走。

wǒ hěn bào qiàn。wǒ xiàn zài
bì xū zǒu。

Where are you going?

你去哪里?

nǐ qù nǎ lǐ?

I have to work early.

我必须早上班。

wǒ bì xū zǎo shàng bān。

I'm flying home in the
morning.

我将在上午乘飞机回家。

wǒ jiāng zài shàng wǔ chéng fēi jī
huí jiā。

I have an early flight.

我得赶早班飞机。

wǒ déi gǎn zǎo bān fēi jī。

I think this was a mistake.	我认为这是一个错误。
	wǒ rèn wéi zhè shì yī gè cuò wù.
Will you make me breakfast too?	您也会为我做早餐吗?
	nín yě huì wéi wǒ zuò zǎo cān ma?
Stay. I'll make you breakfast.	留下来吧。我为您做早餐。
	liú xià lái ba. wǒ wéi nín zuò zǎo cān.

IN THE CASINO

How much is this table?	这张桌子赌注多少钱?
	zhè zhāng zhuō zǐ dǔ zhù duō shǎo qián?
Deal me in.	让我参加。
	ràng wǒ cān jiā.
Put it on red!	放在红色上!
	fàng zài hóng sè shàng!
Put it on black!	放在黑色上!
	fàng zài hēi sè shàng!
Let it ride!	让它转!
	ràng tā zhuàn!
21!	**21!**
	èr shí yī!
Snake-eyes!	蛇眼!
	shé yǎn!
Seven.	七点。
	qī diǎn.

For a full list of numbers, see p7.

Damn, eleven.	该死,十一点。
	gāi sǐ, shí yī diǎn.
I'll pass.	我不投赌注。
	wǒ bù tóu dǔ zhù.
Hit me!	快转到我这儿!
	kuài zhuàn dào wǒ zhè lǐ!
Split.	分牌。
	fēn pái.

Are the drinks complimentary?	饮料是免费赠送吗？
	yǐn liào shì miǎn fèi zèng sòng ma?
May I bill it to my room?	可以把费用转到我的房费上吗？
	kě yǐ bǎ fèi yòng zhuǎn dào wǒ de fáng fèi shàng ma?
I'd like to cash out.	我想兑现。
	wǒ xiǎng duì xiàn。
I'll hold.	我等一下好了。
	wǒ děng yī xià hǎo le。
I'll see your bet.	我看你赌。
	wǒ kàn nǐ dǔ。
I call.	我指挥。
	wǒ zhǐ huī。
Full house!	满堂彩！
	mǎn táng cǎi!
Royal flush.	同花大顺。
	tóng huā dà shùn。
Straight.	顺子。
	shùn zǐ。

PERFORMING ARTS

Acrobatics

Chinese acrobatics are justifiably world famous, their international reputation cemented in no small part by the **Shanghai Acrobatic Troupe**, formed in 1951. While the troupe, one of the world's best, frequently tours internationally, they also perform at home at the **Shanghai Centre Theatre** (☎ 021/6279-8663). The **Shanghai Circus World** (☎ 021/6652-1196) is another good venue for acrobatics performances.

Beijing Opera

A relatively young opera form dating back only 300 years to the early Qing dynasty, Beijing Opera dazzles as much as it grates on the nerves. For the uninitiated, performances can be loud and long, with dialogue sung on a screeching five-note scale, accompanied by a cacophony of gongs, cymbals, drums and strings. This leaves most first-timers exhausted, but the exquisite costumes, elaborate face paint, and martial arts-inspired movements ultimately make it worthwhile. The colorful **Huguang Guild House** (☎ 010/6351-8284), originally built in 1807, is currently Beijing's best opera venue.

Puppets

Puppet shows have been performed in China since the Han dynasty (206 BC–220 AD). Most theatrical performances, including weekend matinees, are held at the **China Puppet Art Theater** in Anhua Xili in Beijing (☎ 010/6424-3698).

Teahouse Theater

Snippets of Beijing opera, stand-up comedy, acrobatics, traditional music, singing and dancing flow across the stage as you sip tea and nibble snacks. If you don't have the time or incentive to see these performances individually, the teahouse is a perfect solution. The most well known teahouse theater in Beijing is the **Lao She Teahouse** (☎ 010/6303-6930), named after a famous Chinese novelist from the early 20th century. Performances change nightly at this somewhat garishly decorated teahouse, but always include authentic opera and acrobatics. All in all, highly recommended.

The Shanghai Symphony
This first-class orchestra was founded in 1879 to entertain the colonialists, taipans, and other Westerners in the city's International Settlement and French Concession. Known then as the Shanghai Municipal Band, it was the first such music group in China. Over the decades, the Shanghainese embraced it, and it has produced many world-class classical musicians (www.sh-symphony.com).

BEIJING AFTER DARK

Beijing's oldest and still most popular drinking district is **Sanlitun**. The name comes from Sanlitun Lu, a strip of drinking establishments east of the Workers' Stadium between the East Second and Third Ring Roads that was once home to practically all the city's bars. Bars here are rowdy and raunchy, and are packed to overflowing on weekends.

Listings for nighttime happenings can be found in magazines such as **That's Beijing**, a free monthly magazine in English (www.thatsbj.com), and **City Weekend** (www.cityweekend.com.cn/beijing). Some recommended bars and clubs in Beijing include:

Bed Bar (Gulou) Carved out of an old traditional home in a *hutong* (Chinese alley), this bar has kang-style bed seating complete with rugs and pillows. It is more of a lounge than a club, but a small dance area exists. © 010/8400-1554.

Buzz Bar (Xidan/Financial Street) Located in the Westin Hotel, this trendy locale is reminiscent of a 70s lounge with a mellow atmosphere. © 010/6606-6866.

Club Obiwan (Houhai) A classy, three-story venue with special theme nights. © 010/6617-3231; www.clubobiwan.com.cn.

East Shore Live Jazz Café (Houhai) A small but authentic live jazz club with floor to ceiling windows looking out on to the Houhai area. ✆ 010/8403-2131.

Frank's Place at Trio (Chaoyang) A lively, neighborhood sports bar bordering on wild and rowdy. Expats regularly gather here for beer and burgers. ✆ 010/6437-8399 x213; www.trio-beijing. com.cn.

Jiadingfang (Houhai) This bar has live music nightly, ranging from traditional Chinese guqing to Western bands. Western food and champagne flow, and lots of big spenders enjoy this club. ✆ 010/6612-9898.

Stone Boat Bar (Ritan Park) Generally frequented by journalists and diplomats, this bar is located in a faux Qing dynasty boat in Ritan Park. ✆ 010/6501-9986.

The Tree (Sanlitun) Known for its pizzas baked in the prominent stone oven, many Europeans hang out here. ✆ 010/6415-1954; www.treebeijing.com.

Beijing Jazz Festivals
China's first (and largest) jazz festival took place in Beijing in 1993, where it ran annually for six years. In 2007 the festival was resurrected in Haidian Park, featuring well known Chinese and Western musicians (www.beijingjazz.cn). Another festival is the **Beijing Ninegates Jazz Festival** (www.ninegate.com.cn).

SHANGHAI AFTER DARK

Shanghai Jazz Bars
Shanghai's pre-revolutionary (before 1949) jazz legacy has been revived for the 21st century. Not only are the old standards being played once again at that most nostalgic of locales—the **Peace Hotel Old Jazz Bar**—but more modern and improvisational sounds can now be heard around town, and there's a greater influx of international jazz artists than ever before. Hotel lounges

NIGHTLIFE

and bars are the most obvious venues for jazz performances, though what you get is mostly easy-listening.

The jazz scene perks up with the **Shanghai International Jazz Concert Series**, a spillover every autumn from the Beijing Jazz Festival. Shanghai's five-day spring jazz festival, known as "**Jazzy Shanghai**," (www.jazzshanghai.com) celebrated its fourth consecutive year in 2007.

Information about jazz events in Shanghai can be found at www.shanghaijazzscene.com. Here are some recommended places to hear jazz in Shanghai:

Club JZ   Established by two musicians as a kind of informal jazz "living room," this spot is known for improvisational jams. ✆ 021/6415-5255.

CJW   This jazz lounge lures the affluent cigar-jazz-and-wine crowd to a dark, moody bar on the top floor of the Bund Center and is strictly for those with expense accounts. ✆ 021/6339-1777.

Cotton Club   The venerable Cotton Club is still the best venue for live jazz and blues. ✆ 021/6437-7110.

Peace Hotel Old Jazz Bar   This place is an institution, with nearly continuous performances since the 1930s and an octogenarian member or two from pre-1949 days still playing. The drinks are predictably expensive and the music (old New Orleans standards) isn't always super, but the atmosphere is sheer nostalgia and no evening could be more Old Shanghai than this. Performances start nightly at 8 p.m. in the historic Art Deco jazz bar at the rear of the main lobby ✆ 021/6321-6888.

CHAPTER ELEVEN

HEALTH & SAFETY

This chapter covers the terms you'll need to maintain your health and safety—including the most useful phrases for the pharmacy, the doctor's office, and the police station.

AT THE PHARMACY

Please fill this prescription.

请填写这张处方。

qǐng tián xiě zhè zhāng chǔ fāng。

Do you have something for _____

a cold?

a cough?

有什么药治_____

yǒu shén me yào zhì _____

感冒？

gǎn mào?

咳嗽？

ké sou?

I need something _____

to help me sleep.

to help me relax.

我需要一些_____

wǒ xū yào yī xiē _____

有助于睡眠的药。

yǒu zhù yú shuì mián de yào。

有助于放松的药。

yǒu zhù yú fàng sōng de yào。

I want to buy _____

condoms.

an antihistamine.

antibiotic cream.

aspirin.

non-aspirin pain reliever.

我想买_____

wǒ xiǎng mǎi _____

避孕套。

bì yùn tào。

抗组胺剂。

kàng zǔ àn jì。

抗生素膏。

kàng shēng sù gāo。

阿司匹林。

ā sī pǐ lín。

非阿司匹林止疼药。

fēi ā sī pǐ lín zhǐ téng yào。

medicine with codeine.	含可待因的药。
	hán kě dài yīn de yào.
insect repellant.	杀虫剂。
	shā chóng jì.
I need something for _____	我需要一些药治_____
	wǒ xū yào yī xiē yào zhì _____
corns.	鸡眼。
	jī yǎn.
congestion.	充血。
	chōng xuè.
warts.	疣。
	yóu.
constipation.	便秘。
	biàn mì.
diarrhea.	腹泻。
	fù xiè.
indigestion.	消化不良。
	xiāo huà bù liáng.
nausea.	反胃。
	fǎn wèi.
motion sickness.	运动病。
	yùn dòng bìng.
seasickness.	晕船。
	yùn chuán.
acne.	痤疮。
	cuó chuāng.

AT THE DOCTOR'S OFFICE

I would like to see _____	我想看_____
	wǒ xiǎng kàn _____
a doctor.	医生。
	yī shēng.
a chiropractor.	脊椎指压治疗医生。
	jǐ zhuī zhǐ yā zhì liáo yī shēng.
a gynecologist.	妇科医生。
	fù kē yī shēng.

an eye / ears / nose / throat specialist.	眼 / 耳 / 鼻 / 喉专家。 *yǎn / ěr / bí / hóu* *zhuān jiā。*
a dentist.	牙医。 *yá yī。*
an optometrist.	验光师。 *yàn guāng shī。*
Do I need an appointment?	我需要预约吗? *wǒ xū yào yù yuē ma?*
I have an emergency.	我有急诊。 *wǒ yǒu jí zhěn。*
I need an emergency prescription refill.	我需要一份续急诊处方。 *wǒ xū yào yī fèn xù jí zhěn chǔ fāng。*
Please call a doctor.	请叫医生。 *qǐng jiào yī shēng。*
I need an ambulance.	我需要救护车。 *wǒ xū yào jiù hù chē。*

SYMPTOMS

For a full list of body parts, see p192.

My ____ hurts.	我的_____受伤了。 *wǒ de _____ shòu shāng le。*
My ____ is stiff.	我的_____僵硬。 *wǒ de _____ jiāng yìng。*
I think I'm having a heart attack.	我认为我心脏病发作了。 *wǒ rèn wéi wǒ xīn zàng bìng fā zuò le。*
I can't move.	我不能动。 *wǒ bù néng dòng。*
I fell.	我跌倒了。 *wǒ diē dǎo le。*
I fainted.	我晕倒了。 *wǒ yūn dǎo le。*
I have a cut on my ____.	我的_____上有伤口。 *wǒ de _____ shàng yǒu shāng kǒu。*

HEALTH & SAFETY

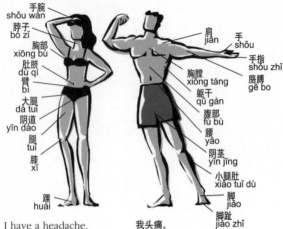

手腕
shǒu wàn

脖子
bó zi

胸部
xiōng bù

肚脐
dù qí

臂
bì

大腿
dà tuǐ

阴道
yīn dào

腿
tuǐ

膝
xī

踝
huái

肩
jiān

手
shǒu

手指
shǒu zhǐ

胳膊
gē bo

胸膛
xiōng táng

躯干
qū gàn

腹部
fù bù

腰
yāo

阴茎
yīn jīng

小腿肚
xiǎo tuǐ dù

脚
jiǎo

脚趾
jiǎo zhǐ

I have a headache.
我头痛。
wǒ tóu tòng。

My vision is blurry.
我的视觉模糊。
wǒ de shì jué mó hu。

I feel dizzy.
我感到眩晕。
wǒ gǎn dào xuàn yūn。

I think I'm pregnant.
我想我怀孕了。
wǒ xiǎng wǒ huái yùn le。

I don't think I'm pregnant.
我想我没怀孕。
wǒ xiǎng wǒ méi huái yùn。

I'm having trouble walking.
我走路困难。
wǒ zǒu lù kùn nán。

I can't get up.
我站不起来。
wǒ zhàn bù qǐ lái。

I was mugged.
我被袭击了。
wǒ bèi xí jī le。

I was raped.
我被强奸了。
wǒ bèi qiáng jiān le。

A dog attacked me.

我被狗咬了。

wǒ bèi gǒu yǎo le。

A snake bit me.

我被蛇咬了。

wǒ bèi shé yǎo le。

I can't move my _____
without pain.

我移动_____时会疼痛。

wǒ yí dòng _____ shí huì téng tòng。

Please fill this prescription.

请按这个处方抓药。

qǐng àn zhè gè chǔ fāng zhuā yào。

I need a prescription for _____

我需要开一剂 _____药。

wǒ xū yào kāi yī jì _____yào。

MEDICATIONS

I need morning-after pills.

我需要一些房事后避孕药。

*wǒ xū yào yī xiē fáng shì hòu
bì yùn yào。*

I need birth control pills.

我需要一些避孕丸。

wǒ xū yào yī xiē bì yùn wán。

I lost my eyeglasses and
need new ones.

我弄丢了眼镜，需要配副新的。

*wǒ nòng diū le yǎn jìng,
xū yào pèi fù xīn de。*

I need new contact lenses.

我需要新的隐形眼镜。

wǒ xū yào xīn de yǐn xíng yǎn jìng。

I need erectile dysfunction
pills.

我需要一些治疗勃起功能障碍的药。

*wǒ xū yào yī xiē zhì liáo bó qǐ
gōng néng zhàng ài de yào。*

It's cold in here!

这里很冷！

zhè lǐ hěn lěng!

I am allergic to _____

我对_____过敏。

wǒ duì _____ guò mǐn。

  penicillin.

  青霉素

  qīng méi sù

  antibiotics.

  抗生素

  kàng shēng sù

  sulfa drugs.

  磺胺药

huáng ān yào

steroids. 类固醇

lèi gù chún

I have asthma. 我有哮喘。

wǒ yǒu xiào chuǎn。

DENTAL PROBLEMS

I have a toothache. 我牙痛。

wǒ yá téng。

I chipped a tooth. 我一颗牙齿有缺口。

wǒ yī kuài yá chǐ yǒu quē kǒu。

My bridge came loose. 我的齿桥松了。

wǒ de chǐ qiáo sōng le。

I lost a crown. 我掉了一个齿冠。

wǒ diào le yī gè chǐ guàn。

I lost a denture plate. 我掉了一个托牙板。

wǒ diào le yī gè tuō yá bǎn。

AT THE POLICE STATION

I'm sorry, did I do something wrong? 很抱歉，我做错了什么事吗？

hěn bào qiàn, wǒ zuò cuò le shén me shì ma?

I am _____ 我是_____

wǒ shì _____

an American. 美国人。

měi guó rén。

British. 英国人。

yīng guó rén。

a Canadian. 加拿大人。

jiā ná dà rén。

Irish. 爱尔兰人。

ài ěr lán rén。

an Australian. 澳大利亚人。

ào dà lì yà rén。

a New Zealander. 新西兰人。

xīn xī lán rén。

Listen Up: Police Lingo

请出示您的执照、登记文件和保单。 *qǐng chū shì nín de zhí zhào、dēng jì wén jiàn hé bǎo dān。*	Your license, registration and insurance, please.
罚款是 **100** 人民币。 *fá kuǎn shì yī bǎi rén mín bì。*	The fine is 100 ¥.
请出示您的护照。 *qǐng chū shì nín de hù zhào。*	Your passport please?
您去哪里? *nín qù nǎ lǐ?*	Where are you going?
您为何那么着急? *nín wèi hé nà me zháo jí?*	Why are you in such a hurry?

The car is a rental.	这车是租来的。 *zhè chē shì zū lái de。*
Do I pay the fine to you?	我付罚款给您吗? *wǒ fù fá kuǎn gěi nín ma?*
Do I have to go to court?	我必须上法庭吗? *wǒ bì xū shàng fǎ tíng ma?*
When?	什么时候? *shén me shí hou?*
I'm sorry, my Chinese isn't very good.	很抱歉,我的汉语不太好。 *hěn bào qiàn, wǒ de hàn yǔ bù tài hǎo。*
I need an interpreter.	我需要一位翻译。 *wǒ xū yào yī wèi fān yì。*
I'm sorry, I don't understand the ticket.	很抱歉,我看不懂这张罚单。 *hěn bào qiàn, wǒ kàn bù dǒng zhè fá dān。*
May I call my embassy?	我可以打电话给我的大使馆吗? *wǒ kě yǐ dǎ diàn huà gěi wǒ de dà shǐ guǎn ma?*

HEALTH & SAFETY

I was robbed.	我被抢劫了。 *wǒ bèi qiǎng jié le。*
I was mugged.	我被袭击了。 *wǒ bèi xí jī le。*
I was raped.	我被强奸了。 *wǒ bèi qiáng jiān le。*
Do I need to make a report?	我需要做份报告吗? *wǒ xū yào zuò fèn bào gào ma?*
Somebody broke into my room.	有人闯入了我的房间。 *yǒu rén chuǎng rù le wǒ de fáng jiān。*
Someone stole my purse / wallet.	有人偷了我的钱包 / 钱夹。 *yǒu rén tōu le wǒ de qián bāo / qián jiā。*

BEFORE YOU LEAVE

Plan well ahead for a trip to mainland China. Depending on the duration and time spent outside larger cities, a few new inoculations may be required, especially if you haven't traveled much in the less developed world before. Start looking into this 3 or 4 months before your trip, since some inoculations need multiple shots separated by a month or two, and some should not be given at the same time. For the latest information on infectious diseases and travel risks, and on the constantly changing situation with malaria, consult the **World Health Organization** (www.who.int) and the **Center for Disease Control** (www.cdc.gov). Check in particular for the latest information on SARS, which may continue long after the media has become bored with reporting it. The standard inoculations, typically for polio, diphtheria, and tetanus, should be up-to date. You may also need inoculations against typhoid fever, meningococcal meningitis, cholera, hepatitis A and B, and Japanese B encephalitis.

The Chinese are generally ignorant about sexually transmitted diseases, which are rife. As with the respiratory disease SARS, the government denied there was any AIDS problem in China until it grew too large to be contained, and it still issues estimates of the spread of infection that are highly conservative. Suffice it to say, condoms are widely available, including Western brands in the larger cities.

If you visit Tibet, you may be at risk from altitude sickness, usually marked by a throbbing headache, loss of appetite, shortness of breath, and overwhelming lethargy. Other than retreating to a lower altitude, avoiding alcohol, and drinking plenty of water, many find a drug called Diamox (acetazolamide) to be effective, if used with caution. For most travelers, one sleepless night is all you will have to endure.

HEALTH & SAFETY

HEALTH

Health Risks

The greatest risk to the enjoyment of a holiday in China is an upset stomach, or more serious illnesses arising from low hygiene standards. Keep your hands frequently washed and away from your mouth. Only eat freshly cooked food, and fruit you can peel yourself. Avoid touching the part to be eaten once it has been peeled. Drink only boiled or bottled water. Never drink from the tap. Use bottled water for brushing your teeth, too.

The second most common cause of discomfort is an upper respiratory tract infection with cold- or flu-like symptoms caused by the heavy pollution. Many standard Western medications (and bogus versions) are available over the counter, but bring a supply of whatever you need.

If you regularly take a nonprescription medication, bring a plentiful supply with you and don't rely on finding it in China. Feminine hygiene products are widely available, but tampons are found mainly in Hong Kong.

Availability of Healthcare

Should you begin to feel unwell in China, your first contact should be your hotel receptionist. Many major hotels have doctors on staff who will try to diagnose and treat minor ailments, and who will know the best place to send foreigners for further treatment.

Be very cautious about what is prescribed for you. Doctors are poorly paid, and many earn kickbacks from pharmaceutical companies for prescribing expensive medicines. Antibiotics are handed out like candy, and indeed, dangerous and powerful drugs of all kinds can be bought over the counter at pharmacies. Mis-prescription is now a significant cause of death in China, including the habit of prescribing a combination of Western drugs and Chinese traditional "medicines," which react badly with each other. In general, the best policy is to stay as far away from Chinese health care as possible.

SAFETY

Crime

China is one of Asia's safest destinations. You must still be cautious about theft in the obvious public places – crowded markets, popular tourist hangouts, bus and railway stations, airports – but the main danger in walking the ill-lit streets at night is of falling down an uncovered manhole or walking into a phone or power wire strung at neck height. Take standard precautions against pickpockets (distribute your valuables around your person, and consider wearing a money belt inside your clothes). There's no need to be concerned about dressing down or not flashing valuables—it's automatically assumed that all foreigners are astonishingly rich anyway—even the scruffiest backpackers. If you are a victim of theft, make a police report, but don't necessarily expect sympathy, cooperation, or action. The main purpose of reporting the crime is to get a theft report to give to your insurers for compensation.

Street crime increases in the period leading up to Chinese New Year as migrants from the country become more desperate to find ways to fund their journeys home. Be especially vigilant at this time of year. Harassment of solo female travelers is slightly more likely if they appear to be of Chinese descent, but is very rare.

Traffic

Traffic is a major hazard for the cautious and the incautious alike. In Hong Kong and Macau, driving is on the left, and road signs and traffic lights are obeyed. In mainland China, however, driving is on the right—at least occasionally. The rules of the road are routinely overridden by one rule: "I'm bigger than you, so get out of my way," and pedestrians are at the bottom of the food chain. Cyclists ride along the sidewalks, and cars mount sidewalks right in front of you as though you don't exist. Watch out for loose paving slabs caused by SUV drivers; usually they only spurt up dirty water, but twisted ankles can occur, too. Cyclists go in both directions along bike lanes at the side of the road, which is also invaded by cars looking to park. The edges of the main lanes also usually have cyclists going in both directions.

Scams

Visitors should be cautious of various scams, especially in areas of high tourist traffic, and of Chinese who approach and speak in English: "Hello friend! Welcome to China!" or similar things. Those who want to practice their English and who suggest moving to some local haunt may leave you with a bill that has two zeros more on it than it should, and there's trouble should you decline to pay.

"Art students" can be pests: They approach you with a story about raising funds for a show overseas, but in fact are merely enticing you into a shop where you will be lied to extravagantly about the authenticity, uniqueness, originality, and true cost of various paintings, which you will be pressured into buying for dozens of times their actual value.

The man who is foolish enough to accept an invitation from pretty girls to sing karaoke deserves all the hot water in which he will find himself, up to being forced by large, well-muscled gentlemen to visit an ATM and withdraw large sums to pay for services not actually provided.

CHAPTER TWELVE

CULTURE GUIDE

THE REGIONS IN BRIEF

Beijing, Tianjin & Hebei

Beijing has far more to offer than several other Chinese cities put together, including some of China's most extravagant monuments, such as the Forbidden City. In addition, there's easy access to the surrounding province of Hebei with its sinuous sections of the Great Wall and vast tomb complexes.

The Northeast

The frigid lands to the northeast, once known as Tartary or Manchuria, represent one of the least-visited and most challenging regions in China, and its last great travel frontier. Despite industrialization, the provinces of Liaoning, Jilin, and Heilong Jiang, and the northern section of Inner Mongolia, still claim China's largest natural forest, its most pristine grasslands, and one of its most celebrated lakes (Tian Chi).

Around The Yellow River

This region comprises an area of northern China that includes Shanxi, Ningxiaa, parts of Shanxi, and Inner Mongolia, roughly following the central loop of the Yellow River north of Xi'an. One of China's "cradles of civilization," the area is home to most of the country's oldest surviving timber-frame buildings, and Pingyao, one of its best-preserved walled cities.

The Silk Routes

From the ancient former capital of Xi'an, famed for the modern rediscovery of the Terra-Cotta Warriors, trade routes ran in all directions, but most famously west and northwest through Gansu and Xinjiang, and on through the Middle East. The Silk Routes are littered with alien monuments and tombs, and with magnificent cave-temple sights such as Dunhuang.

Eastern Central China

Eastern central China, between the Yellow River (Huang He) and the Yangzi River (Chang Jiang), is an area covering the provinces of Henan, Shandong, Jiangsu, and Anhui. Chinese culture developed and flourished with little outside influence here. The hometown of China's most important philosopher, Confucius, is here, as are several of China's holiest mountains, notably Taai Shan and Huang Shan, as well as that watery equivalent of the Great Wall, the Grand Canal.

Shanghai

Shanghai is the country's wealthiest city. The sweep of 19th- and early-20th-century architecture along The Bund and the maze of Art Deco masterpieces in the French Concession behind the Bund, make Shanghai the mainland's top East-meets-West destination, with a more relaxed and open-minded atmosphere to match.

The Southeast

South of Shanghai and the Yangzi River, the coastal provinces of Zhejiang, Fujiaan, and Guangdong have always been China's most outward looking. These areas, which boomed under the relatively open Tang dynasty and which were forced to reopen as "treaty ports" by the guns of the first multinationals in the 19th century, are also those most industrialized under the current "reform and opening" policy.

Hong Kong & Macau

The mixture of Asia's finest hotels, territory-wide duty-free shopping, incense-filled working temples, and British double-decker buses makes this city-state worth flying to Asia to see in its own right. Macau, a little bit of misplaced Mediterranean, is a short ferry ride away.

The Southwest

Encompassing the provinces of Yunnan, Guiizhou, Guangxi, and Hainan Island, this region is home to some of China's most spectacular mountain scenery and three of Asia's mightiest rivers, resulting in some of the most breathtaking gorges and lush river valleys in the country. This region is also the most ethnically diverse in China.

The Yangzi River

In addition to shared borders, the landlocked provinces of Sichuan, Hubei, and Hunan and the municipality of Chongqiing have in common the world's third-longest river, the Chang Jiang ("Long River," aka Yangzi or Yangtze). The home of five holy Buddhist and/or Daoist mountains, this area contains some of China's most beautiful scenery, particularly in northern Siichuan and northern Hunan.

The Tibetan World

The Tibetan plateau is roughly the size of western Europe, with an average elevation of 4,700m (15,400 ft.). Ringed by vast mountain ranges such as the Kunlun range to the north and the Himalayas, the region offers towering scenic splendors as well as some of the richest minority culture within modern China's borders. Lhasa, former seat of the Dalai Lamas, is dominated physically by the vast Potala Palace, and emotionally by the fervor of the pilgrims to the Jokhang Temple.

THE ORIGIN OF CHINESE CHARACTERS

Chinese has the distinction of being the mother tongue of the oldest continuous civilization on earth, as well as being spoken by the greatest number of people. It is also a most intricate language, and by many counts, the most difficult to learn. While many early writing systems went through a pictographic stage, such as Egyptian hieroglyphics, most writing systems eventually developed a phonetic alphabet to represent the sounds of spoken language, rather than visual images perceived in the physical world. Chinese is the only major writing system that has continued its pictograph-based development without interruption, and that is still in use.

The earliest specimens of Chinese writing were found on **oracle bones** dating to the **Shang dynasty** (1766-1122 BC), the first dynasty for which there is literary as well as archaeological evidence. In 1899 some farmers tilling their fields in the village of Xiaotun, outside the city of Anyang in northern Henan Province, found oddly shaped polished bones with cracks on the surface. Believing them to be dragon bones with inherent magical powers, the farmers sold them to local apothecaries, who in turn ground them into powder and offered them for sale as medicine. It is impossible to know just how many oracle bones were turned into dust before they could be deciphered.

Made from tortoise shells or ox scapulae, oracle bones were used for divination purposes by shamans who carved questions into them on behalf of the emperor. The bones were then heated, and answers were ascertained from the formation of the ensuing cracks. From the identifiable characters on oracle bones, which number only a thousand or so, it is apparent that by the second millennium BC, the written language had already attained a solid foundation upon which future generations would expand.

Each Chinese character is a word in and of itself, or, at least, part of a compound word. Characters may therefore be written from right to left, left to right, or top to bottom, since they can be read and understood in any order. Even today Chinese is written in all three directions. Before the invention of paper, however, Chinese was written on **strips of bamboo**—hence, their most commonly seen vertical direction which continued even after paper was in common use.

The characters themselves give little, if any, indication of their sound, there being no alphabet per se in Chinese. It becomes necessary to memorize each and every character and its component parts in order to become literate. Usually this entails mastering several thousand complicated ideographs and their range of different contextual meanings. Because the ideographs are not tied to phonetic patterns of pronunciation, people must learn the sound symbols with which individual ideographs are read. It is estimated that 2,000 characters are required to read a newspaper, and that well-educated Chinese know between 4,000 and 6,000. The most comprehensive Chinese dictionary lists slightly over 49,000 characters, 28,000 of which are already obsolete. This underscores the extent to which spoken Chinese has evolved, compared to its written counterpart.

A lexicographer of the **Han Dynasty** (206 BC-220 AD), **Xu Shen**, was the first to identify six types of written characters, representing meanings and sounds. The two most common are **pictographs** and ideographs. In pictographs, characters are formed according to the shape of the objects themselves. The sun, for example, was originally written as a circle with a dot in the middle (indicating sun spots, which the Chinese identified in ancient times). The character for moon was likewise initially written in the shape of a crescent moon. The horns and legs of a sheep can be seen in the ancient character for that animal.

The second type of character, the **simple ideograph**, represents more abstract concepts, which can't be rendered easily into simply line drawings. For example, a short line drawn either under or on top of a longer, horizontal line stands for "above" or "below."

Complex ideographs comprise the third type of character, with graphic representations formed by combining simpler characters of the first and second types. An example of this is the character meaning "to rest" (*xiu*) which is comprised of the character for a person and the character for a tree, since people sought out trees against which to rest when they were tired.

The fourth of the main types of characters is the **phonetic compound**, also known as logographs. This is a compound character formed by two graphic elements, one giving a hint of the meaning and the other providing a clue to the sound. This last type of character now accounts for over 80% of all characters.

Xu Shen also arranged the characters under hundreds of primitive symbols, which were later arranged into 214 **radicals**– the portion of a character that gives clues to its meaning, such as three dots representing water. These dots appear in almost every character that describes water (such as "moisture," "the ocean," and "tears"). Similarly, the characters for "talk," "speak," and "discuss," all share the radical that means "language."

One way to look up characters in a **dictionary** is to identify its radical, and, if a character contains more than one, to determine which radical is the basic one. You then need to find the section of the dictionary that covers that radical. Here you'll find all the characters in which that radical appears, arranged according to the number of strokes it takes to write them (not including the radical). Other dictionaries allow you to look up characters according to their pronunciation but you must know the tone in which the word is spoken in order to determine which character is the correct one. This gets complicated. Mandarin has four pitched tones and one "neutral" one. The words Gong Li, spoken in the third and fourth tones, refer to a famous Chinese movie star, but "gong li," spoken with the first and third tones, means "kilometer."

Over the centuries words that were once identical in pronunciation came to differ, due primarily to the fact that the written word appealed mainly to the eye, rather than to the ear. It was the written character that kept the country unified for centuries. To this day, two Chinese people speaking different dialects sitting next to each other on a train with the same newspaper would not be able to understand the same article if they read it aloud to each other. If they both read silently, however, they'd be able to understand it. The written word remains the same, regardless of the dialect or the pronunciation.

CHRONOLOGY OF CHINA'S MAJOR DYNASTIES

Dynasty	Period	Inventions - Philosophers
Xia	21st-16th century BC	Silk cultivation
Shang	1600-1045 BC	Bronze metallurgy Chinese writing system Horse-drawn chariots Chopsticks
Zhou Western Zhou Eastern Zhou Spring and Autumn Warring States	1045-256 BC 1045-771 BC 770-256 BC 770-476 BC 475-221 BC	Confucius (551-479 BC) Iron plow Crossbows Mencius (372-289 BC) Laozi (Daoism)
Qin	221-206 BC	Great Wall construction Terra cotta warriors

Han	202 BC-220 AD	
Former Han	202BC-23 AD	Crank handle
		Parachute
Later Han	25-220	Lacquer
		Paper
		Wheelbarrow
		Suspension bridge
		Seismograph
		Rudders
Six Dynasties	220-589	Tea
		Padded horse collar
		Sedan chair
		Kite
Sui	581-618	Porcelain
		Chess
		Segmental arch bridge
Tang	618-907	Block printing
Five Dynasties & Ten Kingdoms	902-979	Gunpowder
Five Dynasties (North)	907-960	
Ten Kingdoms (South)	902-979	Paper money
Song	960-1279	Movable type
Northern Song	960-1127	Magnetic compass
Southern Song	1127-1279	
Yuan (Mongol)	1279-1368	
Ming	1368-1644	Bristle toothbrush
Qing (Manchu)	1644-1911	

CHINESE TRADITIONAL ARTS

Calligraphy

The Chinese regard calligraphy as their highest artistic achievement. The history of calligraphy in China is over 3,000 years old, and all of the basic script forms were fully developed by the 4th century AD.

During the first phase, from the Shang (ca. 1600-1045 BC) to the Six Dynasties periods (220-581), early pictograms were transformed into characters that could be written with greater simplicity and fluency. Changes in both forms and techniques reflect a growing ability to manipulate the traditional Chinese writing brush, which is inherently difficult to maneuver.

As new script forms developed, the older ones remained to influence and inspire students and scholars alike. Some archaic script forms hark back to ancient rituals and therefore continue to be used for commemorative purposes.

Training in the art of calligraphy might begin by copying the styles of the masters. The student must also learn the basics – how to control the brush and how to compose a balanced piece. Emphasis is placed on the ability to interpret early styles and traditions and fill them with the artist's own new, exciting form. What cannot be altered is the arrangement of the written columns, the order of the strokes, and the use of the writing brush itself.

Jade

As early as the **Neolithic era** (ca. 10,000-2,000 BC), jade was used to create ritual objects and personal ornaments. Only two of the various types of semiprecious hardstones comprising jade, however, are recognized as true jade: **nephrite** and **jadeite**.

Nephrite was found in ancient China, having been imported from Khotan in what is currently the northwest region of Xinjiang Province and possibly also from Siberia. Jadeite, however, wasn't used by the Chinese until the 18th century, when it was imported from northern Burma after the Qing Dynasty gained control over the far southwest of the country.

Some early jade objects are modeled on utilitarian stone tools of the Neolithic era such as the ax, the knife and the chisel. Other forms include disks, rings and bracelets, as well as amulets, found in sites of the late Neolithic period.

In the Shang dynasty, jade was made into the shape of spearheads and daggers and other blades. They were presumably used in religious rituals and sacrificial offerings. Some early jade contains emblematic motifs that also appear on large pottery jars excavated from Neolithic sites.

Jade has particular cultural and moral significance for the Chinese, being associated with morality and dignity. Confucius was said to have noted 11 types of virtue embodied in its various physical qualities, including purity, intelligence, justice, music, loyalty, sincerity, chastity and truth. Traditionally people decorated rooms with jade craftworks in patterns of peaches (representing longevity), mandarin ducks (love), deer (high official rank), bats (blessings), fish (affluence), double phoenixes (success), bottles (safety), the lotus (holiness), bamboo (lofty conduct) and fans (benevolence).

CHINESE FESTIVALS & CELEBRATIONS

China's traditional festivals are celebrated according to their dates on the lunar calendar.

January

Chinese New Year The most important of all festivals takes place on the first day of the Chinese lunar year, and ends with the Lantern Festival under a full moon, 15 days later. After the Gregorian calendar was made official with the founding of the Republic of China in 1912, the Chinese New Year came to be called the "**Spring Festival**," to distinguish it from New Year's Day in the West. On the day prior to Spring Festival, known as Chu Xi (pronounced "choo she"), families gather for a large meal and dole out red envelopes to the children, containing "lucky money." On Chinese New Year's Day, family ancestors are honored with food offerings. The gods are also venerated, and the younger generation pays respect to the older one. Families visit a temple to burn incense in a ritual of worship, and then visit friends and relatives with New Year's greetings. Firecrackers and lion dances can be seen and heard everywhere. Since it is a period of national celebration, no business is conducted for three days. *Spring Festival is on the day of the first new moon after January 21, and can be no later than February 20.*

Kurban Bairam Honored by Muslim communities throughout China, this festival, also known as the Festival of Sacrifice, is celebrated in Kashgar with feats of tightrope-walking in the main square and wild dancing outside the Idkah Mosque. *The four-day festival is held 70 days after the end of the fasting month of Ramadan, on the 10th day of the 12th month (Dhul-Hijjah) in the Islamic calendar.*

February

The Lantern Festival Dating to the Han Dynasty (206 BC-221 AD), the Lantern Festival falls on the 15th day of the first month of the Chinese lunar calendar, and marks the end of the Chinese New Year. Under a full moon, people walk about with paper lanterns lit with candles, watch lion dances, and play Chinese riddle games. The traditional food for the Lantern Festival is called "yuanxiao" (pronounced "ywan she yow"), which is a kind of sweet dumpling made of glutinous rice and filled with stuffing. The festival itself is named after this dumpling, whose round shape symbolizes family unity and completeness. *The festival always falls 15 days after Spring Festival.*

April

Tomb Sweeping Festival During the Tomb Sweeping Festival, the Chinese pay respect to their ancestors by going to their graves, sweeping them clean, and burning incense. *April 5.*

Water Splashing Festival This is a particularly colorful festival among the Dai national minority people of Yunnan Province.

Inspired by the Buddhist legend of a dragon sprinkling fragrant showers on Lord Buddha at his birth, this festival is especially popular with tourists, who get sprinkled for good luck. Festivities also include dragon boat racing and local fairs. The Peacock dance is performed by young girls, and both boys and girls throw embroidered purses to those they're interested in. *April 13 to 15.*

May

Saka Dawa   This festival is celebrated by Tibetans to honor the passing away of the Buddha when he attained Nirvana. There is religious dancing and chanting, and giant silk portraits of the Buddha are displayed in public. *The 8th to the 15th days of the fourth lunar month.*

June

The Dragon Boat Festival   This festival commemorates the date when the ancient poet-patriot, Qu Yuan, threw himself into the Miluo River in despair over China's future. People launched boats to search for his body in order to give him a proper burial, and when they couldn't find it, they threw rice dumplings into the river to satiate the hunger of the creatures in the sea in the hopes that they would not mutilate his body. Other traditions associated with this holiday include the eating of *zongzi*, which are dumplings made of glutinous rice wrapped in bamboo leaves. Fragrant herbs are hung in front of homes to ward off evil spirits and invite good fortune in. Children wear colorful herb-filled sachets around their necks, also for good fortune. *Twenty-fourth to 27th day of the fifth lunar month (usually June or early July).*

September

Confucius's Birthday   China's great sage is honored with ritual worship at local Confucian Temples, especially throughout Taiwan and in his hometown of **Qufu** in Shandong Province. *September 28.*

Mid-Autumn Festival   This festival arrives around the time of the autumn equinox. Moon cakes, similar to fruit cakes and plum pudding in English tradition, are eaten on this family holiday as people gather to celebrate family unity. The Chinese also traditionally gaze at the moon (and at each other), which is full on this night. The waxing and waning of the moon is a poignant reminder of the joys and vicissitudes of life. *The 15th day of the eighth lunar month (usually September).*

December

The Ice and Snow Festival   Celebrated in Harbin, this festival is more of a citywide exhibition than a traditional festival. It is the northeast's top winter attraction, centering around hundreds of elaborate ice and snow sculptures representing everything from Tian'anmen Square to Elvis Presley. *From late December to whenever the ice begins to melt (usually late February).*

Miao New Year Festival   Celebrated by the Miao national minority, this festival includes singing, dancing, bullfighting and other competitions. Miao women wear gorgeous silver headdresses and perform various courtship rituals. *End of the 10th lunar month (usually December).*

CHINA'S SACRED MOUNTAINS

China is a mountainous country with spectacular ranges to climb throughout the land. Mountain climbing itself is an ancient tradition, intimately connected with Daoist hermits and Buddhist monks alike, intent on making spiritual journeys to discover enlightenment.

Mountain climbing tours can be booked through reputable Chinese agencies, although locals are the best ones to help you make arrangements with officials and negotiate the best price – no mean feat in China. Advance permission may be required to bring in special gear. For information on tours of China's sacred mountains, check with **China eTours Travel Service**

CULTURE GUIDE

(www.etours.cn), **China Hiking Adventure, Inc.** (www.tibet-hiking.com) and **ChinaTour.Net** (www.chinatour.net).

Heaven and earth were believed to touch atop China's sacred mountains. The mountains themselves were considered pillars separating heaven and earth, and keeping the heavens from falling. In the myth of the "Reparation of Heaven," the **Goddess Nu Wa** repaired the broken sky, killed a huge tortoise, and used its feet as pillars to support the four quarters of the universe. These pillars are considered China's earliest sacred mountains.

Daoist "immortals" (sages and mystics) were thought to make their homes deep in the mountain wilderness, existing on herbs and elixirs, and living to be many hundreds of years old. The dwellings of these immortals came to be regarded as sacred places and the abodes of powerful spirits and deities.

Monasteries built on mountainsides became centers of scholarship, art and philosophy, and the mountains themselves became places for pilgrims throughout the country. The term for **"pilgrimage"** in Chinese literally translates into "paying one's respect to a mountain." The physical exertion it takes to climb them serves as a metaphor for the discipline required for the spiritual journey on the road of life. Vast areas of natural beauty exist, which locals still view with awe.

During China's **Cultural Revolution** (1966-76) and even the earlier **Great Leap Forward** in the 1950s, many Buddhist and Daoist temples and cultural artifacts were destroyed, and the religious observance of monks and nuns suppressed. While some monasteries and temples have been reconstructed, much of the work has been shoddy and the original beauty of those edifices has been compromised.

Unfortunately, the rapid development of tourism has made visits to these holy places problematic. Trails and monasteries, no longer protected by Buddhist and Daoist pilgrims, have deteriorated. Climbing can be dangerous due to the sheer number of visitors. Big business interests have also emerged around China's sacred mountains, and the ancient balance of mountains as wildlife refuge and models of sustainable forestry and agriculture for local communities is now threatened. **Logging, hunting, tourism** and **pollution** are all beginning to take their toll since the land itself is now the state's rather than the monastery's.

For the start of the **2008 Summer Olympics**, the Olympic torch is expected to be taken to the top of **Mount Qomolangma** (known as Mt. Everest in the West), which is regarded as the world's highest peak at 29,017 ft.

Sacred Buddhist Mountains
There are four mountains in China that are associated with the Buddhist tradition and believed to be the homes of **Boddhisattvas** (enlightened beings who have chosen to delay their entrance into Nirvana in order to help others transcend their worldly suffering and attain enlightenment): **Wu Tai Shan** in the north, **Emei Shan** in the West, **Pu Tuo Shan** to the east and **Jiu Hua Shan** to the south, all of which can be visited by tourists. The word "shan" (pronounced "shahn") in Chinese means "mountain."

Buddhism was first introduced to China in the 1st century AD by merchants returning from India along the Silk Road. Over the next few centuries, Chinese pilgrims traveled to India to visit the sacred locations associated with the life of the Buddha, most notably **Xuan Zang** (596-664), who spent 16 years there and returned with translations of Buddhist sutras as well as an affinity for the monastic life. Buddhist monks preferred the mountains and forests for their quiet meditation practices, and, as a result, hermitages and later great monastic complexes sprang up on many peaks.

Wu Tai Shan (Shanxi Province)   This sacred mountain in Shanxi Province in northern China is named for its five flat peaks. It is sacred to the Bodhisattva **Manjushri**, who represents wisdom, intelligence and spiritual realization. Since Manjushri is the special guardian of Tibetan and Mongolian Buddhism, much of the temple architecture of Wu Tai Shan is Tibetan in style. Tibetan monks in maroon and gold robes wander the streets of the small monastic village of Taihuai. This is open to all visitors.

At one time Wu Tai Shan boasted more than 300 temples and monasteries, some dating back to the **Tang Dynasty** (618-907 AD). Most of the remaining ones date to the **Ming Dynasty** (1368-1644). Thanks to its remote location, and its association with Mongolian rather than Chinese Buddhism, it has been better protected under the government's Ethnic Minority Policy. Today 58 temples and monasteries remain.

Both Wu Tai Shan and Emei Shan (see below) are currently being targeted for conservation by environmental protection organizations since they are suffering from the ravages of tourism and pilgrimage, as well as logging and development.

Emei Shan (Sichuan Province)   Only 20 of the original 150 monasteries, some dating back 2,000 years, remain on this sacred Buddhist mountain, whose name translates into "Delicate Eyebrow Mountain." Sacred to the Bodhisattva **Samantabhadra**, who represents the Buddhist ideals of law and compassion, this is the most visited of all Buddhist mountains due to its convenient proximity to Chengdu in Sichuan Province. Today it is a major tourist destination for both foreigners and Chinese, with cable cars for less able-bodied tourists.

Putuo Shan (Zhejiang Province)   The "Potala Mountain," as it is translated, is sacred to the Bodhisattva **Guanyin**, the goddess of compassion, and is the lowest of China's sacred mountains. Its peak follows 1,060 steps along a stone staircase. Located on a small island, Putuo Shan was considered holy even prior to the arrival of Buddhism, perhaps because it's filled with caves, valleys, cliffs and beaches with mystical allure. The three major temples on this island (**Puji**, **Fayu** and **Huiji**) are among the most impressive in all of China.

Jiu Hua Shan (Anhui Province)   Meaning "Nine Glories Mountain," Jiu Hua Shan is sacred to the Bodhisattva **Kshitigarbha**, the savior of the oppressed and the dying. At one point over 200 temples and 5,000 monks could be found on its slopes, but today only 50 temples remain. The most famous are **Huacheng**, **Baisuigong**, **Zhiyuan** and **Ganlu**. Third-century Daoist monks built thatched temples here, but with the rise of Buddhism, stone monasteries gradually replaced them. The trails are generally comfortable to walk, except for those near the summit.

Sacred Daoist Mountains

One of China's mythological rulers, **Xun** (2225-2206 BC) is said to have gone on a pilgrimage to the four mountains which defined the limits of his realm, making ritual sacrifices on each of their summits. The **Classic of History**, compiled around the 5th century, BC, refers to Tai Shan by name. Other mountains highly venerated by Daoists in ancient times were **Heng Shan Bei**, **Hua Shan**, **Heng Shan Nan** and **Song Shan**.

Tai Shan (Shandong Province)   Legend has it that Tai Shan, or "Leading Peaceful Mountain," in the east, was created out of the head of China's first man, **Pangu**. The remaining four peaks were said to come from his shins. Tai Shan, venerated like a god, is China's most sacred peak.

Tai Shan hosts millions of annual pilgrims, who climb its 7,000 steps to visit two key temples located on top: the **Temple of the Jade Emperor**, who is considered to be the heavenly ruler of earth, and the **Temple of the Princess of the Azure Clouds**, who is the Jade Emperor's daughter. The latter temple is visited primarily by Chinese women, including aged ones with bound feet from the pre-Communist era. Those who visit this temple are said to have prayers answered for the successful conception of a child or for curing children's diseases.

In 1987 Tai Shan was designated a world natural and cultural heritage site by UNESCO, and received $1.8 million in 2005, which was used to repair its historic relics and rebuild damaged cultural architecture. The object of an imperial cult for close to 2,000 years, it has been a source of inspiration for Chinese artists scholars and emperors, who ascended it to pray for peace and prosperity.

Heng Shan Bei (Shanxi Province)   "Splendid Mountain," in the north, was a battleground in ancient times, as can be ascertained by a landscape filled with passes, castles, fortresses and beacon towers. It is therefore unique among China's sacred mountains and a must-see for military history buffs. During the Northern Wei Dynasty (386-534), **Overhanging Temple** was built in a virtually unreachable location on a high cliff hemmed in by a precipice on either side. Looking up at it, one can see numerous pavilions supported by wooden pillars. The interior is part house and part cave – a truly unique construction. **Taifeng Summit**, the mountain's highest peak, is covered with pine trees, exotic flowers, rare herbs and odd-shaped stones. Extremes in temperature, from season to season and from day to night, make a visit here a challenge.

Hua Shan (Shaanxi Province)   "Flower Mountain," to the west, is so named because its five peaks resemble the five petals of a flower. A dramatic, steep path leads to the Green Dragon Ridge, where other trails take you to the major peaks. This is a popular hiking destination for the young, who are more up for the arduous task, but it is also trekked by devoted pilgrims and wandering monks alike. It is actually a rather treacherous mountain to scale, with cliffs separated from the abyss below only by a nondescript linked chain.

The **Jade Spring Temple**, at the foot of Hua Shan, is one of China's main Daoist temples. It was built at the foot of Hua Shan in the architectural style of the classical gardens of southern China. Pavilions surround a pond. A walk through the temple gets you to **Huixin Rock** and some 370 precipitous rock steps considered to be the main, breath-taking path of Hua Shan. Another challenging peak is **North Peak** (also known as **Cloud Terrace Peak**).

Heng Shan Nan (Hunan Province)   "Balancing Mountain," in the south, is famous for its magnificent temples. Located 225 miles south of Changsha, capital of Hunan Province, it is often regarded as China's most beautiful mountain, although each of the sacred mountains will elicit the same response.

Song Shan (Henan Province) "Lofty Mountain" is 47 miles southwest of Zhengzhou, the capital of Henan Province. The **Middle Sacred Mountain**, 4,959 feet above sea level, boasts 72 temples on 72 slopes. The **Shaolin Temple**, well known for its role in the development of the Chinese martial art form of kung-fu, is also where the Chan (Zen) sect of Chinese Buddhism began.

RECOMMENDED READING

Accessible modern novelists whose works are available in translation at home include Ha Jin, whose stories tend to be remarkably inconclusive and therefore all the more true to life. *Ocean of Words* (Vintage, 2000), *Waiting* (Vintage, 2001), and *The Bridegroom* (Vintage, 2001), a collection of short stories, offer insights and observation not obvious to the casual visitor. *Soul Mountain* (Harper Collins, 2000), by Gao Xingjian, China's first winner of the Nobel Prize for Literature (although the Chinese populace is kept in ignorance of this), is the tale of a man who embarks on a journey through the wilds of Sichuan and Yunnan in search of his own elusive ling shan (soul mountain).

The Republic of Wine (Arcade, 2001), Mo Yan's graphic satire about a doomed detective investigating a case of officials eating human baby tenderloin, is at once entertaining and disturbing. His *Garlic Ballads* (Viking, 1995) is an unsettling epic of family conflict, doomed love, and government corruption in a small town dependent on the garlic market.

Excellent travel books include Peter Fleming's *News from Tartary* (Northwestern University Press, 1999), originally published in 1936, and still the best travel book ever written about China. Fleming's perceptive account of a hazardous expedition along the southern Silk Route, from Beijing to northern India, is a masterpiece of dry wit.

For good general background reading, Jonathan Spence writes the most readable histories of China, not just the weighty *Search for Modern China* (W.W. Norton, 2001), but gripping and very personal histories such as *The Memory Palace of Matteo Ricci* (Viking, 1994), the story of the clever self-marketing of the first Jesuit to be allowed to reside in Beijing; *God's Chinese Son* (W.W. Norton, 1997), about the leader of the Taiping Rebellion, who thought he was the younger brother of Jesus; and *The Question of Hu* (Vintage, 1989), on the misfortunes of an early Chinese visitor to Europe.

Dover Publications (store.dover.publications.com) reprints handy guides to Chinese history and culture, as well as oddities such as Robert Van Gulik's versions of 18th-century Chinese detective stories featuring a Tang dynasty detective-judge; try *The Haunted Monastery* or *The Chinese Maze Murders* (1977). Dover's two-volume reprint of the 1903 edition of *The Travels of Marco Polo* (1993) is the only edition with copious footnotes from famous explorers and geographers trying to make sense of Polo's route, with fascinating trivia about China that's often more interesting than the original account.

For more recent China watching, anything by the Italian diplomat Tizanio Terzani is a good place to start, but *Behind the Forbidden Door* is particularly compelling. While many books do their best to present the country in a favorable light, Nicholas D. Kristof and Sheryl Wudunn offer a more realistic portrait in *China Wakes* (Vintage, 1995). So does Gordon C. Chang in *The Coming Collapse of China* (Random House, 2001).

More recently, Peter Hessler's *Oracle Bones: A Journey Between China's Past and Present* has met with critical acclaim as one of the best accounts of China's rapid reinvention of itself in the modern era, written by a freelance journalist and *The New Yorker's* Beijing correspondent from 1999 to 2002.

Those interested in China's meteoric economic rise and attendant potential pitfalls involved might want to read *China Shakes the World: A Titan's Rise and Troubled Future – and the Challenge for America* (2007) by James Kynge or *China Road: A Journey Into the Future of a Rising Power* (2007) by Rob Gifford.

DICTIONARY KEY

n	名词 *míng cí*	v	动词 *dòng cí*
adj	形容词 *xíng róng cí*	prep	介词 *jiè cí*
adv	副词 *fù cí*	pron	代词 *dài cí*

Chinese verbs are not conjugated. Here, they are listed in their most basic form. To form tenses, see p26.

For food terms, see the Menu Reader (p89) and Grocery section (p94) in Chapter 4, Dining.

A

able, to be able to (can) *v* 能够 *néng gòu*

above *adj* 上面的 *shàng miàn de*

accept, to accept *v* 接受 *jiē shòu*

> **Do you accept credit cards?** 可以用信用卡吗? *kě yǐ yòng xìn yòng kǎ ma?*

accident *n* 交通事故 *jiāo tōng shì gù*

> **I've had an accident.** 我出了事故。*wǒ chū le shì gù.*

account *n* 账户 *zhàng hù*

> **I'd like to transfer to / from my checking / savings account.** 我想转帐到我的支票账户 / 储蓄账户。/ 我想从我的支票账户 / 储蓄账户转帐。*wǒ xiǎng zhuǎn zhàng dào wǒ de zhī piào zhàng hù / chǔ xù zhàng hù。/ wǒ xiǎng cóng wǒ de zhī piào zhàng hù / chǔ xù zhàng hù zhuǎn zhàng。*

acne *n* 痤疮 *cuó chuāng*

across *prep* 在...对面 *zài ...duì miàn*

> **across the street** 在街道对面 *zài jiē dào duì miàn*

actual *adj* 实际的 *shí jì de*

adapter plug *n* 适配器插头 *shì pèi qì chā tóu*

address *n* 地址 *dì zhǐ*

> **What's the address?** 地址是什么? *dì zhǐ shì shén me?*

admission fee *n* 门票 *mén piào*

in advance 提前 *tí qián*

African-American *adj* 非裔美国人 *fēi yì měi guó rén*

afternoon *n* 下午 *xià wǔ*

> **in the afternoon** 在下午 *zài xià wǔ*

age *n* 年龄 *nián líng*

What's your age? 您多大了?
nín duō dà le?

agency *n* 代理处 *dài lǐ chù*

car rental agency 汽车租赁公司 *qì chē zū lìn gōng sī*

agnostic *adj* 不可知论 *bù kě zhī lùn*

air conditioning *n* 空调 *kōng tiáo*

Would you lower / raise the air conditioning? 您能调低 / 调高空调温度吗? *nín néng tiáo dī / tiáogāo kōng tiáo wēn dù ma?*

airport *n* 机场 *jī chǎng*

I need a ride to the airport. 我需要乘车到机场。 *wǒ xū yào chéng chē dào jī chǎng.*

How far is it from the airport? 离机场有多远? *lí jī chǎng yǒu duō yuǎn?*

airsickness bag *n* 晕机呕吐袋 *yūn jī ǒu tù dài*

aisle (in store) *n* 过道（商店里）*guò dào (shāng diàn lǐ)*

Which aisle is it in? 它在哪一过道? *tā zài nǎ yī guò dào?*

alarm clock *n* 闹钟 *nào zhōng*

alcohol *n* 酒精饮料 *jiǔ jīng yǐn liào*

Do you serve alcohol? 您提供酒精饮料吗? *nín tí gōng jiǔ jīng yǐn liào ma?*

I'd like nonalcoholic beer. 我想要不含酒精的啤酒。 *wǒ xiǎng yào bù hán jiǔ jīng de pí jiǔ.*

all *n* 全部 *quán bù*

all *adj* 所有的 *suǒ yǒu de*

all of the time 一直 *yī zhí*

That's all, thank you. 就那些, 谢谢您。 *jiù nà xiē, xiè xiè nín.*

allergic *adj* 过敏的 *guò mǐn de*

I'm allergic to ____. 我对____过敏。 *wǒ duì ____ guò mǐn.* See p74 and 153 for common allergens.

altitude *n* 海拔 *hǎi bá*

aluminum *n* 铝 *lǚ*

ambulance *n* 救护车 *jiù hù chē*

American *adj* 美国的 *měi guó de*

amount *n* 数量 *shù liàng*

angry *adj* 生气的 *shēng qì de*

animal *n* 动物 *dòng wù*

another *adj* 另外的 *lìng wài de*

answer *n* 答案 *dá àn*

answer, to answer (phone call, question) *v* 回答 *huí dá*

Answer me, please. 请回答我。 *qǐng huí dá wǒ.*

antibiotic *n* 抗生素 *kàng shēng sù*

I need an antibiotic. 我需要抗生素。*wǒ xū yào kàng shēng sù.*

antihistamine n 抗组胺剂 *kàng zǔ àn jì*

anxious adj 焦虑的 *jiāo lǜ de*

any adj 任何的 *rèn hé de*

anything n 任何事 *rèn hé shì*

anywhere adv 任何地方 *rèn hé dì fāng*

April n 四月 *sì yuè*

appointment n 约定 *yuē dìng*

Do I need an appointment? 我需要预约吗? *wǒ xū yào yù yuē ma?*

are v See **be, to be.**

Argentinian adj 阿根廷的 *ā gēn tíng de*

arm n 胳膊 *gē bo*

arrive, to arrive v 到达 *dào dá*

arrival(s) n 到达 *dào dá*

art n 艺术品 *yì shù pǐn*

exhibit of art 艺术品展览 *yì shù pǐn zhǎn lǎn* See for art types.

art adj 艺术的 *yì shù de*

art museum 艺术博物馆 *yì shù bó wù guǎn*

artist n 艺术家 *yì shù jiā*

Asian adj 亚洲的 *yà zhōu de*

ask for (request) v 请求 *qǐng qiú*

ask a question v 问一个问题 *wèn yī gè wèn tí*

aspirin n 阿司匹林 *ā sī pǐ lín*

assist v 援助 *yuán zhù*

assistance n 援助 *yuán zhù*

asthma n 哮喘 *xiāo chuǎn*

I have asthma. 我有哮喘。*wǒ yǒu xiāo chuǎn.*

atheist adj 无神论的 *wú shén-lùn de*

ATM n 自动取款机 *zì dòng qǔ kuǎn jī*

I'm looking for an ATM. 我在找自动取款机。*wǒ zài zhǎo zì dòng qǔ kuǎn jī.*

attend v 参加 *cān jiā*

audio adj 音频的 *yīn pín de*

August n 八月 *bā yuè*

aunt n 姑妈 *gū mā*

Australia n 澳大利亚 *ào dà lì yà*

Australian adj 澳大利亚的 *ào dà lì yà de*

autumn n 秋天 *qiū tiān*

available adj 可得的 *kě dé de*

B

baby n 婴儿 *yīng ér*

baby adj 婴儿的 *yīng ér de*

Do you sell baby food? 卖婴儿食品吗? *mài yīng ér shí pǐn ma?*

babysitter *n* 临时照看幼儿者 *lín shí zhào kàn yòu ér zhě*

> **Do you have babysitters who speak English?** 有会说英语的临时照看幼儿者吗? *yǒu huì shuō yīng yǔ de lín shí zhào kàn yòu ér zhě ma?*

back *n* 背部 *bèi bù*

> **My back hurts.** 我的背部受伤了。*wǒ de bèi bù shòu shāng le。*

back rub *n* 揉背 *róu bèi*

backed up (toilet) *adj* 堵着的 (马桶) *dǔ zhe de (mǎ tǒng)*

> **The toilet is backed up.** 马桶堵上了。*mǎ tǒng dǔ shàng le。*

bag *n* 袋子 *dài zǐ*

> **airsickness bag** 晕机呕吐袋 *yūn jī ǒu tù dài*
>
> **My bag was stolen.** 我的袋子被偷了。*wǒ de dài zǐ bèi tōu le。*
>
> **I lost my bag.** 我的袋子丢了。*wǒ de dài zǐ diū le。*

bag *v* 袋子 *dài zǐ*

baggage *n* 行李 *xíng li*

baggage *adj* 行李的 *xíng li de*

> **baggage claim** 行李领取处 *xíng li lǐng qǔ chù*

bait *n* 饵 *ěr*

balance (on bank account) *n* (银行账户上的) 余额 *(yín háng zhàng hù shàng de) yú é*

balance *v* 平衡 *píng héng*

balcony *n* 阳台 *yáng tái*

ball (sport) *n* 球 (运动) *qiú (yùn dòng)*

ballroom dancing *n* 交际舞 *jiāo jì wǔ*

band (musical ensemble) *n* 乐队 (音乐团体) *yuè duì (yīn yuè tuán tǐ)*

band-aid *n* 创可贴 *chuàng kě tiē*

bank *n* 银行 *yín háng*

> **Can you help me find a bank?** 您能帮我找家银行吗? *nín néng bāng wǒ zhǎo jiā yín háng ma?*

bar *n* 酒吧 *jiǔ bā*

barber *n* 理发师 *lǐ fà shī*

bass (instrument) *n* 贝司 (乐器) *bèi sī (yuè qì)*

bath *n* 洗澡 *xǐ zǎo*

bathroom (restroom) *n* 卫生间 *wèi shēng jiān*

> **Where is the nearest public bathroom?** 最近的公共卫生间在哪里? *zuì jìn de gōng gòng wèi shēng jiān zài nǎ lǐ?*

bathtub *n* 浴缸 *yù gāng*

bathe, to bathe oneself *v* 沐浴 *mù yù*

battery (for flashlight) *n* 电池 (手电筒使用的) *diàn chí (shǒu diàn tǒng shǐ yòng de)*

battery (for car) *n* 蓄电池（汽车使用的）xù diàn chí (qì chē shǐy òng de)

bee *n* 蜜蜂 mì fēng

I was stung by a bee. 我被蜜蜂蛰了。wǒ bèi mì fēng zhé le。

be, to be (temporary state, condition, mood) *v* 处于 chǔ yú

be, to be (permanent quality) *v* 是 shì

beach *n* 海滩 hǎi tān

beach *v* 拖上岸 tuō shàng àn

beard *n* 胡子 hú zǐ

beautiful *adj* 漂亮的 piào liang de

bed *n* 床 chuáng

beer *n* 啤酒 pí jiǔ

beer on tap 扎啤 zhā pí

begin *v* 开始 kāi shǐ

behave *v* 举动 jǔ dòng

behind *adv* 在…后面 zài …hòu miàn

below *adv* 在…下面 zài …xià miàn

belt *n* 带 dài

conveyor belt 传送带 chuán sòng dài

berth *n* 停泊处 tíng bó chù

best 最好的 zuì hǎo de

bet, to bet *v* 打赌 dǎ dǔ

better 更好 gèng hǎo

big *adj* 大的 dà de

bilingual *adj* 双语的 shuāng yǔ de

bill (currency) *n* 票据 piào jù

bill *n* 纸币 zhǐ bì

biography *n* 传记 zhuàn jì

biracial *adj* 混杂种族人 hùn zá zhǒng zú rén

bird *n* 小鸟 xiǎo niǎo

birth control *n* 避孕 bì yùn

birth control *adj* 避孕的 bì yùn de

I'm out of birth control pills. 我没有避孕药丸了。wǒ méi yǒu bì yùn yào wán le。

I need more birth control pills. 我需要更多的避孕药丸。wǒ xū yào gèng duō de bì yùn yào wán。

bit (small amount) *n* 少量 shǎo liàng

black *adj* 黑色的 hēi sè de

blanket *n* 毛毯 máo tǎn

bleach *n* 漂白剂 piǎo bái jì

blind *adj* 盲的 máng de

block *v* 阻塞 zǔ sè

blond(e) *adj* 金发的 jīn fà de

blouse *n* 宽松上衣 kuān sōng shàng yī

blue *adj* 蓝色的 lán sè de

blurry *adj* 模糊的 mó hu de

board n 舱内 cāng nèi

on board 在飞机上 zài fēi jǐ shàng

board v 上飞机 shàng fēi jǐ

boarding pass n 登机牌 dēng jǐ pái

boat n 小船 xiǎo chuán

Bolivian adj 玻利维亚的 bō lì wéi yà de

bomb n 炸弹 zhà dàn

book n 书 shū

bookstore n 书店 shū diàn

boss n 老板 lǎo bǎn

bottle n 瓶子 píng zǐ

May I heat this (baby) bottle someplace? 有地方可以给奶瓶加热吗? yǒu dì fāng kě yǐ gěi nǎi píng jiā rè ma?

box (seat) n 包厢 bāo xiāng

box office n 售票处 shòu piào chù

boy n 男孩 nán hái

boyfriend n 男朋友 nán péng yǒu

braid n 发辫 fà biàn

braille, American n 美国盲人 měi guó máng rén

brake n 刹车 shā chē

emergency brake 紧急刹车 jǐn jí shā chē

brake v 刹车 shā chē

brandy n 白兰地 bái lán dì

bread n 面包 miàn bāo

break v 打断 dǎ duàn

breakfast n 早餐 zǎo cān

What time is breakfast? 早餐时间是几点? zǎo cān shí jiān shì jǐ diǎn?

bridge (across a river, dental) n 桥 (横跨河两岸, 牙齿结构) qiáo (héng kuà hé liǎng àn, yá chǐ jié gòu)

briefcase n 公文包 gōng wén bāo

bright adj 明亮的 míng liàng de

broadband n 宽带 kuān dài

bronze adj 青铜色的 qīng tóng sè de

brother n 兄弟 xiōng di

brown adj 棕色的 zōng sè de

brunette n 黑发女孩 hēi fà nǚ hái

Buddhist n 佛教徒 fó jiào tú

budget n 预算 yù suàn

buffet n 自助餐 zì zhù cān

bug n 虫子 chóng zǐ

bull n 公牛 gōng niú

bullfight n 斗牛 dòu niú

bullfighter n 斗牛士 dòu niú shì

burn v 刻录 kè lù

Can I burn a CD here? 我能在这里刻张 CD 吗? wǒ néng zài zhè lǐ kè zhāng CD ma?

bus n 公共汽车 gōng gòng qì chē

Where is the bus stop? 公共汽车站在哪里？ gōng gòng qì chē zhàn zài nǎ lǐ?

Which bus goes to ____? 哪班公共汽车到_____? nǎ bān gōng gòng qì chē dào _____?

business n 商业 shāng yè

business adj 商业的 shāng yè de

business center 商业中心 shāng yè zhōng xīn

busy adj 忙碌的 máng lù de（饭店）(fàn diàn) 占线的 zhàn xiàn de（电话）(diàn huà)

butter n 黄油 huáng yóu

buy, to buy v 买 mǎi

C

café n 咖啡馆? kā fēi guǎn?

Internet café 网吧 wǎng bā

call, to call v 呼叫 hū jiào（喊）(hǎn) 打电话 dǎ diàn huà（电话）(diàn huà)

camp, to camp v 露营 lù yíng

camper n 露营者 lù yíng zhě

camping adj 露营的 lù yíng de

Do we need a camping permit? 我们需要露营许可吗? wǒ mén xū yào lù yíng xǔ kě ma?

campsite n 露营地 lù yíng dì

can n 罐头 guàn tóu

can (able to) v 能 néng

Canada n 加拿大 jiā ná dà

Canadian adj 加拿大的 jiā ná dà de

cancel, to cancel v 取消 qǔ xiāo

My flight was canceled. 我的航班被取消了。 wǒ de háng bān bèi qǔ xiāo le。

canvas n 画布 huà bù（用于画画）(yòngyú huàhuà), 帆布 fān bù（布）(bù liào)

cappuccino n 卡普契诺咖啡 kǎ pǔ qì nuò kā fēi

car n 小汽车 xiǎo qì chē

car rental agency 汽车租赁公司 qì chē zū lìn gōng sī

I need a rental car. 我需要租一辆小汽车。 wǒ xū yào zū yī liàng xiǎo qì chē。

card n 卡 kǎ

Do you accept credit cards? 可以用信用卡吗? kě yǐ yòng xìn yòng kǎ ma?

May I have your business card? 可以给我您的名片吗? kě yǐ gěi wǒ nín de míng piàn ma?

car seat (child's safety seat) n 汽车座位（儿童的安全座位）qì chē zuò wèi (ér tóng de ān quán zuò wèi)

Do you rent car seats for children? 您租童用汽车座位吗？ nín zū tóng yòng qì chē zuò wèi ma?

carsickness n 晕车 yùn chē

cash n 现金 xiàn jīn

cash only 只收现金 zhī shōu xiàn jīn

cash, to cash v 兑现 duì xiàn

to cash out (gambling) 兑现（赌博）duì xiàn (dǔ bó)

cashmere n 羊绒衫 yáng róng shān

casino n 赌场 dǔ chǎng

cat n 猫 māo

Catholic adj 天主教的 tiān zhǔ jiào de

cavity (tooth cavity) n 蛀洞（牙洞）zhù dòng (yá dòng)

I think I have a cavity. 我想我的牙齿有蛀洞了。wǒ xiǎng wǒ de yá chǐ yǒu zhù dòng le。

CD n CD

CD player n CD 播放器 CD bō fàng qì

celebrate, to celebrate v 庆祝 qìng zhù

cell phone n 移动电话 yí dòng diàn huà

centimeter n 厘米 lí mǐ

chamber music n 室内乐 shì nèi yuè

change (money) n 零钱 líng qián

I'd like change, please. 请给我找零钱。qǐng gěi wǒ zhǎo líng qián。

This isn't the correct change. 找的零钱不对。zhǎo de líng qián bù duì。

change (to change money, clothes) v 换（换钱、衣服）huàn (huàn qián, yī fu)

changing room n 更衣室 gèng yī shì

charge, to charge (money) v 收钱 shōu qián

charge, to charge (a battery) v 充电 chōng diàn

charmed adj 幸会 xìng huì

charred (meat) adj 烤焦的（肉）kǎo jiāo de (ròu)

charter, to charter v 包（船）bāo (chuán)

cheap adj 便宜的 pián yi de

check n 支票 zhī piào

May I use traveler's check? 可以用旅行支票吗？kě yǐ yòng lǚ xíng zhī piào ma?

check, to check v 托运 tuō yùn

checked (pattern) adj 选中的（样式）xuǎn zhōng de (yàng shì)

check-in n 办登机手续 bàn dēng jī shǒu xù

What time is check-in? 什么时间办登机手续? *shén me shí jiān bàn dēng jǐ shǒu xù?*

check-out n 退房 *tuì fáng*

check-out time 退房时间 *tuì fáng shí jiān*

What time is check-out? 什么时间退房? *shén me shí jiān tuì fáng?*

check out, to check out v 退房 *tuì fáng*

cheese n 奶酪 *nǎi lào*

chicken n 鸡肉 *jī ròu*

child n 儿童 *ér tóng*

children n 儿童 *ér tóng*

Are children allowed? 小孩可以吗? *xiǎo hái kě yǐ ma?*

Do you have children's programs? 有小孩的节目吗? *yǒu xiǎo hái de jié mù ma?*

Do you have a children's menu? 有小孩的菜单吗? *yǒu xiǎo hái de cài dān ma?*

Chinese adj 中国的 *zhōng guó de*

chiropractor n 脊椎指压治疗者 *jǐ zhuī zhǐ yā zhì liáo zhě*

church n 教堂 *jiào táng*

cigar n 雪茄 *xuě jiā*

cigarette n 香烟 *xiāng yān*

a pack of cigarettes 一包香烟 *yī bāo xiāng yān*

cinema n 电影院 *diàn yǐng yuàn*

city n 城市 *chéng shì*

claim n 索赔 *suǒ péi*

I'd like to file a claim. 我想提出索赔。 *wǒ xiǎng tí chū suǒ péi.*

clarinet n 竖笛 *shù dí*

class n 等级 *děng jí*

business class 商务舱 *shāng wù cāng*

economy class 经济舱 *jīng jì cāng*

first class 头等舱 *tóu děng cāng*

classical (music) adj 古典的（音乐） *gǔ diǎn de (yīn yuè)*

clean adj 干净的 *gàn jing de*

clean, to clean v 打扫 *dǎ sǎo*

Please clean the room today. 今天请打扫房间。 *jīn tiān qǐng dǎ sǎo fáng jiān.*

clear v 清晰的 *qīng xī de*

clear adj 清澈的 *qīng chè de*

climbing n 攀登 *pān dēng*

climb, to climb v 爬 *pá*

to climb a mountain 爬山 *pá shān*

to climb stairs 爬楼梯 *pá lóu tī*

close, to close v 关闭 *guān bì*

close (near) 靠近的 *kào jìn de*

closed adj 靠近的 *kào jìn de*

cloudy adj 多云的 *duō yún de*

clover n 三叶草 sān yè cǎo

go clubbing, to go clubbing v 露营 lù yíng

coat n 外套 wài tào

cockfight n 斗鸡 dòu jī

coffee n 咖啡 kā fēi

iced coffee 冰咖啡 bīng kā fēi

cognac n 法国白兰地酒 fǎ guó bái lán dì jiǔ

coin n 硬币 yìng bì

cold n 冷 lěng

I have a cold. 我感冒了。 wǒ gǎn mào le.

cold adj 冷的 lěng de

I'm cold. 我很冷。 wǒ hěn lěng.

It's cold out. 外边很冷。 wài biān hěn lěng.

coliseum n 音乐厅 yīn yuè tīng

collect adj 由对方付费的 yóu duì fāng fù fèi de

I'd like to place a collect call. 我想打一个对方付费电话。 wǒ xiǎng dǎ yī gè duì fāng fù fèi diàn huà.

collect, to collect v 收集 shōu jí

college n 大学 dà xué

Colombian adj 哥伦比亚的 gē lún bǐ yà de

color n 颜色 yán sè

color v 变色 biàn sè

computer n 计算机 jì suàn jī

concert n 音乐会 yīn yuè huì

condition n 条件 tiáo jiàn

in good / bad condition 情形 很好 / 差 qíng xíng hěn hǎo / chà

condom n 避孕套 bì yùn tào

Do you have a condom? 您有 避孕套吗? nín yǒu bì yùn tào ma?

not without a condom 没有 避孕套不行 méi yǒu bì yùn tào bù xíng

condor n 秃鹰 tū yīng

confirm, to confirm v 确认 què rèn

I'd like to confirm my reservation. 我想确认我的预 定。 wǒ xiǎng què rèn wǒ de yù dìng.

confused adj 困惑的 kùn huò de

congested adj 拥挤的 yōng jǐ de

connection speed n 连接速度 lián jiē sù dù

constipated adj 患便秘的 huàn biàn mì de

I'm constipated. 我便秘了。 wǒ biàn mì le.

contact lens n 隐形眼镜 yǐn xíng yǎn jìng

I lost my contact lens. 我的隐 形眼镜丢了。 wǒ de yǐn xíng yǎn jìng diū le.

continue, to continue v 继续 jì xù

convertible *n* 兑换 *duì huàn*

cook, to cook *v* 烹饪 *pēng rèn*

> **I'd like a room where I can cook.** 我要一间能做饭的房间。 *wǒ yào yī jiān néng zuò fàn de fáng jiān 。*

cookie *n* 小甜饼 *xiǎo tián bǐng*

copper *adj* 铜的 *tóng de*

corner *n* 角落 *jiǎo luò*

> **on the corner** 在角落 *zài jiǎo luò*

correct *v* 纠正 *jiū zhèng*

correct *adj* 正确的 *zhèng què de*

> **Am I on the correct train?** 我乘的火车对吗? *wǒ chéng de huǒ chē duì ma ?*

cost, to cost *v* 花费 *huā fèi*

> **How much does it cost?** 那得花多少钱? *nà dé huā duō shǎo qián?*

Costa Rican *adj* 哥斯达黎加 *gē sī dá lí jiā*

costume *n* 装束 *zhuāng shù*

cotton *n* 棉线 *mián xiàn*

cough *n* 咳嗽 *ké sou*

cough *v* 咳嗽 *ké sou*

counter (in bar) *n* 吧台 *bā tái*

country-and-western *n* 乡村音乐 *xiāng cūn yīn yuè*

court (legal) *n* 法院 *fǎ yuàn*

court (sport) *n* 球场（运动） *qiú chǎng (yùn dòng)*

courteous *adj* 有礼貌的 *yǒu lǐ mào de*

cousin *n* 姑妈 *gū mā*

cover charge (in bar) *n* 入场最低消费（酒吧） *rù chǎng zuì dī xiāo fèi (jiǔ bā)*

cow *n* 母牛 *mǔ niú*

crack (in glass object) *n* 裂缝（玻璃品上） *liè féng (bō li pǐn shàng)*

craftsperson *n* 手艺人 *shǒu yì rén*

cream *n* 奶油 *nǎi yóu*

credit card *n* 信用卡 *xìn yòng kǎ*

> **Do you accept credit cards?** 可以用信用卡吗? *kě yǐ yòng xìn yòng kǎ ma?*

crib *n* 婴儿床 *yīng ér chuáng*

crown (dental) *n* 齿冠（牙科） *chǐ guàn (yá kē)*

curb *n* 围栏 *wéi lán*

curl *n* 卷发 *juǎn fà*

curly *adj* 卷发的 *juǎn fà de*

currency exchange *n* 货币兑换处 *huò bì duì huàn chù*

> **Where is the nearest currency exchange?** 最近的货币兑换处在哪儿? *zuì jìn de huò bì duì huàn chù zài nǎ er?*

current (water) *n* 流（水） *liú (shuǐ)*

customs *n* 海关 hǎi guān

cut (wound) *n* 伤口 shāng kǒu

> **I have a bad cut.** 我有一个很严重的伤口。 wǒ yǒu yī gè hěn yán zhòng de shāng kǒu。

cut, to cut *v* 切 qiē

cybercafé *n* 网吧 wǎng bā

> **Where can I find a cybercafé?** 哪里有网吧? nǎ lǐ yǒu wǎng bā?

D

damaged *adj* 损坏的 sǔn huài de

Damn! *expletive* 该死! gāi sǐ!

dance *v* 跳舞 tiào wǔ

danger *n* 危险 wēi xiǎn

dark *n* 黑暗 hēi àn

dark *adj* 黑色的 hēi sè de

daughter *n* 女儿 nǚ ér

day *n* 天 tiān

> **the day before yesterday** 前天 qián tiān

> **these last few days** 最后这些日子 zuì hòu zhè xiē rì zǐ

dawn *n* 黎明 lí míng

> **at dawn** 在黎明 zài lí míng

deaf *adj* 聋的 lóng de

deal (bargain) *n* 交易 jiāo yì

> **What a great deal!** 这笔交易真划算! zhè bǐ jiāo yì zhēn huá suàn!

deal (cards) *v* 发牌 fā pái

> **Deal me in.** 让我参加进来。 ràng wǒ cān jiā jìn lái。

December *n* 十二月 shí èr yuè

declined *adj* 拒付的 jù fù de

> **Was my credit card declined?** 我的信用卡被拒付了吗? wǒ de xìn yòng kǎ bèi jù fù le ma?

behave *v* 申报 shēn bào

> **I have nothing to declare.** 我没有要申报的东西。 wǒ méi yǒu yào shēn bào de dōng xí。

deep *adj* 深的 shēn de

delay *n* 延误 yán wù

> **How long is the delay?** 延误时间有多长? yán wù shí jiān yǒu duō cháng?

delighted *adj* 高兴的 gāo xīng de

democracy *n* 民主主义 mín zhǔ zhǔ yì

dent *v* 凹进 āo jìn

> **He / She dented the car.** 他/她把车撞凹了。 tā / tā bǎ chē zhuàng āo le。

dentist *n* 牙医 yá yī

denture *n* 假牙 jiǎ yá

> **denture plate** 托牙板 tuō yá bǎn

departure *n* 离开 lí kāi

designer *n* 设计师 shè jì shī

dessert *n* 餐后甜点 cān hòu tián diǎn

ENGLISH—CHINESE

dessert menu 餐后甜点菜单 cān hòu tián diǎn cài dān

destination n 目的地 mù dì dì

diabetic adj 糖尿病的 táng niào bìng de

dial (a phone) v 拨（电话）bō (diàn huà)

dial direct 直拨 zhí bō

diaper n 尿布 niào bù

Where can I change a diaper? 在哪里可以换尿布? zài nǎ lǐ kě yǐ huàn niào bù?

diarrhea n 痢疾 lì jí

dictionary n 词典 cí diǎn

different (other) adj 不同的（其它的）bù tóng de (qí tā de)

difficult adj 困难的 kùn nán de

dinner n 晚餐 wǎn cān

directory assistance (phone) n 查号服务（电话）chá hào fú wù (diàn huà)

disability n 残疾 cán jí

disappear v 消失 xiāo shī

disco n 迪士高 dí shì gāo

disconnected adj 断线 duàn xiàn

Operator, I was disconnected. 接线员，我的电话断了。jiē xiàn yuán, wǒ de diàn huà duàn le.

discount n 折扣 zhé kòu

Do I qualify for a discount? 我有资格获得折扣吗? wǒ yǒu zī gé huò dé zhé kòu ma?

dish n 盘子 pán zi

dive v 潜水 qián shuǐ

scuba dive 水肺潜水 shuǐ fèi qián shuǐ

divorced adj 离异的 lí yì de

dizzy adj 晕眩的 yūn xuàn de

do, to do v 做 zuò

doctor n 医生 yī shēng

doctor's office n 医生办公室 yī shēng bàn gōng shì

dog n 狗 gǒu

service dog 帮助犬 bāng zhù quǎn

dollar n 美元 měi yuán

door n 门 mén

double adj 双倍的 shuāng bèi de

double bed 双人床 shuāng rén chuáng

double vision 双瞳 shuāng tóng

down adj 下面的 xià miàn de

download v 下载 xià zǎi

downtown n 市区 shì qū

dozen n 一打 yī dá

drain n 消耗 xiāo hào

drama n 戏剧 xì jù

drawing (work of art) n 图画（艺术品）tú huà (yì shù pǐn)

dress (garment) n 服装 fú zhuāng

dress (general attire) n 礼服 lǐ fú

What's the dress code? 有什么着装规则? yǒu shén me zhuó zhuāng guī zé?

dress v 穿衣 chuān yī

Should I dress up for that affair. 这次活动, 我需要穿正装吗? zhè cì huó dòng, wǒ xū yào chuān zhèng zhuāng ma?

dressing (salad) n 调味品 (沙拉) tiáo wèi pǐn (shā lā)

dried adj 干的 gān de

drink n 饮料 yǐn liào

I'd like a drink. 我想要杯饮料。 wǒ xiǎng yào bēi yǐn liào.

drink, to drink v 喝 hē

drip v 滴下 dī xià

drive v 驾驶 jià shǐ

driver n 司机 sī jī

driving range n 高尔夫球练习场 gāo ěr fū qiú liàn xí chǎng

drum n 鼓 gǔ

dry adj 干的 gān de

This towel isn't dry. 这条毛巾不干。 zhè tiáo máo jīn bù gān.

dry, to dry v 使干燥 shǐ gān zào

I need to dry my clothes. 我需要烘干我的衣服。 wǒ xū yào hōng gān wǒ de yī fu.

dry cleaner n 干洗店 gān xǐ diàn

dry cleaning n 干洗 gān xǐ

duck n 鸭子 yā zǐ

duty-free adj 免税 miǎn shuì

duty-free shop n 免税商店 miǎn shuì shāng diàn

DVD n DVD

Do the rooms have DVD players? 房间有 DVD 播放器吗? fáng jiān yǒu DVD bō fàng qì ma?

Where can I rent DVDs or videos? 哪里可以租到 DVD 或录像带? nǎ lǐ kě yǐ zū dào DVD huò lù xiàng dài?

E

early adj 早的 zǎo de

It's early. 时间还早。 shí jiān hái zǎo.

eat v 吃 chī

to eat out 去馆子吃饭 qù guǎn zǐ chī fàn

economy n 经济 jīng jì

Ecuadorian adj 厄瓜多尔的 è guā duō ěr de

editor n 编辑 biān jí

educator n 教育工作者 jiào yù gōng zuò zhě

eight n 八 bā

eighteen n 十八 shí bā

eighth n 第八 dì bā

eighty n 八十 bā shí

election n 选举 xuǎn jǔ

electrical hookup n 电线板 diàn xiàn bǎn

elevator n 电梯 diàn tī

eleven n 十一 shí yī

e-mail n 电子邮件 diàn zǐ yóu jiàn

May I have your e-mail address? 可以给我您的电子邮件地址吗? kě yǐ gěi wǒ nín de diàn zǐ yóu jiàn dì zhǐ ma?

e-mail message 电子邮件消息 diàn zǐ yóu jiàn xiāo xi

e-mail, to send e-mail v 发送电子邮件 fā sòng diàn zǐ yóu jiàn

embarrassed adj 尴尬的 gān gà de

embassy n 大使馆 dà shǐ guǎn

emergency n 紧急情况 jǐn jí qíng kuàng

emergency brake n 紧急刹车 jǐn jí shā chē

emergency exit n 紧急出口 jǐn jí chū kǒu

employee n 雇员 gù yuán

employer n 雇主 gù zhǔ

engine n 引擎 yǐn qíng

engineer n 工程师 gōng chéng shī

England n 英格兰 yīng gé lán

English n, adj 英国的 yīng guó de

Do you speak English? 您说英语吗? nín shuō yīng yǔ ma?

enjoy, to enjoy v 享受 xiǎng shòu

enter, to enter v 进入 jìn rù

Do not enter. 不准进入。bù zhǔn jìn rù.

enthusiastic adj 热情的 rè qíng de

entrance n 入口 rù kǒu

envelope n 信封 xìn fēng

environment n 环境 huán jìng

escalator n 电动扶梯 diàn dòng fú tī

espresso n 浓咖啡 nóng kā fēi

exchange rate n 汇率 huì lǜ

What is the exchange rate for US / Canadian dollars? 美国 / 加拿大元的兑换率是多少? měi guó / jiā ná dà yuán de duì huàn lǜ shì duō shǎo?

excuse (pardon) v 原谅 yuán liàng

Excuse me. 对不起。duì bù qǐ.

exhausted adj 疲惫的 pí bèi de

exhibit n 展览 zhǎn lǎn

exit n 出口 chū kǒu

not an exit 非出口 fēi chū kǒu

exit v 退出 tuì chū

expensive adj 昂贵的 áng guì de

explain v 解释 jiě shì

express adj 急速的 jí sù de

express check-in 快办登机手续 kuài bàn dēng jī shǒu xù

extra (additional) adj 额外的 é wài de

extra-large adj 超大的 chāo dà de

eye n 眼睛 yǎn jīng

eyebrow n 眉毛 méi mao

eyeglasses n 眼镜 yǎn jìng

eyelash n 睫毛 jié máo

F

fabric n 纤维 xiān wéi

face n 脸 liǎn

faint v 晕倒 yūn dǎo

fall (season) n 秋季 qiū jì

fall v 倒下 dǎo xià

family n 家人 jiā rén

fan n 扇子 shàn zi

far 远的 yuǎn de

How far is it to _____? 到_____有多远? dào _____ yǒu duō yuǎn?

fare n 费用 fèi yòng

fast adj 快的 kuài de

fat adj 胖的 pàng de

father n 父亲 fù qīn

faucet n 龙头 lóng tóu

fault n 过错 guò cuò

I'm at fault. 我是过错方。 wǒ shì guò cuò fāng。

It was his fault. 是他的过错。 shì tā de guò cuò。

fax n 传真 chuán zhēn

February n 二月 èr yuè

fee n 费 fèi

female adj 女性的 nǔ xìng de

fiancé(e) n 新娘 xīn niáng

fifteen adj 十五 shí wǔ

fifth adj 第五 dì wǔ

fifty adj 五十 wǔ shí

find v 发现 fā xiàn

fine (for traffic violation) n 罚款（交通违规）fá kuǎn (jiāo tōng wéi guī)

fine 好的 hǎo de

I'm fine. 我很好。 wǒ hěn hǎo。

fire! n 火 huǒ

first adj 第一的 dì yī de

fishing pole n 鱼竿 yú gān

fitness center n 健身中心 jiàn shēn zhōng xīn

fit (clothes) v 合身（衣服）hé shēn (yī fu)

Does this look like it fits? 这件看上去合身吗? zhè jiàn kàn shàng qù hé shēn ma?

fitting room n 试衣间 shì yī jiān

five adj 五 wǔ

flight n 航班 háng bān

ENGLISH—CHINESE

Where do domestic flights arrive / depart? 国内航班在哪里到达 / 离开? *guó nèi háng bān zài nǎ lǐ dào dá / lí kāi?*

Where do international flights arrive / depart? 国际航班在哪里到达 / 离开? *guó jì háng bān zài nǎ lǐ dào dá / lí kāi?*

What time does this flight leave? 这架航班什么时候起飞? *zhè jià háng bān shén me shí hou qǐ fēi?*

flight attendant 航班服务员 *háng bān fú wù yuán*

floor n 层 *céng*

ground floor 底层 *dǐ céng*

second floor 二楼 *èr lóu*

flower n 花 *huā*

flush (gambling) n 顺子（赌博）*shùn zǐ (dǔ bó)*

flush, to flush v 冲刷 *chōng shuā*

This toilet won't flush. 马桶无法冲水。*mǎ tǒng wú fǎ chōng shuǐ。*

flute n 长笛 *cháng dí*

food n 食物 *shí wù*

foot (body part, measurement) n 脚、尺 *jiǎo、chǐ*

forehead n 前额 *qián é*

formula n 配方 *pèi fāng*

Do you sell infants' formula? 卖婴儿配方奶粉吗? *mài yīng ér pèi fāng nǎi fěn ma?*

forty adj 四十 *sì shí*

forward adj 向前 *xiàng qián*

four adj 四 *sì*

fourteen adj 十四 *shí sì*

fourth adj 第四 *dì sì*

one-fourth 四分之一 *sì fēn zhī yī*

fragile adj 易碎的 *yì suì de*

freckle n 雀斑 *què bān*

French adj 法国的 *fǎ guó de*

fresh adj 新鲜的 *xīn xiān de*

Friday n 星期五 *xīng qī wǔ*

friend n 朋友 *péng you*

front adj 前面的 *qián miàn de*

front desk 前台 *qián tái*

front door 前门 *qián mén*

fruit n 水果 *shuǐ guǒ*

fruit juice n 果汁 *guǒ zhī*

full, to be full (after a meal) adj 饱的 *bǎo de*

Full house! n 满堂彩 *mǎn táng cǎi*

fuse n 保险丝 *bǎo xiǎn sī*

G

gallon n 加仑 *jiā lún*

garlic n 大蒜 *dà suàn*

gas n 汽油 *qì yóu*

gas gauge 油表 *yóu biǎos*

out of gas 没油了 *méi yóu le*

gate (at airport) n 登机口（在机场）*dēng jī kǒu (zài jī chǎng)*

German adj 德国的 *dé guó de*

gift n 礼物 *lǐ wù*

gin n 杜松子酒 *dù sōng zǐ jiǔ*

girl n 女孩 *nǚ hái*

girlfriend n 女朋友 *nǚ péng yǒu*

give, to give v 给 *gěi*

glass n 玻璃杯 *bō li bēi*

Do you have it by the glass? 是用玻璃杯喝吗? *shì yòng bō li bēi hē ma?*

I'd like a glass please. 请给我来一杯。*qǐng gěi wǒ lái yī bēi.*

glasses (eye) n 眼镜 *yǎnjìng*

I need new glasses. 我需要配副新眼镜。*wǒ xū yào pèi fù xīn yǎn jìng 。*

glove n 手套 *shǒu tào*

go, to go v 去 *qù*

goal (sport) n 得分（运动）*dé fēn (yùn dòng)*

goalie n 守门员 *shǒu mén yuán*

gold adj 金色的 *jīn sè de*

golf n 高尔夫球 *gāo ěr fū qiú*

golf, to go golfing v 打高尔夫球 *dá gāo ěr fū qiú*

good adj 好的 *hǎo de*

goodbye n 再见 *zài jiàn*

grade (school) n 年级（学校）*nián jí (xué xiào)*

gram n 克 *kè*

grandfather n 祖父 *zǔ fù*

grandmother n 祖母 *zǔ mǔ*

grandparent n 祖父母 *zǔ fù mǔ*

grape n 葡萄 *pú tao*

gray adj 灰色的 *huī sè de*

great adj 美妙的 *měi miào de*

Greek adj 希腊的 *xī là de*

Greek Orthodox adj 希腊正教的 *xī là zhèng jiào de*

green adj 绿色的 *lǜ sè de*

groceries n 杂货 *zá huò*

group n 团体 *tuán tǐ*

grow, to grow (get larger) v 增长 *zēng cháng*

Where did you grow up? 您在哪里长大? *nín zài nǎ lǐ cháng dà?*

guard n 保安 *bǎo ān*

security guard 保安 *bǎo ān*

Guatemalan adj 危地马拉的 *wēi dì mǎ lā de*

guest n 客人 *kè rén*

guide (of tours) n 导游 *dǎo yóu*

guide (publication) n 指南（出版物）*zhǐ nán (chū bǎn wù)*

guide, to guide v 指导 *zhǐ dǎo*

guided tour n 配导游的旅游 *pèi dǎo yóu de lǚ yóu*

guitar n 吉他 jí tā

gym n 体育馆 tǐ yù guǎn

gynecologist n 妇科医生 fù kē yī shēng

H

hair n 头发 tóu fa

haircut n 理发 lǐ fà

> **I need a haircut.** 我需要理发。 wǒ xū yào lǐ fà。
>
> **How much is a haircut?** 理发多少钱? lǐ fà duō shǎo qián?

hairdresser n 美容师 měi róng shī

hair dryer n 吹风机 chuī fēng jī

half n 半个 bàn gè

> **one-half** 二分之一 èr fēn zhī yī

hallway n 走廊 zǒu láng

hand n 手 shǒu

handicapped-accessible adj 残疾人可用的 cán jí rén kě yòng de

handle, to handle v 处理 chǔ lǐ

handsome adj 英俊的 yīng jùn de

hangout (hot spot) n 逛街（热闹的市区）guàng jiē (rè nào de shì qū)

hang out (to relax) v 逛街（休息）guàng jiē (xiū xi)

hang up (to end a phone call) v 挂断电话（结束通话）guà duàn diàn huà (jié shù tōng huà)

hanger n 衣架 yī jià

happy adj 快乐的 kuài lè de

hard adj 艰难的 牢固的 jiān nán de láo gù de

hat n 帽子 mào zi

have v 有 yǒu

hazel adj 淡褐色的 dàn hè sè de

headache n 头痛 tóu tòng

headlight n 前灯 qián dēng

headphones n 耳机 ěr jī

hear v 听见 tīng jiàn

hearing-impaired adj 听障的 tīng zhàng de

heart n 心脏 xīn zàng

heart attack n 心脏病 xīn zàng bìng

hectare n 公顷 gōng qǐng

hello n 您好 nín hǎo

Help! n 帮帮我！ bāng bāng wǒ!

help, to help v 帮助 bāng zhù

hen n 母鸡 mǔ jī

her adj 她的 tā de

herb n 药草 yào cǎo

here n 这里 zhè lǐ

high adj 高的 gāo de

highlights (hair) *n* 挑染（头发）tiāo rǎn (tóu fa)

highway *n* 高速公路 gāo sù gōng lù

hike, to hike *v* 远足 yuǎn zú

him *pron* 他 tā

Hindu *adj* 印度教的 yìn dù jiào de

hip-hop *n* 街舞 jiē wǔ

his *adj* 他的 tā de

historical *adj* 历史性的 lì shǐ xìng de

history *n* 历史 lì shǐ

hobby *n* 爱好 ài hǎo

hold, to hold *v* 握着 wò zhe

to hold hands 牵手 qiān shǒu

Would you hold this for me? 能帮我拿着这个吗? néng bāng wǒ ná zhe zhè gè ma?

hold, to hold (to pause) *v* 暂停 zàn tíng

Hold on a minute! 稍等! shāo děng!

I'll hold. 我等一下好了。wǒ děng yī xià hǎo le。

hold, to hold (gambling) *v* 握着（赌博）wò zhe (dǔ bó)

holiday *n* 假期 jià qī

home *n* 家 jiā

homemaker *n* 家庭主妇 jiā tíng zhǔ fù

Honduran *adj* 洪都拉斯的 hóng dōu lā sī de

horn *n* 角 jiǎo

horse *n* 马 mǎ

hostel *n* 旅社 lǚ shè

hot *adj* 热的 rè de

hot chocolate *n* 热巧克力 rè qiǎo kè lì

hotel *n* 酒店 jiǔ diàn

Do you have a list of local hotels? 您有当地酒店的名单吗? nín yǒu dāng dì jiǔ diàn de míng dān ma?

hour *n* 时间 shí jiān

hours (at museum) *n* 开放时间（博物馆）kāi fàng shí jiān (bó wù guǎn)

how *adv* 多少 duō shǎo

humid *adj* 潮湿的 cháo shī de

hundred *n* 百 bǎi

hurry *v* 赶紧 gǎn jǐn

I'm in a hurry. 我很着急。wǒ hěn zháo jí。

Hurry, please! 请快点! qǐng kuài diàn!

hurt, to hurt *v* 伤害 shāng hài

Ouch! That hurts! 哎唷! 很痛! āi yō! hěn tòng!

husband *n* 丈夫 zhàng fū

I

I *pron* 我 wǒ

ice *n* 冰 bīng

identification *n* 证明 zhèng míng

ENGLISH—CHINESE

inch n 英寸 yīng cùn

indigestion n 消化不良 xiāo huà bùl iáng

inexpensive adj 便宜的 pián yi de

infant n 幼儿 yòu ér

Are infants allowed? 幼儿可以吗? yòu ér kěyǐ ma？

information n 信息 xìn xī

information booth n 信息亭 xìn xī tíng

injury n 伤害 shāng hài

insect repellent n 杀虫剂 shā chóng jì

inside 里边的 lǐ biān de

insult v 侮辱 wǔ rǔ

insurance n 保险 bǎo xiǎn

intercourse (sexual) n 性交 xìng jiāo

interest rate n 利率 lì lǜ

intermission n 兑换 duì huàn

Internet n 网络 wǎng luò

High-speed Internet 高速网络 gāo sù wǎng luò

Do you have Internet access? 可以上网吗? kě yǐ shàng wǎng ma？

Where can I find an Internet café? 哪里有网吧? nǎ lǐ yǒu wǎng bā?

interpreter n 口译人员 kǒu yì rén yuán

I need an interpreter. 我需要一位口译人员。wǒ xū yào yī wèi kǒu yì rén yuán。

introduce, to introduce v 介绍 jiè shào

I'd like to introduce you to ____. 我想把你介绍给——。wǒ xiǎng bǎ nǐ jiè shào gěi____。

Ireland n 爱尔兰 ài ěr lán

Irish adj 爱尔兰的 ài ěr lán de

is v See be (to be)

Italian adj 意大利的 yì dà lì de

J

jacket n 夹克衫 jiā kè shān

January n 一月 yī yuè

Japanese adj 日本的 rì běn de

jazz n 爵士乐 jué shì yuè

Jewish adj 犹太教的 yóu tài jiào de

jog, to run v 慢跑 màn pǎo

juice n 汁 zhī

June n 六月 liù yuè

July n 七月 qī yuè

K

keep, to keep v 保持 bǎo chí

kid n 小孩 xiǎo hái

Are kids allowed? 小孩可以吗? xiǎo hái kě yǐ ma?

Do you have children's programs? 有小孩的节目吗? yǒu xiǎo hái de jiémù ma?

Do you have a kids' menu? 有小孩的菜单吗? yǒu xiǎo hái de cài dān ma?

kilo n 千 qiān

kilometer n 千米 qiān mǐ

kind n 种类 zhǒng lèi

What kind is it? 这是哪一种? zhè shì nǎ yī zhǒng?

kiss n 吻 wěn

kitchen n 厨房 chú fáng

know, to know (something) v 知道（某事）zhī dao (mǒu shi)

know, to know (someone) v 认识（某人）rèn shí (mǒurén)

kosher adj 犹太教的 yóu tài jiào de

L

lactose-intolerant adj 忌乳糖的 jì rǔ táng de

land, to land v 着陆 zhuó lù

landscape n 风景 fēng jǐng

language n 语言 yǔ yán

laptop n 笔记本电脑 bǐ jì běn diàn nǎo

large adj 大的 dà de

last, to last v 持续 chí xù

last adv 最后 zuì hòu

late adj 晚的 wǎn de

Please don't be late. 请不要晚了。qǐng bù yào wǎn le。

later adv 后来 hòu lái

See you later. 回头见。huí tóu jiàn。

laundry n 洗衣店 xǐ yī diàn

lavender adj 淡紫色的 dàn zǐ sè de

law n 法律 fǎ lù

lawyer n 律师 lǜ shī

least n 至少 zhì shǎo

least adj 最少的 zuì shǎo de

leather n 皮革 pí gé

leave, to leave (depart) v 离开 lí kāi

left adj 左边的 zuǒ biān de

on the left 在左边 zài zuǒ biān

leg n 腿 tuǐ

lemonade n 柠檬水 níng méng shuǐ

less adj 少的 shǎo de

lesson n 课程 kè chéng

license n 执照 zhí zhào

driver's license 驾驶执照 jià shǐ zhí zhào

life preserver n 救生用具 jiù shēng yòng jù

light n (lamp) 灯 dēng

light (for cigarette) n 打火机 dǎ huǒ jī

May I offer you a light? n
借个火好吗？ jiè gè huǒ hǎo
ma？

like, desire v 渴望 kě wàng

I would like _____. 我想要____
___。 wǒ xiǎng yào _____。

like, to like v 喜欢 xǐ huān

I like this place. 我喜欢这个
地方。 wǒ xǐ huān zhè gè dì
fāng。

limo n 豪华大巴 háo huá dà bā

liquor n 白酒 bái jiǔ

liter n 升 shēng

little adj 小的（尺寸）少的
（数量）xiǎo de (chǐ cùn)
shǎo de (shù liàng)

live, to live v 居住 jū zhù p23

Where do you live? 您住在哪
里? nín zhù zài nǎ lǐ？

living n 生活 shēng huó

What do you do for a living?
您是做什么工作的? nín shì
zuò shén me gōng zuò de？

local adj 本地 běn dì

lock n 锁 suǒ

lock, to lock v 锁上 suǒ shàng

I can't lock the door. 我锁不上
门。wǒ suǒ bù shàng mén。

I'm locked out. 我被锁在门外
了。wǒ bèi suǒ zài mén
wài le。

locker n 存物柜 cún wù guì

storage locker 储藏柜 chǔ
cáng guì

locker room 存物室 cún wù
shì

long adv 长期地 cháng qī dì

For how long? 多长时间? duō
cháng shí jiān？

long adj 长期的 cháng qī de

look, to look v (to observe)
观看 guān kàn

I'm just looking. 我只是看看。
wǒ zhǐ shì kàn kàn。

Look here! 看这里！ kàn
zhè lǐ！

look, to look v (to appear)
显得 xiǎn dé

How does this look? 这看起
来怎么样? zhè kàn qǐ lái zěn
me yàng？

look for, to look for (to search)
v 寻找 xún zhǎo

I'm looking for a porter. 我在
找搬运工。wǒ zài zhǎo bān
yùn gōng。

loose adj 松的 sōng de

lose, to lose v 遗失 yí shī

I lost my passport. 我的护照
丢了。wǒ de hùzhào diū le。

I lost my wallet. 我的钱夹丢
了。wǒ de qián jiā diū le。

I'm lost. 我迷路了。wǒ mí
lù le。

loud adj 大声的

loudly *adv* 大声地 *dà shēng de*

lounge *n* 休息室 *xiū xī shì*

lounge, to lounge *v* 闲荡 *xián dàng*

love *n* 爱 *ài*

love, to love *v* 爱 *ài*

> **to love (family)** 爱家庭 *ài jiā tíng*
>
> **to love (a friend)** 爱朋友 *ài péng you*
>
> **to love (a lover)** 爱情人 *ài qíng rén*
>
> **to make love** 做爱 *zuò ài*

low *adj* 低的 *dī de*

lunch *n* 午餐 *wǔ cān*

luggage *n* 行李 *xíng li*

> **Where do I report lost luggage?** 我到哪里报告丢失了行李? *wǒ dào nǎ lǐ bào gào diū shī le xíng li?*
>
> **Where is the lost luggage claim?** 丢失行李领取处在哪里? *diū shī xíng li lǐng qǔ chǔzài nǎ lǐ?*

M

machine *n* 机器 *jī qì*

made of *adj* 组成的 *zǔ chéng de*

magazine *n* 杂志 *zá zhì*

maid (hotel) *n* 女仆（酒店）*nǚ pú (jiǔ diàn)*

maiden *adj* 未婚的 *wèi hūn de*

> **That's my maiden name.** 那是我的娘家姓。*nà shì wǒ de niáng jia xìng.*

mail *n* 邮件 *yóu jiàn*

> **air mail** 航空邮件 *háng kōng yóu jiàn*
>
> **registered mail** 挂号邮件 *guà hào yóu jiàn*

mail *v* 邮寄 *yóu jì*

make, to make *v* 制造 *zhì zào*

makeup *n* 组成 *zǔ chéng*

make up, to make up (apologize) *v* 和解（抱歉）*hé jiě (bàoqiàn)*

make up, to make up (apply cosmetics) *v* 化妆（用化妆品）*huà zhuāng (yòng huà zhuāng pǐn)*

male *n* 男性 *nán xìng*

male *adj* 男性的 *nán xìng de*

mall *n* 购物中心 *gòu wù zhōng xīn*

man *n* 男人 *nán rén*

manager *n* 经理 *jīng lǐ*

manual (instruction booklet) *n* 手册 *shǒu cè*

many *adj* 许多的 *xǔ duō de*

map *n* 地图 *dì tú*

March (month) *n* 三月 *sān yuè*

market *n* 市场 *shì chǎng*

> **flea market** 跳蚤市场 *tiào zǎo shì chǎng*

open-air market 露天市场 lù tiān shì chǎng

married adj 已婚的 yǐ hūn de

marry, to marry v 结婚 jié hūn

massage, to massage v 按摩 àn mó

match (sport) n 比赛（运动）bǐ sài (yùndòng)

match n 比赛 bǐ sài

book of matches 一包火柴 yī bāo huǒ chái

match, to match v 匹配 pǐ pèi

Does this ____ match my outfit? ____和我的衣服搭配吗？____ hé wǒ de yīfu dā pèi ma?

May (month) n 五月 wǔ yuè

may v aux 可能 kě néng

May I ____? 我可以____吗？wǒ kě yǐ ____ ma?

meal n 膳食 shàn shí

meat n 肉 ròu

meatball n 肉丸子 ròu wán zī

medication n 药物 yào wù

medium (size) adj 中（号）zhōng (hào)

medium rare (meat) adj 四分熟的（肉）sì fēn shú de (ròu)

medium well (meat) adj 七分熟的（肉）qī fēn shú de (ròu)

member n 成员 chéng yuán

menu n 菜单 cài dān

May I see a menu? 我可以看一下菜单吗？wǒ kě yǐ kàn yī xià cài dān ma?

children's menu 儿童菜单 ér tóng cài dān

diabetic menu 糖尿病人菜单 táng niào bìng rén cài dān

kosher menu 犹太教徒菜单 yóu tài jiào tú cài dān

metal detector n 金属探测器 jīn shǔ tàn cè qì

meter n 米 mǐ

Mexican adj 墨西哥的 mò xī gē de

middle adj 中间的 zhōng jiān de

midnight n 午夜 wǔ yè

mile n 英里 yīng lǐ

military n 军事 jūn shì

milk n 牛奶 niú nǎi

milk shake 奶昔 nǎi xī

milliliter n 毫升 háo shēng

millimeter n 毫米 háo mǐ

minute n 分钟 fēn zhōng

in a minute 马上 mǎ shàng

miss, to miss (a flight) v 错过（航班）cuò guò (háng bān)

missing adj 丢失的 diū shī de

mistake n 错误 cuò wù

moderately priced adj 价格适中的 jià gé shì zhōng de

mole (facial feature) n 痣（脸部特征）zhì (liǎn bù tè zhēng)

Monday n 星期一 xīng qī yī

money n 金钱 jīn qián

money transfer 转帐 zhuǎn zhàng

month n 月 yuè

morning n 早晨 zǎo chén

in the morning 在早晨 zài zǎo chén

mosque n 清真寺 qīng zhēn sì

mother n 母亲 mǔ qīn

mother, to mother v 生育 shēng yù

motorcycle n 摩托车 mó tuō chē

mountain n 山 shān

mountain climbing 爬山 pá shān

mouse n 老鼠 lǎo shǔ

mouth n 嘴 zuǐ

move, to move v 移动 yí dòng

movie n 电影 diàn yǐng

much n 许多 xǔ duō

mug, to mug (someone) v 袭击 xí jǐ

mugged adj 受袭击的 shòu xí jǐ de

museum n 博物馆 bó wù guǎn

music n 音乐 yīn yuè

live music 现场音乐 xiàn chǎng yīn yuè

musician n 音乐家 yīn yuè jiā

muslim adj 穆斯林的 mù sī lín de

mustache n 胡子 hú zǐ

mystery (novel) n 神秘故事 shén mì gù shì

N

name n 名字 míng zi

My name is ___. 我叫_____。wǒ jiào _____.

What's your name? 您叫什么名字? nín jiào shén me míng zi?

napkin n 纸巾 zhǐ jīn

narrow adj 狭窄的 xiá zhǎi de

nationality n 民族 mín zú

nausea n 晕船 yùn chuán

near adj 靠近的 kào jìn de

nearby adj 靠近的 kào jìn de

neat (tidy) adj 干净的 gànjing de

need, to need v 需要 xū yào

neighbor n 邻居 lín jū

nephew n 侄子 zhí zǐ

network n 网络 wǎng luò

new adj 新的 xīn de

newspaper n 报纸 bào zhǐ

newsstand n 报亭 bào tíng

New Zealand *n* 新西兰 *xīn xī lán*

New Zealander *adj* 新西兰的 *xīn xī lán de*

next *prep* 紧邻地 *jǐn lín de*

next to 靠近 *kào jìn*

the next station 下一站 *xià yī zhàn*

Nicaraguan *adj* 尼加拉瓜的 *ní jiā lā guā de*

nice *adj* 美好的 *měi hǎo de*

niece *n* 侄女 *zhí nǚ*

night *n* 夜晚 *yè wǎn*

at night 在夜晚 *zài yè wǎn*

per night 每夜 *měi yè*

nightclub *n* 夜总会 *yè zǒng huì*

nine *adj* 九 *jiǔ*

nineteen *adj* 十九 *shí jiǔ*

ninety *adj* 九十 *jiǔ shí*

ninth *adj* 第九 *dì jiǔ*

no *adv* 不 *bù*

noisy *adj* 噪杂的 *zào zá de*

none *n* 没人 *méi rén*

nonsmoking *adj* 禁止吸烟的 *jìn zhǐ xī yān de*

nonsmoking area 禁烟区 *jìn yān qū*

nonsmoking room 禁烟房间 *jìn yān fáng jiān*

noon *n* 中午 *zhōng wǔ*

nose *n* 鼻子 *bí zǐ*

novel *n* 小说 *xiǎo shuō*

November *n* 十一月 *shí yī yuè*

now *adv* 现在 *xiàn zài*

number *n* 数字 *shù zì*

Which room number? 哪一房间号? *nǎ yī fáng jiān hào?*

May I have your phone number? 可以给我您的电话号码吗? *kě yǐ gěi wǒ nín de diàn huà hào mǎ ma?*

nurse *n* 护士 *hù shì*

nurse *v* 看护 *kān hù*

Do you have a place where I can nurse? 有地方我可以喂奶吗? *yǒu dì fāng wǒ kě yǐ wéi nǎi ma?*

nursery *n* 托儿所 *tuō ér suǒ*

Do you have a nursery? 您这儿有托儿所吗? *nín zhè ér yǒu tuō ér suǒ ma?*

nut *n* 坚果 *jiān guǒ*

O

o'clock *adv* 点钟 *diǎn zhōng*

two o'clock 两点钟 *liǎng diǎn zhōng*

October *n* 十月 *shí yuè*

offer, to offer *v* 提供 *tí gōng*

officer *n* 军官 *jūn guān*

oil *n* 油 *yóu*

okay *adv* 好 *hǎo*

old *adj* 老的 *lǎo de*

olive *n* 橄榄色 *gǎn lǎn sè*

one adj 一个的 yī gè de

one way (traffic sign) adj 单行线（交通标志） dān xíng xiàn (jiāo tōng biāo zhì)

open (business) adj 营业中 yíng yè zhōng

> **Are you open?** 在营业吗? zài yíng yè ma ?

opera n 歌剧 gē jù

operator (phone) n 接线员 jiē xiàn yuán

optometrist n 验光师 yàn guāng shī

orange (color) adj 橙色 chéng sè

orange juice n 橙汁 chéng zhī

order, to order (demand) v 命令 mìng lìng

order, to order (request) v 要求 yāo qiú

organic adj 有机的 yǒu jī de

Ouch! interj 哎唷！ āi yō!

outside n 外面 wài miàn

overcooked adj 煮得过久的 zhǔ dé guò jiǔ de

overheat, to overheat v 过热 guò rè

> **The car overheated.** 车变得过热了。 chē biàn dé guò rè le。

overflowing adv 溢出 yì chū

oxygen tank n 氧气罐 yǎng qì guàn

P

package n 包裹 bāo guǒ

pacifier n 抚慰者 fǔ wèi zhě

page, to page (someone) v 呼叫（某人） hū jiào (mǒu rén)

paint, to paint v 绘画 huì huà

painting n 油画 yóu huà

pale adj 苍白的 cāng bái de

Panamanian adj 巴拿马的 bā ná mǎ de

paper n 纸 zhǐ

parade n 游行 yóu xíng

Paraguayan adj 巴拉圭的 bā lā guī de

parent n 父母 fù mǔ

park n 公园 gōng yuán

park, to park v 停放 tíng fàng

> **no parking** 禁止停车 jìn zhǐ tíng chē

> **parking fee** 停车费 tíng chē fèi

> **parking garage** 停车场 tíng chē chǎng

partner n 伙伴 huǒ bàn

party n 政党 zhèng dǎng

party n 党派 dǎng pai

> **political party** 政党 zhèng dǎng

pass, to pass v 通过 tōng guò

> **I'll pass.** 我会过关的。 wǒ huì guóguān de。

passenger n 乘客 chéng kè

passport n 护照 hù zhào

I've lost my passport. 我的护照丢了。wǒ de hù zhào diū le.

pay, to pay v 支付 zhī fù

peanut n 花生 huā shēng

pedestrian adj 徒步的 tú bù de

pediatrician n 儿科医师 ér kē yī shī

Can you recommend a pediatrician? 您能推荐一位儿科医师吗? nín néng tuī jiàn yī wèi ér kē yī shī ma?

permit n 许可证 xǔ kě zhèng

Do we need a permit? 我们需要许可证吗? wǒmén xū yào xǔkě zhèng ma?

permit, to permit v 允许 yǔn xǔ

Peruvian adj 秘鲁的 mì lǔ de

phone n 电话机 diàn huà jī

May I have your phone number? 可以给我您的电话号码吗? kěyǐ gěi wǒ nín de diàn huà hào mǎ ma?

Where can I find a public phone? 哪里有公用电话? nǎ lǐ yǒu gōng yòng diàn huà?

phone operator 电话接线员 diàn huà jiē xiàn yuán

Do you sell prepaid phones? 卖预付费电话吗? mài yù fù fèi diàn huà ma?

phone adj 电话 diàn huà

Do you have a phone directory? 您有电话号码黄页吗? nín yǒu diàn huà hào mǎ huáng yè ma?

phone call n 电话 diàn huà

I need to make a collect phone call. 我需要打一个对方付费电话。wǒ xū yào dǎ yī gè duì fāng fù fèi diàn huà.

an international phone call 一个国际电话 yī gè guó jì diàn huà

photocopy, to photocopy v 影印 yǐng yìn

piano n 钢琴 gāng qín

pillow n 枕头 zhěn tóu

down pillow 羽绒枕 yǔ róng zhěn

pink adj 粉红色的 fěn hóng sè de

pint n 品脱 pǐn tuō

pizza n 比萨 bǐ sà

place, to place v 放置 fàng zhì

plastic n 塑料 sù liào

play n 游戏 yóu xì

play, to play (a game) v 进行比赛 jìn xíng bǐ sài

play, to play (an instrument) v 演奏 yǎn zòu

playground n 运动场 yùn dòng chǎng

Do you have a playground? 有运动场吗? yǒu yùn dòng chǎng ma?

please (polite entreaty) *adv* 请
（礼貌的请求）qǐng
(lǐ mào de qǐng qiú)

please, to be pleasing to *v* 使
愉快 shǐ yú kuài

pleasure *n* 愉快 yú kuài

It's a pleasure. 见到您很高兴。
jiàn dào nín hěn gāo xīng.

plug *n* 插头 chā tóu

plug, to plug *v* 插上 chā shàng

point, to point *v* 指出 zhǐ chū

Would you point me in the
direction of____? 您能为我
指出_____的方向吗? nín
néng wéi wǒ zhǐ chū_____
de fāng xiàng ma?

police *n* 警察 jǐng chá

police station *n* 警察局 jǐng chá
jú

pool *n* 台球 tái qiú

pool (the game) *n* 台球（游戏）
tái qiú (yóu xì)

pop music *n* 流行音乐 liú xíng
yīn yuè

popular *adj* 受欢迎的 shòu
huān yíng de

port (beverage) *n* 波尔图葡萄
酒 bō ěr tú pú táo jiǔ

port (for ship) *n* 港口 gǎng kǒu

porter *n* 搬运工人 bān yùn
gōng rén

portion *n* 一部分 yī bù fēn

portrait *n* 肖像 xiāo xiàng

postcard *n* 明信片 míng xìn
piàn

post office *n* 邮局 yóu jú

Where is the post office? 哪
里有邮局? nǎ lǐ yǒu yóu jú?

poultry *n* 家禽 jiā qín

pound *n* 磅 páng

prefer, to prefer *v* 更喜欢 gèng
xǐ huān

pregnant *adj* 怀孕的 huái yùn
de

prepared *adj* 准备好的 zhǔn bèi
hǎo de

prescription *n* 处方 chǔ fāng

price *n* 价格 jià gé

print, to print *v* 打印 dǎ yìn

private berth / cabin *n* 私人泊
位 / 舱 sī rén bó wèi / cāng

problem *n* 难题 nán tí

process, to process *v* 处理
chǔ lǐ

product *n* 产品 chǎn pǐn

professional *adj* 专业的 zhuān
yè de

program *n* 节目单 jié mù dān

May I have a program? 可以
给我一份节目单吗? kě yǐ gěi
wǒ yī fèn jié mù dān ma?

Protestant *n* 新教徒 xīn jiào tú

publisher *n* 发行人 fā xíng rén

Puerto Rican *adj* 波多黎各的 bō
duō lí gè de

pull, to pull v 拉 lā

pump n 泵 bèng

purple adj 紫色的 zǐ sè de

purse n 钱包 qián bāo

push, to push v 推 tuī

put, to put v 放 fàng

Q

quarter adj 四分之一的 sì fēn zhī yī de

> **one-quarter** 四分之一 sì fēn zhī yī

quiet adj 安静的 ān jìng de

R

rabbit n 兔子 tù zǐ

radio n 无线电广播 wú xiàn diàn guǎng bō

> **satellite radio** 卫星广播 wèi xīng guǎng bō

rain, to rain v 下雨 xià yǔ

> **Is it supposed to rain?** 天会下雨吗? tiān huì xià yǔ ma?

rainy adj 多雨的 duō yǔ de

> **It's rainy.** 天在下雨。tiān zài xià yǔ。

ramp, wheelchair n 坡道 pō dào

rare (meat) adj 三分熟的（肉）sān fēn shú de (ròu)

rate (for car rental, hotel) n 费用 fèi yòng

> **What's the rate per day?** 每天的费用是多少? měi tiān de fèi yòng shì duō shǎo?

> **What's the rate per week?** 每周的费用是多少? měi zhōu de fèi yòng shì duō shǎo?

rate plan (cell phone) n 收费计划（移动电话）shōu fèi jì huà (yí dòng diàn huà)

rather adv 相当 xiāng dāng

read, to read v 读 dú

really adv 真正地 zhēn zhèng dì

receipt n 收据 shōu jù

receive, to receive v 收到 shōu dào

recommend, to recommend v 推荐 tuī jiàn

red adj 红色的 hóng sè de

redhead n 红头发 hóng tóu fa

reef n 帆 fān

refill (of beverage) n 再斟满 zài zhēn mǎn

refill (of prescription) n 续处方 xù chǔ fāng

reggae adj 瑞格舞的 ruì gé wǔ de

relative (family) n 亲属 qīn shǔ

remove, to remove v 移动 yí dòng

rent, to rent v 租用 zū yòng

> **I'd like to rent a car.** 我想租一辆车。wǒ xiǎng zū yī liàng chē。

repeat, to repeat v 重复 chóng fù

Would you please repeat that? 请您再重复一遍好吗? qǐng nín zài chóng fù yī biàn hǎo ma?

reservation n 预定 yù dìng

I'd like to make a reservation for ____. 我想预定____。 wǒ xiǎng yù dìng ____. See p7 for numbers.

restaurant n 饭店 fàn diàn

Where can I find a good restaurant? 哪里有好的饭店? nǎ lǐ yǒu hǎo de fàn diàn?

restroom n 洗手间 xǐ shǒu jiān

Do you have a public restroom? 有公共洗手间吗? yǒu gōng gòng xǐ shǒu jiān ma?

return, to return (to a place) v 返回 fǎn huí

return, to return (something to a store) v 退货 tuì huò

ride, to ride v 乘 chéng

right adj 右边的 yòu biān de

It is on the right. 在右边。 zài yòu biān.

Turn right at the corner. 在拐角处右转。 zài guǎi jiǎo chù yòu zhuǎn.

rights n pl 权利 quán lì

civil rights 民权 mín quán

river n 河 hé

road n 道路 dào lù

road closed sign n 道路封闭标志 dào lù fēng bì biāo zhì

rob, to rob v 抢夺 qiǎng duó

I've been robbed. 我被抢了。 wǒ bèi qiǎng le.

rock and roll n 摇滚 yáo gǔn

rock climbing n 攀岩 pān yán

rocks (ice) n 冰块 bīng kuài

I'd like it on the rocks. 我想加上冰块。 wǒ xiǎng jiā shàng bīng kuài.

romance (novel) n 爱情小说 ài qíng xiǎo shuō

romantic adj 浪漫的 làng màn de

room (hotel) n 客房（酒店）kè fáng (jiǔ diàn)

room for one / two 单人 / 双人间。 dān rén / shuāng rén jiān.

room service 客房服务 kè fáng fú wù

rope n 绳子 shéng zǐ

rose n 玫瑰 méi guī

royal flush n 同花大顺 tóng huā dà shùn

rum n 朗姆酒 lǎng mǔ jiǔ

run, to run v 运行 yùn xíng

S

sad *adj* 伤心的 shāng xīn de

safe (for storing valuables) *n* 保险箱（存储贵重物品）bǎo xiǎn xiāng (cún chǔ guì zhòng wù pǐn)

> **Do the rooms have safes?** 房间有保险箱吗? fáng jiān yǒu bǎo xiǎn xiāng ma?

safe (secure) *adj* 安全的 ān quán de

> **Is this area safe?** 该地区安全吗? gāi dì qū ān quán ma?

sail *n* 航行 háng xíng

sail, to sail *v* 启航 qǐ háng

> **When do we sail?** 我们什么时候启航? wǒmén shén me shí hou qǐ háng?

salad *n* 沙拉 shā lā

salesperson *n* 销售人员 xiāo shòu rén yuán

salt *n* 盐 yán

> **Is that low-salt?** 那是低盐的吗? nà shì dī yán de ma?

Salvadorian *adj* 萨尔瓦多的 sà ěr wǎ duō de

satellite *n* 卫星 wèi xīng

> **satellite radio** 卫星广播 wèi xīng guǎng bō

> **satellite tracking** 卫星跟踪 wèi xīng gēn zōng

Saturday *n* el 星期六 xīng qī liù

sauce *n* 沙司 shā sī

say, to say *v* 说 shuō

scan, to scan *v* **(document)** 扫描（文档）sǎo miáo (wén dàng)

schedule *n* 时间表 shí jiān biǎo

school *n* 学校 xué xiào

scooter *n* 踏板 tà bǎn

score *n* 得分 dé fēn

Scottish *adj* 苏格兰的 sū gé lán de

scratched *adj* 刮擦的 guā cā de

> **scratched surface** 有刮痕的表面 yǒu guā hén de biǎo miàn

scuba dive, to scuba dive *v* 水肺潜水 shuǐ fèi qián shuǐ

sculpture *n* 雕刻 diāo kè

seafood *n* 海鲜 hǎi xiān

search *n* 搜查 sōu chá

> **hand search** 手工搜查 shǒu gōng sōu chá

search, to search *v* 搜查 sōu chá

seasick *adj* 晕船的 yùn chuán de

> **I am seasick.** 我晕船。 wǒ yùn chuán。 **seasickness pill** *n* 晕船药 yùn chuán yào

seat *n* 座位 zuò wèi

> **child seat** 儿童座位 ér tóng zuò wèi

second *adj* 第二的 dì èr de

security *n* 安全 ān quán

security checkpoint 安检处 *ān jiǎn chú*

security guard 保安 *bǎo ān*

sedan n 箱式小轿车 *xiāng shì xiǎo jiào chē*

see, to see v 看见 *kàn jiàn*

May I see it? 我可以看一下吗? *wǒ kě yǐ kàn yī xià ma?*

self-serve adj 自助的 *zì zhù de*

sell, to sell v 销售 *xiāo shòu*

seltzer n 苏打水 *sū dǎ shuǐ*

send, to send v 发送 *fā sòng*

separated (marital status) adj 分居的(婚姻状态)*fēn jū de (hūn yīn zhuàng tài)*

September n 九月 *jiǔyuè*

serve, to serve v 服务 *fú wù*

service n 服务 *fú wù*

out of service 超出服务范围 *chāo chū fú wù fàn wéi*

services (religious) n 仪式 *yí shì*

service charge n 服务费 *fú wù fèi*

seven adj 七 *qī*

seventy adj 七十 *qī shí*

seventeen adj 十七 *shí qī*

seventh adj 第七 *dì qī*

sew, to sew v 缝制 *féng zhì*

sex (gender) n 性别 *xìng bié*

sex, to have (intercourse) v 性交 *xìng jiāo*

shallow adj 浅薄的 *qiǎn báo de*

sheet (bed linen) n 床单 *chuáng dān*

shellfish n 贝 *bèi*

ship n 轮船 *lún chuán*

ship, to ship v 载运 *zǎi yùn*

How much to ship this to _____? 把这运到_____多少钱? *bǎ zhè yùn dào_____duō shǎo qián?*

shipwreck n 船只失事 *chuán zhī shī shì*

shirt n 衬衫 *chèn shān*

shoe n 鞋子 *xié zǐ*

shop n 商店 *shāng diàn*

shop v 选购 *xuǎn gòu*

I'm shopping for mens' clothes. 我在选购男式衣服。*wǒ zài xuǎn gòu nán shì yī fu.*

I'm shopping for womens' clothes. 我在选购女式衣服。*wǒ zài xuǎn gòu nǔ shì yī fu.*

I'm shopping for childrens' clothes. 我在选购童装。*wǒ zài xuǎn gòu tóng zhuāng.*

short adj 短的 *duǎn de*

shorts n 短裤 *duǎn kù*

shot (liquor) n 口杯 *kǒu bēi*

shout v 喊叫 *hǎn jiào*

show (performance) n 表演 *biǎo yǎn*

What time is the show? 表演
几点开始? biǎo yǎn jǐ diǎn kāi
shǐ?

show, to show v 指示 zhǐshì

Would you show me? 您能
指给我看吗? nín néng zhǐ gěi
wǒ kàn ma?

shower n 淋浴 lín yù

Does it have a shower? 有淋
浴吗? yǒu lín yù ma?

shower, to shower v 淋浴 lín
yù

shrimp n 小虾 xiǎo xiā

shuttle bus n 机场大巴 jī chǎng
dà bā

sick adj 不舒服的 bù shū fú de

I feel sick. 我感觉不舒服。wǒ
gǎn jué bù shū fú.

side n 边缘 biān yuán

**on the side (e.g., salad
dressing)** 在边上（例如，沙
拉油）zài biān shàng (lìrú,
shā lā yóu)

sidewalk n 人行道 rén xíng dào

sightseeing n 观光 guān guāng

sightseeing bus n 观光车 guān
guāng chē

sign, to sign v 签署 qiān shǔ

Where do I sign? 我签在哪里?
wǒ qiān zài nǎ lǐ?

silk n 丝 sī

silver adj 银质的 yín zhì de

sing, to sing v 歌唱 gē chàng

single (unmarried) adj 单身
的（未婚）dān shēn de (wèi
hūn)

Are you single? 您是单身吗?
nín shì dān shēn ma?

single (one) adj 单一的 dān yī
de

single bed 单人床 dān rén
chuáng

sink n 水池 shuǐ chí

sister n 姐妹 jiě mèi

sit, to sit v 坐 zuò

six adj 六 liù

sixteen adj 十六 shí liù

sixty adj 六十 liù shí

size (clothing, shoes) n 尺码
chǐ mǎ

skin n 皮肤 pí fū

sleeping berth n 卧铺 wò pù

slow adj 慢的 màn de

slow, to slow v 减慢 jiǎn màn

Slow down! 慢点开! màn diǎn
kāi!

slow(ly) adv 慢慢地 màn màn
de

Speak more slowly. 请慢
点说。qǐng màn diǎn shuō.

slum n 贫民窟 pín mín kū

small adj 小的 xiǎo de

smell, to smell v 闻 wén

smoke, to smoke v 抽烟 chōu
yān

smoking n 吸烟 xī yān

smoking area 吸烟区 xī yān qū

No Smoking 禁止吸烟 jìn zhǐ xī yān

snack n 小吃 xiǎo chī

Snake eyes! n 蛇眼 shé yǎn

snorkel n 浮潜 fú qián

soap n 肥皂 féi zào

sock n 短袜 duǎn wà

soda n 苏打水 sū dǎ shuǐ

diet soda 减肥苏打水 jiǎn féi sū dǎ shuǐ

soft adj 软的 ruǎn de

software n 软件 ruǎn jiàn

sold out adj 售完的 shòu wán de

some adj 一些 yī xiē

someone n 某人 mǒu rén

something n 某事物 mǒu shì wù

son n 儿子 ér zǐ

song n 歌曲 gē qǔ

sorry adj 抱歉的 bào qiàn de

I'm sorry. 很抱歉。hěn bào qiàn。

soup n 汤 tāng

spa n 水疗 shuǐ liáo

Spain n 西班牙 xī bān yá

Spanish adj 西班牙的 xī bān yá de

spare tire n 备用轮胎 bèi yòng lún tāi

speak, to speak v 说出 shuō chū

Do you speak English? 您说英语吗？nín shuō yīng yǔ ma？

Would you speak louder, please? 您能大声点说吗？nín néng dà shēng diǎn shuō ma？

Would you speak slower, please? 您能说慢点吗？nín néng shuō màn diǎn ma？

special (featured meal) n 特色菜（特色套餐）tè sè cài (tè sè tào cān)

specify, to specify v 详细说明 xiáng xì shuō míng

speed limit n 限速 xiàn sù

What's the speed limit? 限速是多少？xiàn sù shì duō shǎo？

speedometer n 里程计 lǐ chéng jì

spell, to spell v 写出 xiě chū

How do you spell that? 请问它怎么写？qǐng wèn tā zěn me xiě？

spice n 调味品 tiáo wèi pǐn

spill, to spill v 溢出 yì chū

split (gambling) n 平局（赌博）píng jú (dǔ bó)

sports n 运动 yùn dòng

ENGLISH—CHINESE

spring (season) n 春天（季节）
chūn tiān (jì jié)

stadium n 体育场 tǐ yù chǎng

staff (employees) n 员工 yuán
gōng

stamp (postage) n 邮票 yóu
piào

stair n 楼梯 lóu tī

> **Where are the stairs?** 楼梯在
> 哪里? lóu tī zài nǎ lǐ?
>
> **Are there many stairs?** 有许
> 多级楼梯吗? yǒu xǔ duō jí lóu
> tī ma?

stand, to stand v 站起 zhàn qǐ

start, to start (commence) v 开
始 kāi shǐ

start, to start (a car) v 发动 fā
dòng

state n 状态 zhuàng tài

station n 车站 chē zhàn

> **Where is the nearest____?**
> 最近的____在哪里? zuì jìn
> de ____ zài nǎ lǐ?
>
> **gas station** 加油站 jiā yóu
> zhàn
>
> **bus station** 公共汽车站 gōng
> gòng qì chē zhàn
>
> **subway station** 地铁站 dì tiě
> zhàn
>
> **train station** 火车站 huǒ chē
> zhàn

stay, to stay v 停留 tíng liú

> **We'll be staying for ____
> nights.** 我们将停留____
> 晚。 wǒ mén jiāng tíng liú
> ____ wǎn。 See p7 for
> numbers.

steakhouse n 牛排餐厅 niú pái
cān tīng

steal, to steal v 偷窃 tōu qiè

stolen adj 被偷的 bèi tōu de

stop n 站 zhàn

> **Is this my stop?** 这是我要下
> 车的站吗? zhè shì wǒ yào xià
> chē de zhàn ma?
>
> **I missed my stop.** 我坐过
> 站了。 wǒ zuò guò zhàn le。

stop, to stop v 停止 tíng zhǐ

> **Please stop.** 请停下来。 qǐng
> tíng xià lái。
>
> **STOP (traffic sign)** 停车（交通
> 标志）tíng chē (jiāo tōng biāo
> zhì)
>
> **Stop, thief!** 抓小偷! zhuā xiǎo
> tōu!

store n 商店 shāng diàn

straight adj 直的 zhí de（头发）
(tóu fa)

> **straight ahead** 一直向前 yī
> zhí xiàng qián
>
> **straight (drink)** 纯喝（饮料）
> chún hē (yǐn liào)
>
> **Go straight.**（给出方向）(gěi
> chū fāng xiàng) 直走 zhí zǒu

straight (gambling) n 顺子
（赌博）shùn zǐ (dǔ bó)

street n 街道 jiē dào

across the street 街道对面 jiē dào duì miàn

down the street 沿着街道 yán zhe jiē dào

Which street? 哪条街? nǎ tiáo jiē?

How many more streets? 多少街道? duō shǎo jiē dào?

stressed adj 有压力的 yǒu yā lì de

striped adj 有斑纹的 yǒu bān wén de

stroller n 婴儿车 yīng ér chē

Do you rent baby strollers? 您租婴儿手推车吗? nín zū yīng ér shǒu tuī chē ma?

substitution n 替代品 tì dài pǐn

suburb n 郊区 jiāoqū

subway n 地铁 dì tiě

subway line 地铁线 dì tiě xiàn

subway station 地铁站 dì tiě zhàn

Which subway do I take for ____? 到____应乘地铁几号线? dào____ yīng chéng dì tiě jǐ hào xiàn?

subtitle n 字幕 zì mù

suitcase n 手提箱 shǒu tí xiāng

suite n 套间 tào jiān

summer n 夏季 xià jì

sun n 太阳 tài yáng

sunburn n 晒斑 shai bān

I have a bad sunburn. 我有很严重的晒斑。wǒ yǒu hěn yán zhòng de shai bān.

Sunday n 星期天 xīng qī tiān

sunglasses n 太阳镜 tài yáng jìng

sunny adj 晴朗的 qíng lǎng de

It's sunny out. 外边天气很晴朗。wài biān tiān qì hěn qíng lǎng.

sunroof n 天窗 tiān chuāng

sunscreen n 遮光剂 zhē guāng jì

Do you have sunscreen SPF ____? 有 SPF____ 的遮光剂吗? yǒu SPF____ de zhē guāng jì ma? 参见第七页的数字。 See p7 for numbers.

supermarket n 超市 chāo shì

surf v 冲浪 chōng làng

surfboard n 冲浪板 chōng làng bǎn

suspiciously adv 令人怀疑地 lìng rén huái yí de

swallow, to swallow v 吞咽 tūn yàn

sweater n 套衫 tào shān

swim, to swim v 游泳 yóu yǒng

Can one swim here? 可以在这里游泳吗? kě yǐ zài zhè lǐ yóu yǒng ma?

swimsuit n 泳衣 yǒng yī

swim trunks n 泳裤 yǒng kù

symphony n 交响乐 jiāo xiǎng yuè

T

table n 桌子 zhuō zi

> **table for two** 两人餐桌 liǎng rén cān zhuō

tailor n 裁缝 cái feng

> **Can you recommend a good tailor?** 能推荐一位好的裁缝吗? néng tuī jiàn yī wèi hǎo de cái feng ma?

take, to take v 带领 dài lǐng

> **Take me to the station.** 带我到车站吧。dài wǒ dào chē zhàn bā。

> **How much to take me to _____?** 到_____需要多少钱? dào _____ xū yào duō shǎo qián?

takeout menu n 外卖菜单 wài mài cài dān

talk, to talk v 谈论 tán lùn

tall adj 高的 gāo de

tanned adj 茶色的 chá sè de

taste (flavor) n 风味 fēng wèi

taste n (discernment) 品位 pǐn wèi

taste, to taste v 品尝 pǐn cháng

tax n 税 shuì

value-added tax (VAT) 增值税 zēng zhí shuì

taxi n 出租车 chū zū chē

> **Taxi!** 出租车！chū zū chē！

> **Would you call me a taxi?** 您能帮我叫辆出租车吗? nín néng bāng wǒ jiào liàng chū zū chē ma?

tea n 茶 chá

team n 队 duì

Techno n 电子音乐 diàn zǐ yīn yuè

television n 电视 diàn shì

temple n 寺庙 sì miào

ten adj 十 shí

tennis n 网球 wǎng qiú

> **tennis court** 网球场 wǎng qiú chǎng

tent n 帐篷 zhàng péng

tenth adj 第十 dì shí

terminal n (airport) 候机楼 (机场) hòu jī lóu (jī chǎng)

Thank you. 谢谢您。xiè xiè nín

that (near) adj 那个 nà gè

that (far away) adj 那个 nà gè

theater n 剧院 jù yuàn

them (m / f) 他们 tā mén

there (demonstrative) adv 那里 nà lǐ (nearby), allí (far)

> **Is / Are there?** 有? yǒu?

> **over there** 在那里 zài nà lǐ

these adj 这些 zhè xiē

thick adj 厚的 hòu de

thin adj 瘦的 shòu de

third adj 第三 dì sān

thirteen adj 十三 shí sān

thirty adj 三十 sān shí

this adj 这个 zhè gè

those adj 那些 nà xiē

thousand 千 qiān

three 三 sān

Thursday n 星期四 xīng qī sì

ticket n 票 piào

> **ticket counter** 售票台 shòu piào tái
>
> **one-way ticket** 单程票 dān chéng piào
>
> **round-trip ticket** 往返票 wǎng fǎn piào

tight adj 紧的 jǐn de

time n 时间 shí jiān

> **Is it on time?** 准时吗? zhǔn shí ma?
>
> **At what time?** 在几点? zài jǐ diǎn?
>
> **What time is it?** 现在几点了? xiàn zài jǐ diǎn le?

timetable n (train) 时刻表 shí kè biǎo

tip (gratuity) n 小费 xiǎo fèi

tire n 轮胎 lún tāi

> **I have a flat tire.** 爆胎了。 bào tāi le。

tired adj 疲惫的 pí bèi de

today n 今天 jīn tiān

toilet n 马桶 mǎ tǒng

> **The toilet is overflowing.** 马桶溢水了。 mǎ tǒng yì shuǐ le.
>
> **The toilet is backed up.** 马桶堵上了。 mǎ tǒng dǔ shàng le.

toilet paper n 卫生纸 wèi shēng zhǐ

> **You're out of toilet paper.** 您的卫生纸用完了。 nín de wèi shēng zhǐ yòng wán le。

toiletries n 化妆品 huà zhuāng pǐn

toll n 通行费 tōng xíng fèi

tomorrow n 明天 míng tiān

ton n 吨 dūn

too (excessively) adv 太(过分) tài (guò fēn)

too (also) adv 也 yě

tooth n 牙 yá

> **I lost my tooth.** 我的牙掉了。 wǒ de yá diào le.

toothache n 牙痛 yá tòng

> **I have a toothache.** 我牙疼。 wǒ yá téng.

total n 总数 zǒng shù

> **What is the total?** 总数是多少? zǒng shù shì duō shǎo?

tour n 旅游 lǚ yóu

> **Are guided tours available?** 有配导游的旅游吗? yǒu pèi dǎo yóu de lǚ yóu ma?

Are audio tours available? 有用英文解说的语音导览设备吗? *yǒu yòng yīng wén jié shuō de yǔ yīn dǎo lǎn shè bèi ma?*

towel *n* 毛巾 *máo jīn*

May we have more towels? 可以多给我们几条毛巾吗? *kě yǐ duō gěi wǒ mén jǐ tiáo máo jīn ma?*

toy *n* 玩具 *wán jù*

toy store *n* 玩具店 *wán jù diàn*

Do you have any toys for the children? 您有儿童玩具吗? *nín yǒu ér tóng wán jù ma?*

traffic *n* 交通 *jiāo tōng*

How's traffic? 交通怎么样? *jiāo tōng zěn me yàng?*

traffic rules 交通规则 *jiāo tōng guī zé*

trail *n* 小径 *xiǎo jìng*

Are there trails? 有些小径吗? *yǒu xiē xiǎo jìng ma?*

train *n* 火车 *huǒ chē*

express train 特快火车 *tè kuài huǒ chē*

local train 普通火车 *pǔ tōng huǒ chē*

Does the train go to _____? 这列火车到_____吗? *zhè liè huǒ chē dào _____ ma?*

May I have a train schedule? 可以给我一份火车时刻表吗? *kě yǐ gěi wǒ yī fèn huǒ chē shí kè biǎo ma?*

Where is the train station? 火车站在哪里? *huǒ chē zhàn zài nǎ lǐ?*

train, to train *v* 训练 *xùn liàn*

transfer, to transfer *v* 转移 *zhuǎn yí*

I need to transfer funds. 我需要转帐。 *wǒ xū yào zhuǎn zhàng。*

transmission *n* 传输 *chuán shū*

automatic transmission 自动传输 *zì dòng chuán shū*

standard transmission 标准传输 *biāo zhǔn chuán shū*

travel, to travel *v* 旅行 *lǚxíng*

travelers' check *n* 旅行支票 *lǚ xíng zhī piào*

Do you cash travelers' checks? 您兑现旅行支票吗? *nín duì xiàn lǚ xíng zhī piào ma?*

trim, to trim (hair) *v* 修剪(头发) *xiū jiǎn (tóu fa)*

trip *n* 旅程 *lǚ chéng*

triple *adj* 三倍的 *sān bèi de*

trumpet *n* 喇叭 *lǎ ba*

trunk *n* 大衣箱 *dà yī xiāng*

try, to try (attempt) *v* 试 *shì*

try, to try on (clothing) *v* 试穿 *shì chuān*

try, to try (food) *v* 尝试 *cháng shì*

Tuesday *n* 星期二 *xīng qī èr*

turkey n 火鸡 huǒ jī

turn, to turn v 转动 zhuàn dòng

to turn left / right 左 / 右转 zuǒ / yòu zhuǎn

to turn off / on 关 / 开 guān / kāi

twelve adj 十二 shí èr

twenty adj 二十的 èr shí de

twine n 细绳 xì shéng

two adj 两个的 liǎng gè de

U

umbrella n 伞 sǎn

uncle n 叔叔 shū shū

undercooked adj 未做熟的 wèi zuò shú de

understand, to understand v 理解 lǐ jiě

I don't understand. 我不理解。 wǒ bù lǐ jiě 。

Do you understand? 您理解 吗？ nín lǐ jiě ma?

underwear n 内衣裤 nèi yī kù

university n 大学 dà xué

up adv 向上 xiàng shàng

update, to update v 更新 gēng xīn

upgrade n 升级 shēng jí

upload, to upload v 上传 shàng chuán

upscale adj 最高级的 zuì gāo jí de

Uruguayan adj 乌拉圭的 wū lā guī de

us pron 我们 wǒ mén

USB port n USB 接口 USB jiē kǒu

use, to use v 使用 shǐ yòng

V

vacation n 假期 jià qī

on vacation 在休假 zài xiū jià

to go on vacation 去度假 qù dù jià

vacancy n 空房 kōng fáng

van n 面包车 miàn bāo chē

VCR n 录像机 lù xiàng jī

Do the rooms have VCRs? 房 间有录像机吗？ fáng jiān yǒu lù xiàng jī ma?

vegetable n 蔬菜 shū cài

vegetarian n 素食主义者 sù shí zhǔ yì zhě

vending machine n 自动售货机 zì dòng shòu huò jī

Venezuelan adj 委内瑞拉的 wěi nèi ruì lā de

version n 版本 bǎn běn

very 很 *hěn*

video n 录像 *lù xiàng*

> **Where can I rent videos or DVDs?** 哪里可以租到录像带或 DVD？ *nǎ lǐ kě yǐ zū dào lù xiàng dài huò DVD?*

view n 风景画 *fēng jǐng huà*

> **beach view** 海滩景观 *hǎi tān jǐng guān*

> **city view** 城市景观 *chéng shì jǐng guān*

vineyard n 葡萄园 *pú tao yuán*

vinyl n 乙烯树脂 *yǐ xī shù zhī*

violin n 小提琴 *xiǎo tí qín*

visa n 签证 *qiān zhèng*

> **Do I need a visa?** 我需要签证吗？ *wǒ xū yào qiān zhèng ma?*

vision n 视觉 *shì jué*

visit, to visit v 参观 *cān guān*

visually-impaired adj 视障的 *shì zhàng de*

vodka n 伏特加酒 *fú tè jiā jiǔ*

voucher n 优惠券 *yōu huì quàn*

W

wait, to wait v 等待 *děng dài*

> **Please wait.** 请等一下。 *qǐng děng yī xià.*

> **How long is the wait?** 要等多长时间？ *yào děng duō cháng shí jiān?*

waiter n 服务员 *fú wù yuán*

waiting area n 等候区 *děng hòu qū*

wake-up call n 电话叫醒服务 *diàn huà jiào xǐng fú wù*

wallet n 钱夹 *qián jiā*

> **I lost my wallet.** 我的钱夹丢了。 *wǒ de qián jiā diu le.*

> **Someone stole my wallet.** 有人偷了我的钱夹。 *yǒu rén tōu le wǒ de qián jiā.*

walk, to walk v 走 *zǒu*

walker (ambulatory device) n 助行器（助行设备）*zhù xíng qì (zhù xíng shèbèi)*

walkway n 人行道 *rén xíng dào*

> **moving walkway** 自动人行道 *zì dòng rén xíng dào*

want, to want v 想要 *xiǎng yào*

war n 战争 *zhàn zhēng*

warm adj 温暖的 *wēn nuǎn de*

watch, to watch v 观看 *guān kàn*

water n 水 *shuǐ*

> **Is the water potable?** 这水可以饮用吗？ *zhè shuǐ kě yǐ yǐn yòng ma?*

> **Is there running water?** 有自来水吗？ *yǒu zì lái shuǐ ma?*

wave, to wave *v* 摇动 *yáo dòng*

waxing *n* 去毛 *qù máo*

weapon *n* 武器 *wǔ qì*

wear, to wear *v* 穿 *chuān*

weather forecast *n* 天气预报 *tiān qì yù bào*

Wednesday *n* 星期三 *xīng qī sān*

week *n* 周 *zhōu*

> **this week** 这周 *zhè zhōu*
>
> **last week** 上周 *shàng zhōu*
>
> **next week** 下周 *xià zhōu*

weigh *v* 重 *zhòng*

> **I weigh ____.** 我的体重是____。 *wǒ de tǐ zhòng shì ____.*
>
> **It weighs ____.** 它重____。 *tā zhòng ____. See p7 for numbers.*

weights *n* 重量 *zhòng liàng*

welcome *adv* 欢迎 *huān yíng*

> **You're welcome.** 不用谢。 *bù yòng xiè.*

well *adv* 好 *hǎo*

> **well done (meat)** 煮熟的 (肉) *zhǔ shú de (ròu)*
>
> **well done (task)** 做的很好 (任务) *zuò de hěn hǎo (rènwù)*
>
> **I don't feel well.** 我感觉不舒服。 *wǒ gǎn jué bù shū fú.*

western *adj* 西方的 *xī fāng de*

whale *n* 鲸 *jīng*

what *adv* 什么 *shén me*

> **What sort of ____?** 哪种____? *nǎ zhǒng ____ ?*
>
> **What time is ____?** 什么时间____? *shén me shí jiān ____ ?*

wheelchair *n* 轮椅 *lún yǐ*

> **wheelchair access** 轮椅通道 *lún yǐ tōng dào*
>
> **wheelchair ramp** 轮椅坡道 *lún yǐ pō dào*
>
> **power wheelchair** 电轮椅 *diàn lún yǐ*

wheeled (luggage) *adj* 带轮的 (行李) *dài lún de (xíng li)*

when *adv* 何时 *hé shí*

where *adv* 哪里 *nǎ lǐ*

> **Where is it?** 这是哪里? *zhè shì nǎ lǐ?*

which *adv* 哪个 *nǎ gè*

> **Which one?** 哪一个? *nǎ yī gè?*

white *adj* 白色的 *bái sè de*

who *adv* 谁 *shuí*

whose *adj* 谁的 *shuí de*

wide *adj* 宽的 *kuān de*

widow, widower *n* 寡妇, 鳏夫 *guǎ fù, guān fū*

wife *n* 妻子 *qī zǐ*

wi-fi *n* 无线保真 *wú xiàn bǎo zhēn*

window *n* 窗户 *chuāng hu*

> **drop-off window** 邮件投入窗口 *yóu jiàn tóu rù chuāng kǒu*

> **pickup window** 领取窗口 *lǐng qǔ chuāng kǒu*

windshield *n* 挡风玻璃 *dǎng fēng bō li*

windshield wiper *n* 档雨雪刷 *fēng dàng yǔ xuě shuā*

windy *adj* 有风的 *yǒu fēng de*

wine *n* 葡萄酒 *pú tao jiǔ*

winter *n* 冬天 *dōng tiān*

wiper *n* 雨刷 *yǔ shuā*

with *prep* 和 *hé*

withdraw *v* 提款 *tí kuǎn*

> **I need to withdraw money.** 我需要取钱。 *wǒ xū yào qǔ qián.*

without *prep* 没有 *méi yǒu*

woman *n* 妇女 *fù nǚ*

work, to work *v* 工作 *gōng zuò*

> **This doesn't work.** 它坏了。 *tā huài le.*

workout *n* 测验 *cè yàn*

worse 更坏 *gèng huài*

worst 最坏 *zuì huài*

write, to write *v* 写出 *xiě chū*

> **Would you write that down for me?** 您能给我写下那个吗? *nín néng gěi wǒ xiě xià nà gè ma?*

writer *n* 作家 *zuò jiā*

X

x-ray machine *n* x 射线机 *x shè xiàn jǐ*

Y

yellow *adj* 黄色的 *huáng sè de*

Yes. *adv* 是 *shì*

yesterday *n* 昨天 *zuó tiān*

the day before yesterday
前天 *qián tiān*

yield sign *n* 避让标志 *bì ràng biāo zhì*

you *pron* 您 *nín*

you (singular, informal) 你 *nǐ*
you (singular, formal) 您 *nín*
you (plural informal) 你们 *nǐ mén*
you (plural formal) 你们 *ní mén*

your, yours *adj* 您的 *nín de*

young *adj* 年轻的 *nián qīng de*

Z

zoo *n* 动物园 *dòng wù yuán*

A

阿根廷的 ā gēn tíng de
Argentinian adj

阿司匹林 ā sī pǐ lín *aspirin n*

哎唷！āi yō! *Ouch! interj*

哎唷！很痛！āi yō! hěn tòng!
Ouch! That hurts!

爱 ài *love n*

爱 ài *to love v*

爱尔兰 ài ěr lán *Ireland n*

爱尔兰的 ài ěr lán de *Irish adj*

爱好 ài hào *hobby n*

安静的 ān jìng de *quiet adj*

安全 ān quán *security n*

> 安检处 ān jiǎn chù *security checkpoint*
>
> 保安 bǎo ān *security guard*

安全的 ān quán de *safe (secure) adj*

按摩 àn mó *to massage v*

昂贵的 áng guì de *expensive adj*

盎司 àng sī *ounce n*

凹陷 āo xià *dent n*

澳大利亚 ào dà lì yà
Australia n

澳大利亚的 ào dà lì yà de
Australian adj

B

八 bā *eight n adj*

八十 bā shí *eighty n adj*

八月 bā yuè *August n*

巴拉圭的 bā lā guī de
Paraguayan adj

巴拿马的 bā ná mǎ de
Panamanian adj

吧台 bā tái *counter (in bar) n*

利口酒 lì kǒu jiǔ *liqueur, liquor n*

白兰地 bái lán dì *brandy n*

白色的，黄白的 bái sè de,
huáng bái de *white, off-white adj*

百 bǎi *hundred n adj*

版本 bǎn běn *version n*

办登机手续 bàn dēng jī shǒu
xù *check-in n*

> 电子登机服务 diàn zǐ dēng jī
> fú wù *electronic check-in*
>
> 快办登机手续服务 kuài bàn
> dēng jī shǒu xù fú wù
> *express check-in*
>
> 路边办理登机服务 lù biān
> bàn lǐ dēng jī fú wù *curbside check-in*

半磅 bàn bàng *half-pound*

半个 bàn gè *half n*

帮帮我！bāng bāng wǒ!
Help! n

搬运工人 bān yùn gōng rén
porter n

帮助 bāng zhù *help n*

帮助 bāng zhù *to help v*

磅 bàng *pound n*

包（交通工具）**bāo (jiāo tōng gōng jù)** to charter (transportation) v

包裹 **bāo guǒ** package n

包厢 **bāo xiāng** box (seat) n

保安 **bǎo ān** security guard n

保持 **bǎo chí** to keep v

保卫 **bǎo wèi** guard n

保险 **bǎo xiǎn** insurance n

碰撞险 **pèng zhuàng xiǎn** collision insurance

责任险 **zé rèn xiǎn** liability insurance

保险丝 **bǎo xiǎn sī** fuse n

保险箱（存储贵重物品）**bǎo xiǎn xiāng (cún chǔ guì zhòng wù pǐn)** safe (for storing valuables) n

报亭 **bào tíng** newsstand n

报纸 **bào zhǐ** newspaper n

杯（饮用）**bēi (yǐn yòng)** glass (drinking) n

贝 **bèi** shellfish n

贝司（乐器）**bèi sī (yuè qì)** bass (instrument) n

背 **bèi** back n

被偷的 **bèi tōu de** stolen adj

本地 **běn dì** local adj

泵 **bèng** pump n

鼻子 **bí zi** nose n

比萨 **bǐ sà** pizza n

比赛 **bǐ sài** to match v

比赛（运动）**bǐ sài (yùn dòng)** match (sport) n

笔记本电脑 **bǐ jì běn diàn nǎo** laptop n

避让标志 **bì ràng biāo zhì** yield sign n

避孕 **bì yùn** birth control n

避孕套 **bì yùn tào** condom n

避孕中的 **bì yùn zhōng de** birth control adj

我没有避孕药丸了。**wǒ méi yǒu bì yùn yào wán le.** I'm out of birth control pills.

边缘 **biān yuán** side n

在边上（例如，沙拉油）**zài biān shàng (lì rú, shā lā yóu)** on the side (e.g., salad dressing)

编辑，出版商 **biān jí, chū bǎn shāng** editor, publisher n

变色 **biàn sè** to color v

表哥 / 弟 / 姐 / 妹 **biǎo gē / dì / jiě / mèi** cousin n

表演 **biǎo yǎn** show (performance) n

冰 **bīng** ice n

冰咖啡 **bīng kā fēi** iced coffee n

浓咖啡 **nóng kā fēi** espresso n

拨（电话）**bō (diàn huà)** to dial (a phone number) v

直拨 **zhí bi** to dial direct

波多黎各的 **bō duō lí gè de** Puerto Rican adj

波尔图葡萄酒 bō ěr tú pú táo jiǔ *port (beverage) n*

玻利维亚的 bō lì wéi yà de *Bolivian adj*

博物馆 bó wù guǎn *museum n*

不 bù *no adj adv*

不叫牌（赌博）bù jiào pái (dǔ bó) *to pass (gambling) v*

不可知论 bù kě zhī lùn *agnostic n adj*

不舒服的 bù shū fú de *sick adj*

不同的（其它的）bù tóng de (qí tā de) *different (other) adj*

不用谢。bù yòng xiè. *You're welcome.*

不准进入。bù zhǔn jìn rù. *Do not enter.*

美国盲人 měi guó máng rén *braille (American) n*

C

CD 播放器 CD bō fàng qì *CD player n*

裁缝 cái feng *tailor n*

菜单 cài dān *menu n*

> 儿童菜单 ér tóng cài dān *children's menu*
>
> 糖尿病人菜单 táng niào bìng rén cài dān *diabetic menu*
>
> 外卖菜单 wài mài cài dān *takeout menu*

参观 cān guān *to visit v*

参加、协助 cān jiā , xié zhù *to attend v / to assist v*

餐后甜点 cān hòu tián diǎn *dessert n*

> 餐后甜点菜单 cān hòu tián diǎn cài dān *dessert menu*

残疾 cán ji *disability n*

苍白的 cāng bái de *pale adj*

舱内 cāng nèi *board n*

层 céng *floor n*

> 底层 dǐ céng *ground floor, first floor*

插上 chā shàng *to plug v*

插头 chā tóu *plug n*

查号服务 chá hào fú wù *directory assistance n*

茶 chá *tea n*

> 草药茶 cǎo yào chá *herbal tea*
>
> 加了牛奶和糖的茶 jiā le niú nǎi hé táng de chá *tea with milk and sugar*
>
> 加了柠檬的茶 jiā le níng méng de chá *tea with lemon*

茶色 chá sè *tanned adj*

产品 chǎn pǐn *product n*

长笛 cháng dí *flute n*

长的 cháng de *long adj*

> 更长 gèng cháng *longer*
>
> 最长 zuì cháng *longest*

尝试 **cháng shì** *to taste v, to try (food) v*

场地（运动）**chǎng dì (yùn dòng)** *court (sport) n*

敞篷汽车 **chǎng péng qì chē** *convertible n*

超大的 **chāo dà de** *extra-large adj*

超市 **chāo shì** *supermarket n*

潮湿的 **cháo shī de** *humid adj*

车站 **chē zhàn** *station n*

最近的加油站在哪里？**zuì jìn de jiā yóu zhàn zài nǎ lǐ?** *Where is the nearest gas station?*

衬衫 **chèn shān** *shirt n*

成员 **chéng yuán** *member n*

城市 **chéng shì** *city n*

乘客 **chéng kè** *passenger n*

橙、橙色的 **chéng, chéng sè de** *orange n, orange (color) adj*

橙汁 **chéng zhī** *orange juice n*

吃 **chī** *to eat v*

持续 **chí xù** *to last v*

尺码 **chǐ mǎ** *size (clothing, shoes) n*

齿冠（牙科）**chǐ guàn (yá kē)** *crown (dental) n*

充电 **chōng diàn** *to charge (a battery) v*

充血（窦）**chōng xuè (dòu)** *congestion (sinus) n*

冲浪 **chōng làng** *to surf v*

冲浪板 **chōng làng bǎn** *surfboard n*

冲刷 **chōng shuā** *to flush v*

重复 **chóng fù** *to repeat v*

抽烟 **chōu yān** *smoking n to smoke v*

出租车 **chū zū chē** *taxi n*

出租车！**chū zū chē!** *Taxi!*

出租车停靠点 **chū zū chē tíng kào diǎn** *taxi stand*

初中/高中 **chū zhōng/gāo zhōng** *junior high / middle school*

厨房 **chú fáng** *kitchen n*

储藏柜 **chǔ cáng guì** *storage locker*

处方 **chǔ fāng** *prescription n*

处理 **chǔ lǐ** *to handle v*

轻拿轻放。**qīng ná qīng fàng。** *Handle with care.*

处理 **chǔ lǐ** *to process (a transaction) v*

处于 **chǔ yú** *to be (temporary state, condition, mood) v*

触及、演奏 **chù jí, yǎn zòu** *to touch v / to play (an instrument) v*

穿衣 **chuān yī** *to dress v*

传输 **chuán shū** *transmission n*

标准传输 **biāo zhǔn chuán shū** *standard transmission*

自动传输 **zì dòng chuán shū** *automatic transmission*

传送带 **chuán sòng dài** *conveyor belt* n

传真 **chuán zhēn** *fax* n

船只失事 **chuán zhǐ shī shì** *shipwreck* n

窗口 **chuāng kǒu** *window* n

领取窗口 **lǐng qǔ chuāng kǒu** *pickup window*

邮件投入窗口 **yóu jiàn tóu rù chuāng kǒu** *drop-off window*

窗口 **chuāng kǒu** *window* n

床 **chuáng** *bed* n

床单 **chuáng dān** *sheet (bed linen)* n

床铺加早餐 **chuáng pù jiā zǎo cān** *bed-and-breakfast (B & B)* n

吹风机 **chuī fēng jī** *hair dryer* n

春天（季节）**chūn tiān (jì jié)** *spring (season)* n

词典 **cí diǎn** *dictionary* n

匆忙 **cōng máng** *to hurry* v

存物柜 **cún wù guì** *locker* n

存物室 **cún wù shì** *locker room* n

痤疮 **cuó chuāng** *acne* n

错过 **cuò guò** *to lose* v / *to miss (a flight)* v

错误 **cuò wù** *mistake* n

D

DVD *DVD* n

答案 **dá àn** *answer* n

打（电话）**dǎ (diàn huà)** *to call (to phone)* v

打赌 **dǎ dǔ** *to bet* v

打断 **dǎ duàn** *to break* v

打高尔夫球 **dǎ gāo ěr fū qiú** *to go golfing* v

打火机 **dǎ huǒ jī** *light (for cigarette)* n

我能帮您点火吗？**wǒ néng bāng nín diǎn huǒ ma?** *May I offer you a light?*

打火机 **dǎ huǒ jī** *lighter (cigarette)* n

打扫 **dǎ sǎo** *to clean* v

打印 **dǎ yìn** *to print* v

大的 **dà de** *big* adj, *large* adj

更大的 **gèng dà de** *bigger, larger*

最大的 **zuì dà de** *biggest, largest*

大使馆 **dà shǐ guǎn** *embassy* n

大蒜 **dà suàn** *garlic* n

大象 **dà xiàng** *elephant* n

大学 **dà xué** *university* n

大衣箱（行李）**dà yī xiāng (xíng li)** *trunk (luggage)* n

带 **dài** *belt* n

带领 **dài lǐng** *to take* v

这将用多长时间？ **zhè jiāng yòng duō cháng shí jiān?** *How long will this take?*

带轮的（行李）**dài lún de（xíng li）** *wheeled (luggage)* adj

袋子 **dài zǐ** *bag* n

单程票 **dān chéng piào** *one-way ticket* n

单个的、简单的 **dān gè de, jiǎn dān de** *single* n adj / *simple* adj

纯喝（饮料）**chún hē（yǐn liào）** *straight up (drink)*

单身的（未婚）**dān shēn de（wèi hūn）** *single (unmarried)* adj

您是单身吗？ **nín shì dān shēn ma?** *Are you single?*

单身酒吧 **dān shēn jiǔ bā** *singles bar* n

单行线（交通标志）**dān xíng xiàn（jiāo tōng biāo zhì）** *one way (traffic sign)* n

淡紫色的 **dàn zǐ sè de** *lavender* adj

档雨雪刷 **dǎng fēng bō li** *windshield wiper* n

导游 **dǎo yóu** *guide (of tours)* n

倒下 **dǎo xià** *to fall* v

到_____应乘地铁几号线？ **dào _____ yīng chéng dì tiě jǐ hào xiàn?** *Which subway do I take for _____?*

到达 **dào dá** *arrivals* n *to arrive* v

道路 **dào lù** *road* n

道路封闭标志 **dào lù fēng bì biāo zhì** *road closed sign* n

得分 **dé fēn** *score* n

得分（运动）**dé fēn（yùn dòng）** *goal (sport)* n

德国人，德国的 **dé guó rén, dé guó de** *German* n adj

灯 **dēng** *light (lamp)* n

灯 **dēng** *light (on car dashboard)*

机油灯 **jī yóu dēng** *oil light*

前灯 **qián dēng** *headlight*

刹车灯 **shā chē dēng** *brake light*

引擎检验灯 **yǐn qíng jiǎn yàn dēng** *check engine light*

登机牌 **dēng jī pái** *boarding pass* n

等待 **dēng dài** *wait* n

等候 **dēng hòu** *to hold (to pause)* v, *to wait* v

等候区 **dēng hòu qū** *waiting area* n

等级 **dēng jí** *class* n

低的 **dī de** *low* adj

滴下 **dī xià** *to drip* v

迪士高 **dí shì gāo** *disco* n

地铁 **dì tiě** *subway* n

地铁线 **dì tiě xiàn** *subway line*

地图 **dì tú** *map n*

> 车载地图 **chē zǎi dì tú** *onboard map*

地址 **dì zhǐ** *address n*

> 地址是什么？**dì zhǐ shì shén me?** *What's the address?*

第八 **dì bā** *eighth n adj*

> 八分之三 **bā fēn zhī sān** *three eighths*

第二的 **dì èr de** *second adj*

第九的 **dì jiǔ de** *ninth n adj*

第七的 **dì qī de** *seventh n adj*

第三的 **d ìsān de** *third n adj*

第十的 **dì shí de** *tenth adj*

第四的 **dì sì de** *fourth n adj*

第五的 **dì wǔ de** *fifth adj*

第一的 **dì yī de** *first adj*

点钟 **diǎn zhōng** *o'clock adv*

> 两点钟 **liǎng diǎn zhōng** *two o'clock*

电池（手电筒使用的）**diàn chí (shǒu diàn tǒng shǐ yòng de)** *battery (for flashlight) n*

电动扶梯 **diàn dòng fú tī** *escalator n*

电话 **diàn huà** *phone adj*

> 电话号码簿 **diàn huà hào mǎ bù** *phone directory*

电话 **diàn huà** *phone, phone call n*

> 长途电话 **cháng tú diàn huà** *long-distance phone call*

对方付费电话 **duì fāng fù fèi diàn huà** *collect phone call*

国际电话 **guó jì diàn huà** *international phone call*

电话机 **diàn huà jī** *phone n*

> 电话接线员 **diàn huà jiē xiàn yuán** *phone operator*

> 可以给我您的电话号码吗？**kě yǐ gěi wǒ nín de diàn huà hào mǎ ma?** *May I have your phone number?*

> 移动电话 **yí dòng diàn huà** *cell phone*

> 预付费电话 **yù fù fèi diàn huà** *prepaid phones*

电话叫醒服务 **diàn huà jiào xǐng fú wù** *wake-up call n*

电视 **diàn shì** *television n*

> 有线电视 **yǒu xiàn diàn shì** *cable television*

> 卫星电视 **wèi xīng diàn shì** *satellite television*

电梯 **diàn tī** *elevator n*

电线板 **diàn xiàn bǎn** *electrical hookup n*

电影 **diàn yǐng** *movie n*

电影院 **diàn yǐng yuàn** *cinema n*

电子音乐 **diàn zǐ yīn yuè** *techno n (music)*

电子邮件 **diàn zǐ yóu jiàn** *e-mail n*

> 电子邮件消息 **diàn zǐ yóu jiàn xiāo xi** *e-mail message*

可以给我您的电子邮件地址吗？ **kě yǐ gěi wǒ nín de diàn zǐ yóu jiàn dì zhǐ ma?** *May I have your e-mail address?*

雕刻 **diāo kè** *sculpture n*

顶部 **dǐng bù** *roof n*

天窗 **tiān chuāng** *sunroof*

顶楼房间 **dǐng lóu fáng jiān** *penthouse n*

丢失的 **diū shī de** *missing adj, lost adj*

冬天 **dōng tiān** *winter n*

动物 **dòng wù** *animal n*

动物园 **dòng wù yuán** *zoo n*

斗鸡 **dòu jī** *cockfight n*

斗牛 **dòu niú** *bullfight n*

斗牛士 **dòu niú shì** *bullfighter n*

读 **dú** *to read v*

赌 **dǔ** *bet n*

我看你押。 **wǒ kàn nǐ yā.** *I'll see your bet.*

赌场 **dǔ chǎng** *casino n*

杜松子酒 **dù sōng zǐ jiǔ** *gin n*

短的 **duǎn de** *short adj*

短袜 **duǎn wà** *sock n*

断开连接 **duàn kāi lián jiē** *to disconnect v*

锻炼 **duàn liàn** *workout n*

队、设备 **duì、shè bèi** *team n / equipment n*

对不起 **duì bù qǐ** *sorry adj*

我很抱歉。 **wǒ hěn bào qiàn.** *I'm sorry.*

兑现 **duì xiàn** *to cash v*

兑现（赌博）**duì xiàn (dǔ bó)** *to cash out (gambling) v*

吨 **dūn** *ton n*

多长时间？ **duō cháng shí jiān?** *For how long?*

多少 **duō shǎo** *how (many) adv*

多少 **duō shǎo** *how (much) adv*

多少钱？ **duō shǎo qián?** *How much?*

多雨的 **duō yǔ de** *rainy adj*

多云的 **duō yún de** *cloudy adj*

E

额外的 **é wài de** *extra adj*

厄瓜多尔的 **è guā duō ěr de** *Ecuadorian adj*

儿科医师 **ér kē yī shī** *pediatrician n*

儿童 **ér tóng** *children n pl*

儿子 **ér zi** *son n*

耳机 **ěr jī** *headphones n*

饵 **ěr** *bait n*

二 **èr** *two n adj*

二分之一的 **èr fēn zhī yī de** *adj, one-half adj*

二十的 **èr shí de** *twenty n adj*

二月 **èr yuè** *February n*

F

发辫 **fā biàn** *braid n*

发动 **fā dòng** *to start (a car) v, to turn on v*

发牌 **fā pái** *to deal (cards) v*

> 让我参加。**ràng wǒ cān jiā.** *Deal me in.*

发送 **fā sòng** *to send v*

发送电子邮件 **fā sòng diàn zǐ yóu jiàn** *to send e-mail v*

发现 **fā xiàn** *to find v*

罚款（交通违规）**fá kuǎn (jiāo tōng wéi guī)** *fine (for traffic violation) n*

法国的 **fǎ guó de** *French adj*

法律 **fǎ lǜ** *law n*

法学院 **fǎ xué yuàn** *law school n*

法院 **fǎ yuàn** *court (legal) n*

帆 **fān** *reef n*

帆布（纤维）**fān bù (xiān wéi)** *canvas (fabric) n*

返回 **fǎn huí** *to return (to a place) v*

饭店 **fàn diàn** *restaurant n*

> 牛排餐厅 **niú pái cān tīng** *steakhouse*

方向 **fāng xiàng** *direction*

放置 **fàng zhì** *to place v*

非裔美国人 **fēi yì měi guó rén** *African American adj*

非洲的 **fēi zhōu de** *afro adj*

肥皂 **féi zào** *soap n*

费 **fèi** *fee n*

费用 **fèi yòng** *fare n / rate n*

分居的（婚姻状态）**fēn jū de (hūn yīn zhuàng tài)** *separated (marital status) adj*

分钟 **fēn zhōng** *minute n*

> 马上 **mǎ shàng** *in a minute*

粉红的 **fěn hóng de** *pink adj*

风帆冲浪 **fēng fān chōng làng** *to windsurf v*

风景画 **fēng jǐng huà** *landscape (painting) n*

风景 **fēng jǐng** *view n / vision n*

> 城市景观 **chéng shì jǐng guān** *city view*
>
> 海滩景观 **hǎi tān jǐng guān** *beach view*

风味 **fēng wèi** *taste, flavor n*

> 巧克力味 **qiǎo kè lì wèi** *chocolate flavor*

缝制 **féng zhì** *to sew v*

佛教徒 **fó jiào tú** *Buddhist n*

伏特加酒 **fú tè jiā jiǔ** *vodka n*

服务 **fú wù** *service n*

> 超出服务范围 **chāo chū fú wù fàn wéi** *out of service*

服务 **fú wù** *to serve v*

服务费 **fú wù fèi** *service charge n*

服务员 **fú wù yuán** *waiter n*

服装 **fú zhuāng** *dress (garment) n*

浮潜（呼吸管）**fú qián (hū xī guǎn)** *snorkel (breathing tube)* n

抚慰者 **fǔ wèi zhě** *pacifier* n

父亲 **fù qīn** *father, parent* n

妇科医生 **fù kē yī shēng** *gynecologist* n

妇女 **fù nǚ** *woman* n

附近的 **fù jìn de** *near, nearby* adj

G

该死！**gāi sǐ!** *Damn! expletive*

干的 **gān de** *dried* adj

干的 **gān de** *dry* adj

干净的 **gān jìng de** *clean, neat (tidy)* adj

干洗 **gān xǐ** *dry cleaning* n

干洗店 **gān xǐ diàn** *dry cleaner* n

尴尬的 **gān gà de** *embarrassed* adj

干邑酒 **gān yì jiǔ** *cognac* n

感冒 **gǎn mào** *cold (illness)* n

橄榄色 **gǎn lǎn sè** *olive* n

钢琴 **gāng qín** *piano* n

钢琴酒吧 **gāng qín jiǔ bā** *piano bar*

港口 **gǎng kǒu** *port (for ship mooring)* n

高的 **gāo de** *high* adj

更高的 **gèng gāo de** *higher*

高尔夫球 **gāo ěr fū qiú** *golf* n

高尔夫球场 **gāo ěr fū qiú chǎng** *golf course*

高尔夫球练习场 **gāo ěr fū qiú liàn xí chǎng** *driving range* n

高级的 **gāo jí de** *upscale* adj

高速公路 **gāo sù gōng lù** *highway* n

高兴的 **gāo xìng de** *delighted* adj

高中 **gāo zhōng** *high school* n

哥伦比亚的 **gē lún bǐ yà de** *Colombian* adj

哥斯达黎加的 **gē sī dá lí jiā de** *Costa Rican* n adj

胳膊 **gē bo** *arm* n

歌唱 **gē chàng** *to sing* v

歌剧 **gē jù** *opera* n

歌剧院 **gē jù yuàn** *opera house* n

歌曲 **gē qǔ** *song* n

格式 **gé shi** *format* n

给 **gěi** *to give* v

更便宜 **gèng pián yi** *cheaper* adj

更低 **gèng dī** adj *lower*

更好的 **gèng hǎo de** *better* adj See *good*

更坏 **gèng huài** *worse* adj See *bad*

更近 **gèng jìn** *closer* adj

更近的（对比）**gèng jìn de (duì bǐ)** *nearer* (comparative) adj

更适宜的 **gèng shì yí de** *preferably* adj

更喜欢 **gèng xǐ huān** to *prefer* v

更新 **gēng xīn** to *update* v

更衣室 **gēng yī shì** *changing room* n

工程师 **gōng chéng shī** *engineer* n

工作 **gōng zuò** to *work* v

我为＿＿＿工作。**wǒ wèi ＿＿＿ gōng zuò.** I *work for ＿＿＿*.

公共汽车 **gōng gòng qì chē** *bus* n

公共汽车站 **gōng gòng qì chē zhàn** n *bus stop*

机场大巴 **jī chǎng dà bā** *shuttle bus*

公牛 **gōng niú** *bull* n

公顷 **gōng qǐng** *hectare* n

公文包 **gōng wén bāo** *briefcase* n

公园 **gōng yuán** *park* n

狗 **gǒu** *dog* n

帮助犬 **bāng zhù quǎn** *service dog*

购物 **gòu wù** to *shop* v

购物 **gòu wù** to *shop* v

购物中心 **gòu wù zhōng xīn** *mall* n

姑妈 **gū mā** *aunt* n

古典的（音乐）**gǔ diǎn (yīn yuè)** *classical (music)* adj

鼓 **gǔ** *drum* n

雇员 **gù yuán** *employee* n

雇主 **gù zhǔ** *employer* n

刮擦 **guā cā** to *scratch* v

刮擦的 **guā cā de** *scratched* adj

刮痕 **guā hén** *scratch mark* n

刮水片 **guā shuǐ piàn** *wiper blade* n

寡妇 **guǎ fù** *widow* n

挂断电话（结束通话）**guà duàn diàn huà (jié shù tōng huà)** *hang up (to end a phone call)* v

关掉（灯）**guān diào (dēng)** to *turn off (lights)* v

观光 **guān guāng** *sightseeing* n

观光车 **guān guāng chē** n *sightseeing bus*

观看 **guān kàn** to *look (observe)* v

看这里！**kàn zhè lǐ!** *Look here!*

观看 **guān kàn** to *watch* v

鳏夫 **guān fū** *widower* n

罐头 **guàn tóu** *can* n

光盘 **guāng pán** *CD* n

逛街（热闹的市区）**guàng jiē (rè nào de shì qū)** *hangout (hot spot)* n

逛街（休息）**guàng jiē (xiū xi)** to *hang out (relax)* v

果汁 **guǒzhī** *fruit juice n*

过错 **guòcuò** *fault n*

过道（商店）**guò dào (shāng diàn)** *aisle (in store) n / hallway n*

过敏 **guò mǐn** *allergy n*

过敏的 **guò mǐn de** *allergic adj*

过热 **guò rè** *to overheat v*

H

海拔 **hǎi bá** *altitude n*

海关 **hǎi guān** *customs n*

海滩 **hǎi tān** *beach n*

海鲜 **hǎi xiān** *seafood n*

喊叫 **hǎn jiào** *to call (shout) v*

喊叫 **hǎn jiào** *to shout v*

航班 **háng bān** *flight n*

航班乘务员 **háng bān chéng wù yuán** *flight attendant*

航空邮件 **háng kōng yóu jiàn** *n air mail*

第一类邮件 **dì yī lèi yóu jiàn** *first class mail*

挂号邮件 **guà hào yóu jiàn** *certified mail*

挂号邮件 **guà hào yóu jiàn** *registered mail*

邮局在哪里？**yóu jú zài nǎ lǐ?** *Where is the post office?*

邮政特快 **yóu zhèng tè kuài** *express mail*

航行 **háng xíng** *sail n*

毫米 **háo mǐ** *millimeter n*

毫升 **háo shēng** *milliliter n*

豪华大巴 **háo huá dà bā** *limo n*

好 **hǎo** *fine, good, Okay adj well, Okay adv*

喝 **hē** *to drink v*

何时 **hé shí** *when adv*

和 **hé** *with prep*

和蔼的 **hé ǎi de** *kind (nice) adj*

和解（抱歉）**hé jiě (bào qiàn)** *to make up (apologize) v*

河 **hé** *river n*

黑暗 **hēi àn** *darkness n*

黑发的 **hēi fā de** *brunette n*

黑暗的 **hēi sè de** *black adj*

黑色的 **hēi àn de** *dark adj*

很 **hěn** *very adv*

很少的 **hěn shǎo de** *little adj*

红发人 **hóng fā rén** *redhead n adj*

红色的 **hóng sè de** *red adj*

洪都拉斯的 **hóng dū lā sī de** *Honduran adj*

后来 **hòu lái** *later adv*

回见。**huí jiàn.** *See you later.*

后面的 **hòu miàn de** *behind adj*

候机楼（机场）**hòu jī lóu (jī chǎng)** *terminal (airport) n*

呼叫（某人）**hū jiào (mǒu rén)** *to page (someone) v*

护士 **hù shì** *nurse n*

护照 **hù zhào** *passport n*

花 **huā** *flower* n

花费 **huā fèi** *to cost* v

花生 **huā shēng** *peanut* n

化妆（用化妆品）**huà zhuāng (yòng huà zhuāng pǐn)** *to make up (apply cosmetics)* v

化妆品 **huà zhuāng pǐn** *toiletries* n

怀孕的 **huái yùn de** *pregnant* adj

环境 **huán jìng** *environment* n

换钱／衣服 **huàn qián / yī fu** *to change (money)* v / *to change (clothes)* v

患便秘症的 **huàn biàn bì zhèng de** *constipated* adj

黄白的 **huáng bái de** *off-white* adj

黄金 **huáng jīn** *gold* n

黄色的 **huáng sè de** *yellow* adj

黄油 **huáng yóu** *butter* n

灰色的 **huī sè de** *gray* adj

汇率 **huì lǜ** *exchange rate* n

会员 **huì yuán** *membership* n

绘画（活动）**huì huà (huó dòng)** *to paint, drawing (activity)* v

混杂种族人 **hùn zá zhǒng zú rén** *biracial* adj

火 **huǒ** *fire* n

火柴 **huǒ chái** *match (fire)* n

火车 **huǒ chē** *train* n

普通火车 **pǔ tōng huǒ chē** *local train*

特快火车 **tè kuài huǒ chē** *express train*

火鸡 **huǒ jī** *turkey* n

伙伴 **huǒ bàn** *partner* n

货币兑换处 **huò bì duì huàn chù** *currency exchange* n

J

机场 **jī chǎng** *airport* n

机构 **jī gòu** *agency* n

机器 **jī qì** *machine* n

x 射线机 **x shè xiàn jī** *x-ray machine*

自动售货机 **zì dòng shòu huò jī** *vending machine*

鸡肉 **jī ròu** *chicken* n

吉他 **jí tā** *guitar* n

极瘦的 **jí shòu de** *thin (skinny)* adj

急速的 **jí sù de** *express* adj

快速登机 **kuài sù dēng jī** *express check-in*

脊椎指压治疗者 **jǐ zhuī zhǐ yā zhì liáo zhě** *chiropractor* n

计算机 **jì suàn jī** *computer* n

忌乳糖的 **jì rǔ táng de** *lactose-intolerant* adj

继续 **jì xù** *to continue* v

加冰块 **jiā bīng kuài** *on the rocks*

加仑 **jiā lún** *gallon* n

加拿大 jiā ná dà Canada n

加拿大的 jiā ná dà de Canadian adj

夹克衫 jiā kè shān jacket n

家 jiā home n

家禽 jiā qín poultry n

家人 jiā rén family n

家庭的 jiā tíng de home adj

家庭地址 jiā tíng dì zhǐ home address

家庭电话号码 jiā tíng diàn huà hào mǎ home telephone number

家庭主妇 jiā tíng zhǔ fù homemaker n

价格 jià gé price n

价格适中的 jià gé shì zhōng de moderately priced

门票 mén piào admission fee n

驾驶 jià shǐ to drive v

驾驶执照 jià shǐ zhí zhào driver's license

假期 jià qī holiday n

假期 jià qī vacation n

在休假 zài xiū jià on vacation

去度假 qù dù jià to go on vacation n

坚果 jiān guǒ nut n

间断 jiàn duàn intermission n

减慢 jiǎn màn to slow v

慢点开！màn diǎn kāi! Slow down!

减慢 jiǎn màn to slow v

健身房 jiàn shēn fáng fitting room n

健身中心 jiàn shēn zhōng xīn fitness center n

交际舞 jiāo jì wǔ ballroom dancing n

交通 jiāo tōng traffic n

交通怎么样？jiāo tōng zěn me yàng? How's traffic?

交通很糟。jiāo tōng hěn zāo。 Traffic is terrible.

交通 jiāo tōng traffic n

交通规则 jiāo tōng guī zé traffic rules

交通法庭 jiāo tōng fǎ tíng traffic court n

交响乐 jiāo xiǎng yuè symphony n

交易 jiāo yì deal (bargain), transaction n

郊区 jiāo qū suburb n

焦虑的 jiāo lǜ de anxious adj

角 jiǎo horn n

角落 jiǎo luò corner n

脚、尺 jiǎo、chǐ foot (body part) n, foot (unit of measurement) n

教堂 jiào táng church n

教育工作者 jiào yù gōng zuò zhě educator n

接（电话），回答（问题）jiē (diàn huà), huí dá (wèn tí) *to answer (phone call) v, to answer (respond to a question) v*

接受 jiē shòu *to accept v*

接线员 jiē xiàn yuán *operator (phone) n*

街道 jiē dào *street n*

街道对面 jiē dào duì miàn *across the street n*

街舞 jiē wǔ *hip-hop n*

节目单 jié mù dān *program n*

节日 jié rì *festival n*

结婚 jié hūn *to marry v*

睫毛 jié máo *eyelash n*

她 tā *she pron*

她的 tā de *hers adj*

姐妹 jiě mèi *sister n*

解释 jiě shì *to explain v*

介绍 jiè shào *to introduce v*

我想把您介绍给———。wǒ xiǎng bǎ nín jiè shào gěi ———. *I'd like to introduce you to ____.*

今天 jīn tiān *today n*

金发的 jīn fā de *blond(e) n adj*

金钱 jīn qián *money n*

金色的 jīn sè de *gold (color), golden adj*

金属探测器 jīn shǔ tàn cè qì *metal detector n*

紧的 jǐn de *tight adj*

紧急联络人 jǐn jí lián luò rén *emergency contact n*

紧急情况 jǐn jí qíng kuàng *emergency n*

紧邻地 jǐn lín dì *next prep*

靠近 kào jìn *next to*

近的 jìn de *near adj*

进入 jìn rù *to enter v*

进行比赛 jìn xíng bǐ sài *to play (a game) v*

禁止进入。jìn zhǐ jìn rù。*Entry forbidden.*

禁止停车 jìn zhǐ tíng chē *no parking v*

禁止吸烟的 jìn zhǐ xī yān de *non-smoking adj*

禁烟车 jìn yān chē *non-smoking car*

禁烟房间 jìn yān fáng jiān *non-smoking room*

禁烟区 jìn yān qū *non-smoking area*

经济 jīng jì *economy n*

经济舱 jīng jì cāng *economy class n*

经理 jīng lǐ *manager n*

警察 jǐng chá *police n*

警察局 jǐng chá jú *police station n*

纠正 jiū zhèng *to correct v*

九 jiǔ *nine n adj*

九十 jiǔ shí *ninety n adj*

九月 jiǔ yuè *September n*

酒吧 **jiǔ bā** *bar* n

酒店 **jiǔ diàn** *hotel* n

酒精 **jiǔ jīng** *alcohol* n

救护车 **jiù hù chē** *ambulance* n

救生用具 **jiù shēng yòng jù** *life preserver* n

居住 **jū zhù** *to live* v

> 您住在哪里？ **nín zhù zài nǎ lǐ?** *Where do you live?*

举动 **jǔ dòng** *to behave* v

拒付的 **jù fù de** *declined* adj

> 您的信用卡被拒付了。 **nín de xìn yòng kǎ bèi jù fù le.** *Your credit card was declined.*

剧院 **jù yuàn** *theater* n

卷发 **juàn fā** *curly hair* n, adj

爵士乐 **jué shì yuè** *jazz* n

军官 **jūn guān** *officer* n

军事 **jūn shì** *military* n

K

咖啡 **kā fēi** *coffee* n

卡 **kǎ** *card* n

> 可以用信用卡吗？ **kě yǐ yòng xìn yòng kǎ ma?** *Do you accept credit cards?*
>
> 名片 **míng piàn** *business card*
>
> 信用卡 **xìn yòng kǎ** *credit card*

卡里普索（音乐）**kǎ lǐ pǔ suǒ (yīn yuè)** *calypso (music)* n

卡普契诺咖啡 **kǎ pǔ qì nuò kā fēi** *cappuccino* n

开放时间（博物馆）**kāi fàng shí jiān (bó wù guǎn)** *hours (at museum)* n

开始 **kāi shǐ** *to begin* v, *to start (commence)* v

开帐单 **kāi zhàng dān** *to bill* v

看见 **kàn jiàn** *to see* v

> 我可以看一下吗？ **wǒ kě yǐ kàn yī xià ma?** *May I see it?*

看起来 **kàn qǐ lái** *to look (appear)* v

抗生素 **kàng shēng sù** *antibiotic* n

抗组胺剂 **kàng zǔ àn jì** *antihistamine* n

烤焦的（肉）**kǎo jiāo de (ròu)** *charred (meat)* adj

靠近 **kào jìn** *to close* v

靠近的 **kào jìn de** *close, near* adj

靠近的 **kào jìn de** *closed* adj

咳嗽 **ké sou** *cough* n *to cough* v

可得的 **kě dé de** *available* adj

> 可以用信用卡。 **kě yǐ yòng xìn yòng kǎ.** *Credit cards accepted.*

克 **kè** *gram* n

客房（酒店）**kè fáng (jiǔ diàn)** *room (hotel)* n

客人 **kè rén** *guest* n

课程 **kè chéng** *lesson n*

空调 **kōng tiáo** *air conditioning n*

空房 **kōng fáng** *vacancy n*

没有空房 **méi yǒu kōng fáng** *no vacancy*

口杯 **kǒu bēi** *shot (liquor) n*

口译人员 **kǒu yì rén yuán** *interpreter n*

裤子 **kù zi** *pair of pants n*

短裤 **duǎn kù** *shorts*

泳裤 **yǒng kù** *swim trunks n*

夸脱 **kuā tuō** *quart n*

快的 **kuài de** *fast adj*

快乐的 **kuài lè de** *happy adj*

宽带 **kuān dài** *broadband n*

宽的 **kuān de** *wide adj*

宽松上衣 **kuān sōng shàng yī** *blouse n*

困惑的 **kùn huò de** *confused adj*

困难的 **kùn nán de** *difficult adj*

L

拉 **lā** *to pull v*

喇叭 **lǎ ba** *trumpet n*

蓝色的 **lán sè de** *blue adj*

朗姆酒 **lǎng mǔ jiǔ** *rum n*

浪漫的 **làng màn de** *romantic adj*

牢固的 **láo gù de** *hard (firm) adj*

老板 **lǎo bǎn** *boss n*

老的 **lǎo de** *old adj*

老年人折扣 **lǎo nián rén zhé kòu** *senior discount n*

老鼠 **lǎo shǔ** *mouse n*

乐队 **yuè duì** *band n*

冷的 **lěng de** *cold adj*

冷水 **lěng shuǐ** *cold water n*

厘米 **lí mǐ** *centimeter n*

离开 **lí kāi** *to leave (depart) v*

离异的 **lí yì de** *divorced adj*

黎明 **lí míng** *dawn n*

礼服 **lǐ fú** *dress (general attire) n*

礼物 **lǐ wù** *gift n*

里边的 **lǐ biān de** *inside adj*

里程计 **lǐ chéng jì** *speedometer n*

理发 **lǐ fā** *haircut n*

理发师 **lǐ fā shī** *barber n*

理发师 **lǐ fā shī** *hairdresser n*

理解 **lǐ jiě** *to understand v*

您理解吗? **nín lǐ jiě ma?** *Do you understand?*

我不理解。 **wǒ bù lǐ jiě。** *I don't understand.*

历史 **lì shǐ** *history n*

历史的 **lì shǐ de** *historical adj*

立体派 **lì tǐ pài** *Cubism n*

利率 **lì lǜ** *interest rate n*

痢疾 **lì jí** *diarrhea n*

连接速度 **lián jiē sù dù** *connection speed n*

脸 **liǎn** *face n*

裂缝（玻璃品上）**liè féng (bō li pǐn shàng)** *crack (in glass object) n*

邻居 **lín jū** *neighbor n*

临时照顾幼儿者 **lín shí zhào gù yòu ér zhě** *babysitter n*

淋浴 **lín yù** *shower n* to shower v

零钱 **líng qián** *change (money) n*

令人怀疑地 **lìng rén huái yí dì** *suspiciously adv*

另一个 **lìng yī gè** *another adj*

流（水）**liú (shuǐ)** *current (water) n*

六 **liù** *six n adj*

六十 **liù shí** *sixty n adj*

六月 **liù yuè** *June n*

龙头 **lóng tóu** *faucet n*

聋的 **lóng de** *deaf adj*

露营 **lù yíng** *to camp v to go camping v*

露营地 **lù yíng dì** *campsite n*

露营者 **lù yíng zhě** *camper n*

录像 **lù xiàng** *video n*

录像机 **lù xiàng jī** *VCR n*

驴子 **lú zǐ** *donkey n*

旅程 **lǚ chéng** *trip n*

旅社 **lǚ shè** *hostel n*

旅行 **lǚ xíng** *to travel v*

旅行支票 **lǚ xíng zhī piào** *travelers' check n*

旅游 **lǚ yóu** *tour n*

铝 **lǚ** *aluminum n*

律师 **lǜ shī** *lawyer n*

绿色的 **lǜ sè de** *green adj*

轮胎 **lún tāi** *tire n*

> 备用轮胎 **bèi yòng lún tāi** *spare tire n*

轮椅 **lún yǐ** *wheelchair n*

> 电轮椅 **diàn lún yǐ** *power wheelchair*
>
> 轮椅通道 **lún yǐ tōng dào** *wheelchair access*
>
> 轮椅坡道 **lún yǐ pō dào** *wheelchair ramp*

M

妈妈 **mā ma** *mom n, mommy n*

马 **mǎ** *horse n*

马桶 **mǎ tǒng** *toilet n*

满堂彩！**mǎn táng cǎi!** *Full house! n*

慢 **màn** *slowly adv slow adj*

忙碌的（饭店）**máng lù de (fàn diàn)** *busy (restaurant) adj*

盲的 **máng de** *blind adj*

猫 **māo** *cat n*

毛巾 **máo jīn** *towel n*

毛毯 **máo tǎn** *blanket n*

毛衣 **máo yī** *sweater n*

帽子 **mào zǐ** *hat n*

没人 **méi rén** none n

没油了 **méi yóu le** out of gas

没有 **méi yǒu** without prep

没有避孕套不行 **méi yǒu bì yùn tào bù xíng** not without a condom

玫瑰 **méi guì** rose n

眉毛 **méi mao** eyebrow n

美国的 **měi guó de** American adj

美好的 **měi hǎo de** nice adj

美元 **měi yuán** dollar n

门 **mén** door n

登机口（在机场）**dēng jī kǒu (zài jī chǎng)** gate (at airport)

弥补 **mí bǔ** to make up (compensate) v

迷你酒吧 **mí nǐ jiǔ bā** minibar n

秘鲁人、秘鲁的 **mì lǔ rén、mì lǔ de** Peruvian n adj

密码 **mì mǎ** password n

蜜蜂 **mì fēng** bee n

棉布 **mián bù** cotton n

免费赠送的饮料 **miǎn fèi zèng sòng de yǐn liào** complimentary drink n

免税 **miǎn shuì** duty-free adj

面包 **miàn bāo** bread n

面包车 **miàn bāo chē** van n

民事权利 **mín shì quán lì** civil rights n

民主 **mín zhǔ** democracy n

民族 **mín zú** nationality n

名字 **míng zi** name n

我叫_____。**wǒ jiào _____。** My name is ____.

明亮的 **míng liàng de** bright adj

明天 **míng tiān** tomorrow n adv

明信片 **míng xìn piàn** postcard n

模糊的 **mó hu de** blurry adj

摩托车 **mó tuō chē** motorcycle n

墨西哥的 **mò xī gē de** Mexican adj

某人 **mǒu rén** someone n

某事物 **mǒu shì wù** something n

母牛 **mǔ niú** cow n

母亲 **mǔ qīn** mother n

母乳喂养 **mǔ rǔ wèi yǎng** to breastfeed v

木块 **mù kuài** block n

目的地 **mù dì dì** destination n

沐浴 **mù yù** to bathe v

穆斯林教 **mù sī lín jiào** Muslim n adj

N

哪个 **nǎ ge** which adv

哪里 **nǎ lǐ** where adv

内衣裤 **nèi yī kù** underwear n

那个 **nà ge** *that adj*

那里 **nà lǐ** *there (far) adv*
(demonstrative)

那里 **nà lǐ** *there (nearby) adv*
(demonstrative)

那些 **nà xiē** *those adj*

奶酪 **nǎi lào** *cheese n*

奶油 **nǎi yóu** *cream n*

男朋友 **nán péng yǒu**
boyfriend n

男人 **nán rén** *man n*

男洗手间 **nán xǐ shǒu jiān**
men's restroom n

男性（人）**nán xìng (rén)** *male
(person) n*

男性的 **nán xìng de** *male adj*

难题 **nán tí** *problem n*

能够 **néng gòu** *to be able to
(can) v, may v aux*

我可以_____吗？**wǒ kě yǐ
_____ ma?** *May I ____?*

尼加拉瓜的 **ní jiā lā guā de**
Nicaraguan adj

你 **nǐ** *you pron sing (informal)*

你的 **nǐ de** *your, yours adj sing
(informal)*

你们 **nǐ mén** *you pron pl
(informal)*

年 **nián** *year n*

您多大了？**nín duō dà le?**
What's your age?

年级（学校）**nián jí (xué xiào)**
grade (school) n

年龄 **nián líng** *age n*

年轻的 **nián qīng de** *young adj*

尿布 **niào bù** *diaper n*

布尿布 **bù niào bù** *cloth
diaper*

一次性尿布 **yī cì xìng niào bù**
disposable diaper

您 **nín** *you pron (formal)*

您的 **nín de** *your, yours adj
(formal)*

您的年龄多大？**nín de nián líng
duō dà?** *What's your age?*

您好 **nín hǎo** *hello n*

您还好吗？**nín hái hǎo ma?**
Are you okay?

您叫什么名字？**nín jiào shén
me míng zi?** *What's your
name?*

名字 **míng zi** *first name*

您们 **nín mén** *you pron pl
(formal)*

您有避孕套吗？**nín yǒu bì yùn
tào ma?** *Do you have a
condom?*

您在哪里长大？**nín zài nǎ lǐ
zhǎng dà?** *Where did you
grow up?*

柠檬水 **níng méng shuǐ**
lemonade n

牛奶 **niú nǎi** *milk n*

奶昔 **nǎi xī** *milk shake n*

浓的 **nóng de** *thick adj*

女儿 **nǚ ér** *daughter n*

女孩 **nǚ hái** *girl* n

女朋友 **nǚ péng yǒu** *girlfriend* n

女仆（酒店）**nǚ pú (jiǔ diàn)** *maid (hotel)* n

女洗手间 **nǚ xǐ shǒu jiān** *women's restroom*

P

爬楼梯 **pá lóu tī** *to climb stairs* v

爬山 **pá shān** *mountain climbing* n, *to climb a mountain* v

攀登 **pān dēng** *climbing* n *to climb* v

攀登的 **pān dēng de** *climbing* adj

攀登设备 **pān dēng shè bèi** *climbing gear*

攀岩 **pān yán** *rock climbing*

盘子 **pán zǐ** *dish* n

胖的 **pàng de** *fat* adj

跑 **pǎo** *to run* v

跑步机 **pǎo bù jī** *treadmill* n

配导游的旅游 **pèi dǎo yóu de lǚ yóu** *guided tour* n

配方 **pèi fāng** *formula* n

烹饪 **pēng rèn** *to cook* v

朋友 **péng yǒu** *friend* n

皮肤 **pí fū** *skin* n

皮革 **pí gé** *leather* n

疲惫的 **pí bèi de** *tired* adj

啤酒 **pí jiǔ** *beer* n

便宜的 **pián yi de** *cheap, inexpensive* adj

漂白剂 **piǎo bái jì** *bleach* n

漂亮的 **piào liàng de** *beautiful* adj

票 **piào** *ticket* n

贫民窟 **pín mín kū** *slum* n

品尝室 **pǐn cháng shì** *tasting room* n

品脱 **pǐn tuō** *pint* n

品位（识别力）**pǐn wèi (shí bié lì)** *taste (discernment)* n

平衡 **píng héng** *to balance* v

平局（赌博）**píng jú (dǔ bó)** *split (gambling)* n

瓶子 **píng zǐ** *bottle* n

葡萄 **pú tao** *grape* n

葡萄酒 **pú tao jiǔ** *wine* n

葡萄园 **pú tao yuán** *vineyard* n

Q

七 **qī** *seven* n adj

七分熟的（肉）**qī fēn shú de (ròu)** *medium well (meat)* adj

七十 **qī shí** *seventy* n adj

七月 **qī yuè** *July* n

妻子 **qī zǐ** *wife* n

启航 **qǐ háng** *to sail* v

我们什么时候启航? **wǒ mén shén me shí hou qǐ háng?** *When do we sail?*

汽车 qì chē *car n*

汽车牌照 qì chē pái zhào *automobile license plate*

汽车租赁公司 qì chē zū lìn gōng sī *car rental agency*

汽油 qì yóu *gas n*

器官 qì guān *organ n*

千 qiān *kilo n*

千 qiān *thousand n adj*

千米 qiān mǐ *kilometer n*

签署 qiān shǔ *to sign v*

在这里签字。zài zhè lǐ qiān zì。*Sign here.*

前灯 qián dēng *headlight n*

前额 qián é *forehead n*

前面的 qián miàn de *front adj*

前台 qián tái *front desk n*

前天 qián tiān *the day before yesterday adv*

钱包 qián bāo *purse n*

钱包 qián bāo *purse n, wallet n*

钱夹 qián jiā *wallet n*

潜水 qián shuǐ *to dive v*

浅薄的 qiǎn báo de *shallow adj*

抢夺、偷窃 qiǎng duó 、tōu qiè *to rob v, to steal v*

桥（横跨河两岸，牙齿结构）qiáo (héng kuà hé liǎng àn, yá chǐ jié gòu) *bridge (across a river) n / bridge (dental structure) n*

切 qiē *to cut v*

切口 qiē kǒu *cut (wound) n*

亲属 qīn shǔ *relative n*

青铜色的 qīng tóng sè de *bronze (color) adj*

清澈的 qīng chè de *clear adj*

清晰的 qīng xī de *to clear v*

清真寺 qīng zhēn sì *mosque n*

情况 qíng kuàng *condition n*

情形很好 / 差 qíng xíng hěn hǎo / chà *in good / bad condition*

晴朗的 qíng lǎng de *sunny adj*

请（礼貌的请求）qǐng (lǐ mào de qǐng qiú) *please (polite entreaty) adv*

请回答我。qǐng huí dá wǒ。*Answer me, please.*

请快点！qǐng kuài diǎn！*Hurry, please!*

庆祝 qìng zhù *to celebrate v*

秋季 qiū jì *autumn (fall season) n*

球（运动）qiú (yùn dòng) *ball (sport) n*

取消 qǔxiāo *to cancel v*

去 qù *to go v*

去馆子吃饭 qù guǎn zǐ chī fàn *to eat out v*

去毛 qù máo *waxing n*

权利 quán lì *rights n pl*

雀斑 què bān *freckle n*

确认 què rèn *confirmation n to confirm v*

R

热的，温暖的 **rè de，wēn nuǎn de** hot *adj*, warm *adj*

热巧克力 **rè qiǎo kè lì** hot chocolate *n*

热情的 **rè qíng de** enthusiastic *adj*

热水 **rè shuǐ** hot water *n*

人 **rén** person *n*

视障人士 **shì zhàng rén shì** visually-impaired person

人行道 **rén xíng dào** sidewalk *n*

人行道 **rén xíng dào** walkway *n*

自动人行道 **zì dòng rén xíng dào** moving walkway

认识（某人）**rèn shí (mǒu rén)** to know (someone) *v*

任何的 **rèn hé de** any *adj*

任何地方 **rèn hé dì fāng** anywhere *adv*

任何事 **rèn hé shì** anything *n*

日本的 **rì běn de** Japanese *adj*

日晒 **rì shài** sunburn *n*

揉背 **róu bèi** back rub *n*

肉 **ròu** meat *n*

肉丸子 **ròu wán zǐ** meatball *n*

如何 **rú hé** how *adv*

入场最低消费（酒吧）**rù chǎng zuì dī xiāo fèi (jiǔ bā)** cover charge (in bar) *n*

入口 **rù kǒu** entrance *n*

软的 **ruǎn de** soft *adj*

软件 **ruǎn jiàn** software *n*

瑞格舞 **ruì gé wǔ** reggae *n*

S

萨尔瓦多的 **sà ěr wǎ duō de** Salvadoran *adj*

三 **sān** three *n adj*

三倍的 **sān bèi de** triple *adj*

三分熟的 **sān fēn shú de** rare (meat) *adj*, undercooked *adj*

三十 **sān shí** thirty *n adj*

三月 **sān yuè** March (month) *n*

伞 **sǎn** umbrella *n*

散步 **sàn bù** walk *n*

扫描 **sǎo miáo** to scan (document) *v*

色彩 **sè cǎi** color *n*

杀虫剂 **shā chóng jì** insect repellent *n*

沙拉 **shā lā** salad *n*

沙司 **shā sī** sauce *n*

刹车 **shā chē** brake *n* to brake *v*

山 **shān** mountain *n*

爬山 **pá shān** mountain climbing

山羊 **shān yáng** goat *n*

扇子（手握的）**shàn zi (shǒu wò de)** fan (hand-held) *n*

膳食 **shàn shí** meal *n*

伤害 **shāng hài** injury *n*

伤害（感到痛苦）shāng hài (gǎn dào tòng kǔ) to hurt (to feel painful) v

伤心的 shāng xīn de sad adj

商店 shāng diàn shop n, store n

帐篷 zhàng péng tent n

商务舱 shāng wù cāng business class n

商业 shāng yè business n business adj

商业中心 shāng yè zhōng xīn business center

上传 shàng chuán to upload v

上飞机 shàng fēi jī to board v

上面的 shàng miàn de above adj

烧制 shāo zhì to burn v

少量 shǎo liàng bit (small amount) n

蛇眼！shé yǎn! Snake eyes! n

设计师 shè jì shī designer n

社会主义 shè huì zhǔ yì socialism n

申报 shēn bào to declare v

深的 shēn de deep adj

升 shēng liter n

升级 shēng jí upgrade n

生活 shēng huó life n

您是做什么工作的？nín shì zuò shén me gōng zuò de? What do you do for a living?

生气的 shēng qì de angry adj

生育 shēng yù to mother v

十 shí ten n adj

十八 shí bā eighteen n adj

十二 shí èr twelve n adj

十二月 shí èr yuè December n

十九 shí jiǔ nineteen n adj

十六 shí liù sixteen n adj

十七 shí qī seventeen n adj

十三 shí sān thirteen n adj

十四 shí sì fourteen n adj

十五 shí wǔ fifteen n adj

十一 shí yī eleven n adj

十一月 shí yī yuè November n

十月 shí yuè October n

什么 shén me what adv

怎么了？zěn me le? What's up?

时间 shí jiān hour n, time n

时刻表 shí kè biǎo schedule n, timetable (train) n

实际的 shí jì de actual adj

食品 shí pǐn groceries n

食物 shí wù food n

使干燥 shǐ gān zào to dry v

使合身（衣服）shǐ hé shēn (yī fu) to fit (clothes) v

使愉快 shǐ yú kuài to please v, to be pleasing to v

市场 shì chǎng market n

露天市场 lù tiān shì chǎng open-air market

跳蚤市场 tiào zǎo shì chǎng *flea market*

市区 **shì qū** *downtown n*

事故 **shì gù** *accident n*

事件 **shì jiàn** *matter, affair*

别多管闲事。**bié duō guǎn xián shì**。 *Mind your own business.*

试 **shì** *to try (attempt) v*

试穿 **shì chuān** *to measure v / to try on (clothing) v*

是 **shì** *to be (permanent quality) v*

是的 **shì de** *yes adv*

是他的过错。**shì tā de guò cuò**。 *It was his fault.*

是用玻璃杯喝吗? **shì yòng bō li bēi hē ma?** *Do you have it by the glass?*

请给我来一杯。**qǐng gěi wǒ lái yī bēi**。 *I'd like a glass please.*

适配器插头 **shì pèi qì chā tóu** *adapter plug n*

收到 **shōu dào** *to receive v*

收费计划（移动电话）**shōu fèi jì huà (yí dòng diàn huà)** *rate plan (cell phone)*

有收费计划吗? **yǒu shōu fèi jì huà ma?** *Do you have a rate plan?*

收回 **shōu huí** *to withdraw v, withdrawal n*

收集 **shōu jí** *to collect v*

收据 **shōu jù** *receipt n*

收钱 **shōu qián** *to charge (money) v*

手 **shǒu** *hand n*

手册 **shǒu cè** *manual (instruction booklet) n*

手工搜索 **shǒu gōng sōu suǒ** *hand search v*

手套 **shǒu tào** *glove n*

手提箱 **shǒu tí xiāng** *suitcase n*

守门员 **shǒu mén yuán** *goalie n*

受欢迎的 **shòu huān yíng de** *popular adj, welcome adj*

售票处 **shòu piào chù** *box office n*

售票台 **shòu piào tái** *ticket counter*

瘦的（苗条）**shòu de (miáo tiáo)** *thin (fine) adj*

瘦的（苗条）**shòu de (miáo tiáo)** *thin (slender) adj*

书 **shū** *book n*

书店 **shū diàn** *bookstore n*

叔叔 **shū shū** *uncle n*

蔬菜 **shū cài** *vegetable n*

竖笛 **shù dí** *clarinet n*

数量 **shù liàng** *amount n*

数字 **shù zì** *number n*

双倍的 **shuāng bèi de** *double adj*

双语的 **shuāng yǔ de** *bilingual adj*

谁 **shéi** *who adv*

——是谁的? ——**shì shuí de?** *Whose is ____?*

水 **shuǐ** *water n*

水池 **shuǐ chí** *sink n*

水肺潜水 **shuǐ fèi qián shuǐ** *to scuba dive v*

水果 **shuǐ guǒ** *fruit n*

水疗 **shuǐ liáo** *spa n*

税 **shuì** *tax n*

增值税 **zēng zhí shuì** *value-added tax (VAT)*

顺子 **shùn zǐ** *stair n / flush, straight (gambling) n*

说出 **shuō chū** *to say v*

丝 **sī** *silk n*

司机 **sī jī** *driver n*

四 **sì** *four n adj*

四分熟的（肉）**sì fēn shú de (ròu)** *medium rare (meat) adj*

四分之一 **sì fēn zhī yī** *one quarter, one fourth*

四十 **sì shí** *forty n adj*

四月 **sì yuè** *April n*

寺庙 **sì miào** *temple n*

松的 **sōng de** *loose adj*

搜索 **sōu suǒ** *search n*

苏打水 **sū dǎ shuǐ** *seltzer, soda n*

减肥苏打水 **jiǎn féi sū dǎ shuǐ** *diet soda*

苏格兰的 **sū gé lán de** *Scottish adj*

素餐 **sù cān** *vegetarian meal*

素食者、素食的 **sù shí zhě、sù shí de** *vegetarian n adj*

塑料 **sù liào** *plastic n*

损坏的 **sǔn huài de** *damaged adj*

所有的 **suǒ yǒu de** *all adj*

索赔 **suǒ péi** *claim n*

锁 **suǒ** *lock n*

锁上 **suǒ shàng** *to lock v*

T

他 **tā** *him pron*

他的 **tā de** *his adj*

他们 **tā mén** *them pron pl*

踏板 **tà bǎn** *scooter n*

这是哪里? **tā zài nar?** *Where is it?*

台球（游戏）**tái qiú (yóu xì)** *pool (the game) n*

太（过分）**tài (guò fèn)** *too (excessively) adv*

太阳 **tài yáng** *sun n*

太阳镜 **tài yáng jìng** *sunglasses n*

谈论 **tán lùn** *to speak v, to talk v*

这里说英语。**zhè lǐ shuō yīng yǔ。** *English spoken here.*

汤 **tāng** *soup n*

糖尿病的 **táng niào bìng de** *diabetic adj*

糖尿病人餐 **táng niào bìng rén cān** *diabetic meal n*

烫（头发）**tàng (tóu fa)** *permanent (hair) n*

套间 **tào jiān** *suite n*

特色菜（特色套餐）**tè sè cài (tè sè tào cān)** *special (featured meal) n*

提供 **tí gōng** *to offer v*

提前 **tí qián** *advance n, in advance adv*

体育场 **tǐ yù chǎng** *stadium n*

体育馆 **tǐ yù guǎn** *gym n*

体育馆存物柜 **tǐyù guǎn cún wù guì** *gym locker*

替代品 **tì dài pǐn** *substitution n*

天 **tiān** *day n*

天鹅 **tiān é** *swan n*

天气预报 **tiān qì yù bào** *weather forecast n*

天主教的 **tiān zhǔ jiào de** *Catholic n adj*

挑染（头发）**tiāo rǎn (tóu fa)** *highlights (hair) n*

调味品 **tiáo wèi pǐn** *spice n*

调味品（沙拉）**tiáo wèi pǐn (shā lā)** *dressing (salad) n*

听 **tīng** *to listen v*

听见 **tīng jiàn** *to hear v*

听障的 **tīng zhàng de** *hearing-impaired adj*

停泊 **tíng bó** *berth n*

停车（交通标志）**tíng chē (jiāo tōng biāo zhì)** *STOP (traffic sign) n*

停车的 **tíng chē de** *parking adj*

停放 **tíng fàng** *to park v*

停留 **tíng liú** *to stay v*

停止 **tíng zhǐ** *to stop v*

请停下来。**qǐng tíng xià lái。** *Please stop.*

通行费 **tōng xíng fèi** *toll n*

同花大顺 **tóng huā dà shùn** *royal flush n*

铜的 **tóng de** *copper adj*

桶装啤酒，生啤 **tǒng zhuāng pí jiǔ, shēng pí** *beer on tap, draft beer n*

头等舱 **tóu děng cāng** *first class*

头发 **tóu fa** *hair n*

头痛 **tóu tòng** *headache n*

投票 **tóu piào** *to vote v*

图画（艺术品）**tú huà (yì shù pǐn)** *drawing (work of art) n*

徒步的 **tú bù de** *pedestrian adj*

步行购物区 **bù xíng gòu wù qū** *pedestrian shopping district*

兔子 **tù zǐ** *rabbit n*

团体 **tuán tǐ** *group n*

推 **tuī** *to push v*

推荐 **tuī jiàn** *to recommend v*

腿 **tuǐ** *leg n*

退房 **tuì fáng** *check-out n / departure n / exit n*

非出口 **fēi chū kǒu** *not an exit*

紧急出口 **jǐn jí chū kǒu** *emergency exit*

退房时间 **tuì fáng shí jiān** *check-out time*

退房（酒店）**tuì fáng (jiǔ diàn)** *to check out (of hotel) v*

退还（某物）**tuì huán (mǒu wù)** *to return (something) v*

吞咽 **tūn yàn** *to swallow v*

托儿所 **tuō ér suǒ** *nursery n*

托牙板 **tuō yá bǎn** *dentures, denture plate n*

托运 **tuō yùn** *to check v*

拖上岸 **tuō shàng àn** *to beach v*

脱销的 **tuō xiāo de** *sold out (thing) adj*

U

USB 接口 **USB jiē kǒu** *USB port n*

V

签证 **qiān zhèng** *visa n*

W

外面 **wài miàn** *outside n*

外套 **wài tào** *coat n*

完全的 **wán quán de** *full adj*

玩具 **wán jù** *toy n*

玩具店 **wán jù diàn** *toy store n*

晚安 **wǎn ān** *good night*

晚的 **wǎn de** *late adj*

请不要晚了。**qǐng bù yào wǎn le .** *Please don't be late.*

晚饭 **wǎn fàn** *dinner n*

晚上好 **wǎn shàng hǎo** *good evening*

网吧 **wǎng bā** *Internet café n*

网络 **wǎng luò** *Internet n*

哪里有网吧？**nǎ lǐ yǒu wǎng bā?** *Where can I find an Internet café?*

网络 **wǎng luò** *network n*

网球 **wǎng qiú** *tennis n*

往返票 **wǎng fǎn piào** *round-trip ticket*

危地马拉的 **wēi dì mǎ lā de** *Guatemalan adj*

危险 **wēi xiǎn** *danger n*

围栏 **wéi lán** *curb n*

委内瑞拉的 **wěi nèi ruì lā de** *Venezuelan adj*

卫生间 **wèi shēng jiān** *bathroom, restroom n*

卫生纸 **wèi shēng zhǐ** *toilet paper n*

卫星 **wèi xīng** *satellite n*

卫星跟踪 **wèi xīng gēn zōng** *satellite tracking*

卫星广播 wèi xīng guǎng bō
satellite radio

未婚夫（妇）wèi hūn fū (fù)
fiancé(e) n

闻 wén to smell v

吻 wěn kiss n

问 wèn to ask v

问讯台 wèn xùn tái
information booth n

我 wǒ I pron

我保留娘家姓。wǒ bǎo liú
niáng jia xìng。 I kept my
maiden name.

我的钱包丢了。wǒ de qián
bāo diū le。 I lost my wallet.

我对＿＿＿过敏。wǒ duì
＿＿＿guò mǐn。 I'm allergic
to ＿＿. See p74 and p153
for common allergens.

我很好。wǒ hěn hǎo。 I'm fine.

我们 wǒmén we, us pron pl

我是过错方。wǒ shì guò cuò
fāng。 I'm at fault.

我想要杯饮料。wǒ xiǎng yào
bēi yǐn liào。 I'd like a drink.

我需要抗生素。wǒ xū yào
kàng shēng sù。 I need an
antibiotic.

我要进行水肺潜水。wǒ yào jìn
xíng shuǐ fèi qián shuǐ。 I
scuba dive.

浮潜 fú qián to snorkel v

我有哮喘。wǒ yǒu xiào
chuǎn。 I have asthma.

我在避孕。wǒ zài bì yùn。 I'm
on birth control.

卧铺车 wò pù chē sleeping
car n

握着 wò zhe to hold v

牵手 to hold hands

握着（赌博）wò zhe (dǔ bó) to
hold (gambling) v

乌拉圭人 wū lā guī rén
Uruguayan n

无神论 wú shén lùn atheist adj

无线保真 wú xiàn bǎo zhēn
wi-fi n

无线广播 wú xiàn guǎng bō
radio n

卫星广播 wèi xīng guǎng bō
satellite radio

五 wǔ five n adj

五十 wǔ shí fifty n adj

五月 wǔyuè May (month) n

午餐 wǔ cān lunch n

午夜 wǔyè midnight adv

武器 wǔqì weapon n

武装力量 wǔ zhuāng lì liàng
armed forces n pl

侮辱 wǔrǔ to insult v

X

西班牙（的）xī bān yá (de)
Spanish n adj

西方的 xī fāng de western adj

西方的（电影）xī fāng de (diàn
yǐng) western adj (movie)

吸烟区 **xī yān qū** *smoking area*

禁止吸烟 **jìn zhǐ xī yān** *no smoking*

希腊的 **xī là de** *Greek adj*

希腊正教的 **xī là zhèng jiào de** *Greek Orthodox adj*

袭击 **xí jī** *to mug (assault) v*

洗衣店 **xǐ yī diàn** *laundry n*

喜欢参见（关于喜欢的解释） **xǐhuān cān jiàn (guān yú xǐ huān de jiě shì)** *to please v*

戏剧 **xì jù** *drama n*

细绳 **xì shéng** *rope n, twine n*

狭窄的 **xiá zhǎi de** *narrow adj*

下面的 **xià miàn de** *below adj*

下午 **xià wǔ** *afternoon n*

在下午 **zài xià wǔ** *in the afternoon*

下午好 **xià wǔ hǎo** *Good afternoon!*

下一站 **xià yī zhàn** *the next station*

下雨 **xià yǔ** *to rain v*

下载 **xià zǎi** *to download v*

夏季 **xià jì** *summer n*

纤维 **xiān wéi** *fabric n*

闲荡 **xián dàng** *to lounge v*

现金 **xiàn jīn** *cash n*

只收现金 **zhī shōu xiàn jīn** *cash only*

现在 **xiàn zài** *now adv*

限速 **xiàn sù** *speed limit n*

乡村音乐 **xiāng cūn yīn yuè** *country-and-western music adj*

香烟 **xiāng yān** *cigarette n*

箱式小轿车 **xiāng shì xiǎo jiào chē** *sedan n*

详细说明 **xiáng xì shuō míng** *to specify v*

享受 **xiǎng shòu** *to enjoy v*

想法 **xiǎng fǎ** *thought n*

想要 **xiǎng yào** *to want v*

向 **xiàng** *toward prep*

向前的 **xiàng qián de** *forward adj*

向上 **xiàng shàng** *up adv*

向下 **xiàng xià** *down adv*

消耗 **xiāo hào** *drain n*

消化不良 **xiāo huà bù liáng** *indigestion n*

消失 **xiāo shī** *to disappear v*

销售 **xiāo shòu** *to sell v*

销售人员 **xiāo shòu rén yuán** *salesperson n*

街头小贩 **jiē tóu xiǎo fàn** *street vendor*

小吃 **xiǎo chī** *snack n*

小虫 **xiǎo chóng** *bug n*

小厨房 **xiǎo chú fáng** *kitchenette n*

小船 **xiǎo chuán** *boat n, ship n*

小的、短的 **xiǎo de、duǎn de** *small adj, short adj, little adj*

更小的 **gèng xiǎo de** *smaller, littler*

最小的 **zuì xiǎo de** *smallest, littlest*

小费 **xiǎo fèi** *tip (gratuity)*

包含小费 **bāo hán xiǎo fèi** *tip included*

小孩 **xiǎo hái** *boy n, kid n*

小径 **xiǎo jìng** *trail n*

小鸟 **xiǎo niǎo** *bird n*

小女孩 **xiǎo nǚhái** *little girl n*

小跑 **xiǎo pǎo** *jogging n*

小说 **xiǎo shuō** *novel n*

爱情小说 **ài qíng xiǎo shuō** *romance novel*

神秘故事 **shén mì gù shì** *mystery novel*

小提琴 **xiǎo tí qín** *violin n*

小甜饼 **xiǎo tián bǐng** *cookie n*

小虾 **xiǎo xiā** *shrimp n*

小学 **xiǎo xué** *primary school n*

肖像 **xiào xiàng** *portrait n*

哮喘 **xiào chuǎn** *asthma n*

鞋子 **xié zi** *shoe n*

写出 **xiě chū** *to spell v*

请问它怎么写? **qǐng wèn tā zěn me xiě?** *How do you spell that?*

写出 **xiě chū** *to write v*

您能给我写下那个吗? **nín néng gěi wǒ xiě xià nà ge ma?** *Would you write that down for me?*

谢谢您 **xiè xiè nín** *thank you*

心脏 **xīn zàng** *heart n*

心脏病 **xīn zàng bìng** *heart attack n*

新的 **xīn de** *new adj*

新教 **xīn jiào** *Protestant n adj*

新西兰 **xīn xī lán** *New Zealand n*

新西兰的 **xīn xī lán de** *New Zealander adj*

新鲜的 **xīn xiān de** *fresh adj*

信封 **xìn fēng** *envelope n*

信息 **xìn xī** *information n*

信用局 **xìn yòng jú** *credit bureau n*

星期二 **xīng qī èr** *Tuesday n*

星期六 **xīng qī liù** *Saturday n*

星期三 **xīng qī sān** *Wednesday n*

星期四 **xīng qī sì** *Thursday n*

星期天 **xīng qī tiān** *Sunday n*

星期五 **xīng qī wǔ** *Friday n*

星期一 **xīng qī yī** *Monday n*

行李 **xíng lǐ** *baggage, luggage n*

行李丢了 **xíng lǐ diū le** *lost baggage*

行李车 **xíng lǐ chē** *trunk (of car) n*

行李领取处 **xíng lǐ lǐng qǔ chù** *baggage claim*

姓 **xìng** *last name*

幸会 **xìng huì** *charmed adj*

性别 **xìng bié** *sex (gender) n*

性交 **xìng jiāo** *intercourse (sexual) n*

兄弟 **xiōng dì** *brother n*

休息室 **xiū xī shì** *lounge n*

修剪（头发）**xiū jiǎn (tóu fa)** *to trim (hair) v*

需要 **xū yào** *to need v*

许多 **xǔ duō** *a lot n/many adj*

许多的 **xǔ duō de** *much adj*

许可证 **xǔ kě zhèng** *permit n*

续处方 **xù chǔ fāng** *refill (of prescription) n*

蓄电池（汽车使用的）**xù diàn chí (qì chē shǐ yòng de)** *battery (for car) n*

选举 **xuǎn jǔ** *election n*

选中的（样式）**xuǎn zhōng de (yàng shì)** *checked (pattern) adj*

学生折扣 **xué shēng zhé kòu** *student discount*

学校 **xué xiào** *school n*

学院，高中 **xué yuàn, gāo zhōng** *college n, high school n*

雪茄 **xuě jiā** *cigar n*

寻找 **xún zhǎo** *to look for (to search) v*

训练 **xùn liàn** *to train v*

Y

押注（赌博）**yā zhù (dǔ bó)** *to put (gambling) v*

放在红色 / 黑色上！**fàng zài hóng sè / hēi sè shàng!** *Put it on red / black!*

鸭子 **yā zǐ** *duck n*

牙 **yá** *tooth n*

牙痛 **yá tòng** *toothache n*

我牙疼。**wǒ yá téng。** *I have a toothache.*

牙医 **yá yī** *dentist n*

亚洲的 **yà zhōu de** *Asian adj*

延误 **yán wù** *delay n*

岩石 **yán shí** *rock n*

沿着街道 **yán zhe jiē dào** *down the street*

盐 **yán** *salt n*

低盐 **dī yán** *low-salt*

眼睛 **yǎn jīng** *eye n*

眼镜 **yǎn jing** *eyeglasses, glasses (spectacles) n*

验光师 **yàn guāng shī** *optometrist n*

羊绒衫 **yáng róng shān** *cashmere n*

阳台 **yáng tái** *balcony n*

氧气罐 **yǎng qì guàn** *oxygen tank n*

摇滚 **yáo gǔn** *rock and roll n*

药草 **yào cǎo** *herb n*

药片 **yào piàn** *pill n*

晕船药 yùn chuán yào *seasickness pill*

药物 yào wù *medicine n, medication n*

要求 yāo qiú *to order, request, demand v*

也 yě *too (also) adv*

夜晚 yè wǎn *night n*

每夜 měi yè *per night*

在夜晚 zài yè wǎn *at night*

夜总会 yè zǒng huì *nightclub n*

一 yī *one n adj*

一包香烟 yī bāo xiāng yān *pack of cigarettes*

一打 yī dá *dozen n*

一份 yī fēn *portion (of food) n*

一些 yī xiē *some adj*

一月 yī yuè *January n*

一直 yī zhí *all the time*

就那些。 jiù nà xiē。 *That's all.*

衣架 yī jià *hanger n*

医生 yī shēng *doctor n*

医生办公室 yī shēng bàn gōng shì *doctor's office n*

医学院 yī xué yuàn *medical school n*

仪式 yí shì *service (religious) n*

移动 yí dòng *to move, to remove v*

乙烯基 yǐ xī jī *vinyl n*

已婚的 yǐ hūn de *married adj*

艺术 yì shù *art n*

艺术展 yì shù zhǎn *exhibit of art*

艺术博物馆 yì shù bó wù guǎn *art museum*

手艺人 shǒu yì rén *craftsperson / artisan n*

艺术的 yì shù de *art adj*

艺术家 yì shù jiā *artist n*

易碎的 yì suì de *fragile adj*

意大利的 yì dà lì de *Italian adj*

溢出 yì chū *to spill v*

音乐 yīn yuè *music n*

流行音乐 liú xíng yīn yuè *pop music*

音乐的 yīn yuè de *musical adj*

音乐会 yīn yuè huì *concert n*

音乐家 yīn yuè jiā *musician n*

音乐厅 yīn yuè tīng *coliseum n*

音乐喜剧（音乐流派）yīn yuè xǐ jù（yīn yuè liú pai）*musical (music genre) n*

音频 yīn pín *audio n*

音频的 yīn pín de *audio adj*

银 yín *silver n*

银色的 yín sè de *silver (color) adj*

银行 yín háng *bank n*

银行卡 yín háng kǎ *bank card n*

银行账户 yín háng zhàng hù *bank account n*

银质的 **yín zhì de** silver adj

引擎 **yǐn qíng** engine n

饮料 **yǐn liào** drink n

隐形眼镜 **yǐn xíng yǎn jìng** contact lens n

印度教教徒 **yìn dù jiào jiào tú** Hindu n

印象流派 **yìn xiàng liú pài** Impressionism n

英寸 **yīng cùn** inch n

英格兰 **yīng gé lán** England n

英俊的 **yīng jùn de** handsome adj

英里 **yīng lǐ** mile n

英语的 **yīng yǔ de** English adj

婴儿 **yīng ér** baby n

婴儿车 **yīng ér chē** stroller n

婴儿床 **yīng ér chuáng** crib n

婴儿的 **yīng ér de** infantile adj

婴儿食品 **yīng ér shí pǐn** baby food

婴儿推车 **yīng ér tuī chē** baby stroller

鹰 **yīng** eagle n

营业中 **yíng yè zhōng** open (business) adj

影印 **yǐng yìn** to photocopy v

硬币 **yìng bì** coin n

拥挤的 **yōng jǐ de** congested adj

拥塞（交通）**yōng sāi (jiāo tōng)** congestion (traffic) n

泳衣 **yǒng yī** swimsuit n

用 **yòng** to use v

优惠券 **yōu huì quàn** voucher n

就餐优惠券 **jiù cān yōu huì quàn** meal voucher

住宿优惠券 **zhù sù yōu huì quàn** room voucher

由对方付费的 **yóu duì fāng fù fèi de** collect adj

犹太教的 **yóu tài jiào de** Jewish adj Judaism n

犹太教的 **yóu tài jiào de** kosher adj

犹太教食品 **yóu tài jiào shí pǐn** kosher meal n

邮件 **yóu jiàn** mail

邮局 **yóu jú** post office n

邮票 **yóu piào** stamp (postage) n

油 **yóu** oil n

油表 **yóu biǎo** gas gauge n

油画 **yóu huà** painting n

疣 **yóu** wart n

游戏 **yóu xì** play n

游戏控制台 **yóu xì kòng zhì tái** game console n

游行 **yóu xíng** parade n

游泳 **yóu yǒng** to swim v

禁止游泳。**jìn zhǐ yóu yǒng.** Swimming prohibited.

游泳池 yóu yǒng chí pool (swimming) n

有 yǒu to have v

性交 xìng jiāo to have sex (intercourse)

有____吗? yǒu ____ ma? Is / Are there ____?

有斑纹的 yǒu bān wén de striped adj

有风的 yǒu fēng de windy adj

有公共洗手间吗? yǒu gōng gòng xǐ shǒu jiān ma? Do you have a public restroom?

有机的 yǒu jī de organic adj

有礼貌的 yǒu lǐ mào de courteous adj

有人偷了我的钱包。 yǒu rén tōu le wǒ de qián bāo Someone stole my wallet.

有压力的 yǒu yā lì de stressed adj

幼儿 yòu ér infant n

鱼竿 yú gān fishing pole n

愉快 yú kuài pleasure n

见到您很愉快。 jiàn dào nín hěn yú kuài. It's a pleasure.

羽绒枕 yǔ róng zhěn down pillow

语言 yǔ yán language n

浴缸 yù gāng bathtub n

预定 yù dìng reservation n

预算 yù suàn budget n

员工 yuán gōng staff (employees) n

原谅 yuán liàng to excuse (pardon) v

对不起。 duì bù qǐ. Excuse me.

援助 yuán zhù assistance n

远的 yuǎn de far adj

更远的 gèng yuǎn de farther

最远的 zuì yuǎn de farthest

远足 yuǎn zú to hike v

约会 yuē huì appointment n

月 yuè month n

允许 yǔn xǔ to permit v

运动 yùn dòng sports n

运动场 yùn dòng chǎng playground n

运行 yùn xíng to ride v / to run v

晕车 yùn chē carsickness n

晕船 yùn chuán nausea n

晕倒 yūn dǎo to faint v

晕眩的/晕船 yūn xuàn de/yùn chuán dizzy adj / seasick adj

Z

杂志 zá zhì magazine n

载运 zǎi yùn to ship v

再见 zài jiàn goodbye n

再斟满 zài zhēn mǎn refill (of beverage) n

在飞机上 **zài fēi jī shàng** *on board*

在角落 **zài jiǎo luò** *on the corner*

在黎明 **zài lí míng** *at dawn*

在那边 **zài nà biān** *over there adv*

遭袭击 **zāo xí jī** *to get mugged*

早餐 **zǎo cān** *breakfast n*

早晨 **zǎo chén** *morning n*

在早晨 **zài zǎo chén** *in the morning*

早的 **zǎo de** *early adj*

早上好 **zǎo shàng hǎo** *Good morning!*

噪杂的 **zào zá de** *loud, noisy adj*

增长 **zēng zhǎng** *to grow (get larger) v*

炸弹 **zhà dàn** *bomb n*

展览 **zhǎn lǎn** *exhibit n*

占线的，占用的 **zhàn xiàn de, zhàn yòng de** *busy adj (phone line), occupied adj*

战争 **zhàn zhēng** *war n*

站 **zhàn** *stop n*

公共汽车站 **gōng gòng qì chē zhàn** *bus stop*

站起 **zhàn qǐ** *to stand v*

丈夫 **zhàng fū** *husband n*

账户 **zhàng hù** *account n*

障碍 **zhàn gài** *handicap n*

遮光剂 **zhē guāng jì** *sunscreen n*

折扣 **zhé kòu** *discount n*

儿童折扣 **ér tóng zhé kòu** *children's discount*

这个 **zhè gè** *this adj this n*

这里 **zhè lǐ** *here adv*

这是哪一种? **zhè shì nǎ yī zhǒng?** *What kind is it?*

这些 **zhè xiē** *these n adj pl*

真棒! **zhēn bàng!** *Great! interj*

真的 **zhēn de** *really adj*

枕头 **zhěn tóu** *pillow n*

正确的 **zhèng què de** *correct adj*

证明 **zhèng míng** *identification n*

政党 **zhèng dǎng** *political party n*

支付 **zhī fù** *to pay v*

支票 **zhī piào** *check n*

汁 **zhī** *juice n*

知道（某事） **zhī dao (mǒu shì)** *to know (something) v*

执照 **zhí zhào** *license n*

侄女 **zhí nǚ** *niece n*

侄子 **zhí zi** *nephew n*

直 **zhí** *straight adv*

在拐角处右转。**zài guǎi jiǎo chù yòu zhuǎn。** *Turn right at the corner.*

在右侧。**zài yòu cè。** *It is on the right.*

直走（指示方向）。**zhí zǒu (zhǐ shì fāng xiàng)** Go straight. (giving directions)

直 **zhí** straight adj

直（头发）**zhí (tóu fa)** straight (hair) adj

纸 **zhǐ** paper n

> 餐巾纸 **cān jīn zhǐ** paper napkin

> 纸盘 **zhǐ pán** paper plate

纸币（货币）**zhǐ bì (huò bì)** bill (currency) n

纸巾 **zhǐ jīn** napkin n

指出 **zhǐ chū** to point v

指南（出版物）**zhǐ nán (chū bǎn wù)** guide (publication) n

指示 **zhǐ shì** to show v

> 您能指给我吗? **nín néng zhǐ gěi wǒ ma?** Would you show me?

至少 **zhì shǎo** at least n

制冰机 **zhì bīng jī** ice machine

制造 **zhì zào** to make v

痣（脸部特征）**zhì (liǎn bù tè zhēng)** mole (facial feature) n

中（号）**zhōng (hào)** medium adj (size)

中国的 **zhōng guó de** Chinese adj

中间的 **zhōng jiān de** middle adj

中午 **zhōng wǔ** noon n

钟 **zhōng** clock n, watch n

> 闹钟 **nào zhōng** alarm clock

种类 **zhǒng lèi** kind (type) n

重 **zhòng** to weigh v

> 请您再重复一遍好吗? **qǐng nín zài chóng fù yī biàn hǎo ma?** Would you please repeat that?

重量 **zhòng liàng** weights n

周 **zhōu** week n

> 从现在起一周 **cóng xiàn zài qǐ yī zhōu** a week from now

> 上周 **shàng zhōu** last week

> 下周 **xià zhōu** next week

> 一周 **yī zhōu** one week

> 这周 **zhè zhōu** this week

猪 **zhū** pig n

煮得过久的 **zhǔ dé guò jiǔ de** overcooked adj

助行器（助行设备）**zhù xíng qì (zhù xíng shè bèi)** walker (ambulatory device) n

蛀洞（牙洞）**zhù dòng (yá dòng)** cavity (tooth cavity) n

抓小偷! **zhuā xiǎotōu!** Stop, thief!

专业的 **zhuān yè de** professional adj

转动 **zhuàn dòng** to turn v

> 左/右转。**zuǒ/yòu zhuǎn。** Turn left / right.

转移 **zhuǎn yí** to transfer v
transfer n

转帐 **zhuǎn zhàng** money
transfer

装入 **zhuāng rù** to bag v

装束 **zhuāng shù** costume n

状态 **zhuàng tài** state n

准备好的 **zhǔn bèi hǎo de**
prepared adj

桌子 **zhuō zǐ** table n

啄木鸟 **zhuó mù niǎo**
woodpecker n

着陆 **zhuó lù** to land v

紫色的 **zǐ sè de** purple adj

字幕 **zì mù** subtitle n

自动取款机 **zì dòng qǔ kuǎn jī**
ATM n

自助餐 **zì zhù cān** buffet n

自助的 **zì zhù de** self-serve adj

自助形式的 **zì zhù xíng shì de**
buffet-style adj

棕色的 **zōng sè de** brown adj

总数 **zǒng shù** total n

总数是多少? **zǒng shù shì
duō shǎo?** What is the
total?

走 **zǒu** to walk v

租赁 **zū lìn** to rent v

租用中的 **zū yòng zhōng de**
charter adj

包机 **bāo jī** charter flight

阻塞 **zǔsè** to block v

组成 **zǔ chéng** makeup n

组成的 **zǔ chéng de** made
of adj

祖父 **zǔ fù** grandfather n

祖母 **zǔ mǔ** grandmother n

嘴 **zuǐ** mouth n

最便宜 **zuì pián yi** cheapest

最低 **zuì dī** lowest

（银行账户上的）余额 **(yín
háng zhàng hù shàng de)
yú é** balance (on bank
account) n

最高的 **zuì gāo de** highest

最好的 **zuì hǎo de** best See
good

最后 **zuì hòu** last adv

最后这些日子 **zuì hòu zhè xiē rì
zǐ** these last few days

最坏 **zuì huài** worst
See bad adj

最近 **zuì jìn** closest adj

最近的（最高级）**zuì jìn de (zuì
gāo jí)** nearest (superlative)

最少的 **zuì shǎo de** least
See little

昨天 **zuó tiān** yesterday adv

左边的 **zuǒ biān de** left adj

作家 **zuò jiā** writer n

坐 **zuò** *to sit v*

座位 **zuò wèi** *seat n*

做预算 **zuò yù suàn** *to budget v*

前排座位 **qián pái zuò wèi** *orchestra seat*

NOTES